Religion, the Body, and Sexuality

D1603680

How does religion relate to bodies and sexualities? Many people would answer, simply, "through repression," but the relationship is much more complicated than that. While many religions draw boundaries between what they consider to be appropriate and inappropriate use of the human body, especially in the realm of sexuality, the same religions often celebrate human sexuality and even expect sexual partners to provide each other with sexual pleasure. Celibacy, too, is more than just repression, and sometimes it is even seen as providing the practitioner with great spiritual power; in other settings, the sex act itself is understood to provide this power.

Religion, the Body, and Sexuality offers students and general readers a sophisticated and accessible exploration of the connections between religion, sexuality, and the body, through case studies and overviews in the following thematic chapters:

- Celibacy
- Regulation
- Controversy
- Violence
- Innovation
- Instrumentalization
- Ecstasy

Each chapter includes suggestions for further reading, questions for further thought, and a list of relevant media resources.

This engaging book is an excellent addition to introductory courses on religion or sexuality and is a much-needed new volume for advanced courses on the intersections of these areas of human experience.

Nina Hoel is Associate Professor of Religion and Society at the University of Oslo, Norway.

Melissa M. Wilcox is Professor and Holstein Family and Community Chair of Religious Studies at the University of California, Riverside, USA.

Liz Wilson is Professor of Comparative Religion at Miami University of Ohio, USA.

Engaging with Religion

Religion, the Body, and Sexuality
An Introduction
Nina Hoel, Melissa M. Wilcox, and Liz Wilson

For more information about this series, please visit:
https://www.routledge.com/religion/series/EWR

Religion, the Body, and Sexuality

An Introduction

Nina Hoel, Melissa M. Wilcox, and Liz Wilson

Routledge
Taylor & Francis Group

LONDON AND NEW YORK

First published 2021
by Routledge
2 Park Square, Milton Park, Abingdon, Oxon OX14 4RN

and by Routledge
52 Vanderbilt Avenue, New York, NY 10017

Routledge is an imprint of the Taylor & Francis Group, an informa business

British Library Cataloguing-in-Publication Data
A catalogue record for this book is available from the British Library

Library of Congress Cataloging-in-Publication Data
Names: Hoel, Nina, author. | Wilcox, Melissa M., 1972- author. | Wilson, Liz, 1961- author.
Title: Religion, the body, and sexuality : an introduction / Nina Hoel, Melissa M. Wilcox, and Liz Wilson.
Description: Abingdon, Oxon ; New York, NY : Routledge, 2020. |
Series: Engaging with religion | Includes bibliographical references and index.
Identifiers: LCCN 2020014235 | ISBN 9781138728103 (hardback) |
ISBN 9781138728127 (paperback) | ISBN 9781315190594 (ebook)
Subjects: LCSH: Human body--Religious aspects. | Sex--Religious aspects.
Classification: LCC BL65.B63 H64 2020 | DDC 202/.2--dc23
LC record available at https://lccn.loc.gov/2020014235

ISBN: 978-1-138-72810-3 (hbk)
ISBN: 978-1-138-72812-7 (pbk)
ISBN: 978-1-315-19059-4 (ebk)

Typeset in Bembo
by Taylor & Francis Books

Contents

Acknowledgments   vi
Preface for instructors   viii

Introduction   1

1 Celibacy   23

2 Regulation   40

3 Controversy   55

4 Violence   73

5 Innovation   92

6 Instrumentalization   111

7 Ecstasy   130

Glossary   142

Resources for teaching   146

Bibliography   152
Index   159

Acknowledgments

This book is the result of several years of planning, researching, writing, editing, pilot-testing, and revisions. At Routledge, the idea was initially floated by Eve Mayer; Rebecca Shillabeer took over the project when Eve moved on to another position. Amy Doffegnies has handled all of the production details with patience and alacrity. We are grateful to Eve, Rebecca, and Amy, as well as to four anonymous reviewers whose enthusiastic comments on the initial proposal contributed to the final form of the book. Rebecca Alpert heroically read a penultimate draft in its entirety, for which we offer deepest thanks.

Talented artist and seminary student Immanuel Paul Karunakaran generously offered to create a new work specifically for the cover of this book. We are honored to be able to feature his gorgeous and complex work on the cover, and deeply grateful for his time, talents, and generosity.

Major planning of the book took place at the University of Oslo, where we were able to spend two days moving from initial visions to a full outline and proposal. We are grateful to the university for hosting us, and to Miami University and the University of California, Riverside – especially the Holstein Family and Community Chair in Religious Studies – for making this opportunity possible. Finally, we are deeply thankful to our graduate and undergraduate students at the University of Oslo, the University of California, Riverside, and Miami University for reading a draft of the book as part of their coursework and their teaching, and for providing us with further insights and feedback that helped us to make the final version even clearer and more accessible.

Each of us would also like to offer a few individual acknowledgments:

Nina Hoel: I am grateful to the graduate students at the Faculty of Theology, University of Oslo, who partook in the course piloting the book. Your enthusiasm, reflections and critical engagement was not only invaluable, but also provided an opportunity for important clarifications. Thank you for your rich and creative contributions.

A special thanks to Federico Settler, whose sabbatical spent at the Faculty of Theology, provided a unique and long-overdue opportunity for meaningful conversations. Your critical and complex insights (as usual!) contributed to the deepening of central perspectives and provided me with a keen sense of direction in the writing up of this book. Moreover, I am deeply grateful to Sa'diyya Shaikh, Elaine Nogueira-Godsey, and Gabeba Baderoon. Although geographically distant, you continue to be profound sources of inspiration when it comes to teaching, writing and living.

Finally, in many ways the prolonged birthing of this book is deeply intertwined with the birthing of Dennis Mathias in 2017 and, Samuel Marley – who still has two months to go in the womb at the time of this writing. I am deeply thankful to my husband Dennis for his patience, strength and love during this wonderful, yet incredibly exhausting time. A warm thanks also to bestemor, bestefar and ouma, for their love and generosity.

Melissa Wilcox: I am deeply grateful to more than two decades of students at UC Santa Barbara, Whitman College, and UC Riverside for their unending questions and curiosities that have helped me to hone my teaching abilities, piqued my interest, and ceaselessly pushed me toward greater insight and inclusion in my teaching. Special thanks to Danielle Dempsey and Kathryn Phillips, who served as the teaching assistants for the course in which this book was piloted at UCR. They were on the front lines as our students grappled with the ideas presented here, and they were the ones who gave me the clearest sense of what was working well and what was not. Dani and Katie, it's always a pleasure to work and learn with you!

I grew up watching my parents in the classroom, and learned much of my teaching style and pedagogical principles from them. Although we lost my dad in 2018 his lessons live on, and I still have the joy of occasionally having my mom visit my classes. My brother comes too, sometimes! Thanks for teaching inspiration to W. Wayne Wilcox, Margaret R. Wilcox, Wynn Gadkar-Wilcox, and my sister-in-law Sujata Gadkar-Wilcox.

Nicole Pitsavas gives me strength, courage, and laughter. May family members yet to come finally make it into our lives.

And finally, as always, a heartbroken trail of bread crumbs for J., lost but never forgotten, should they ever choose to question the stories they've been told and come searching for the truth.

Liz Wilson: I'm grateful to Miami University for providing support to travel to the University of Oslo early on, when face-to-face collaboration for this project was especially needed. The Miami University Humanities Center helped the process along with a grant that funded a research apprentice to help me track down sources. I'm grateful to students in my Marriage Across Cultures classes who have, over the years, helped me think through much of the material presented here. Gratitude is also due to my departmental colleagues at Miami University, who have been extremely helpful in their comments on key ideas and approaches. Colleague and ride-share companion Hillel Gray proved to be a great conversation partner, carefully considering issues and problems on the way to work and back. Others have made the research process fun by their enthusiastic support. Lisa Sommer, in particular, took a keen interest in many of the topics covered here and dug up some lovely research gems. Finally, Jenn Grant gives me so many things a researcher needs: poetry and contemplative practice every day, ecstatic dance on Sunday mornings, and a kitchen filled with spices from every continent on the planet.

Preface for instructors

Thank you for selecting *Religion, the Body and Sexuality* for your course. In this Preface we discuss the layout of the book, the reasoning behind the book's design, suggestions for teaching with our thematic approach, and the teaching tools we have woven into the book. As seasoned instructors of religion and sexuality courses, we have designed the book we wanted to use in the classroom and have even pilot-tested a draft in our own courses. We hope you find it as engaging and pedagogically useful as we do, and we encourage you to send us feedback on what works well and what could use further fine-tuning.

Teaching religious studies thematically

The thematic design of this book is a response to the widespread critique of the "world religions" paradigm in religious studies (e.g., Asad 1993; Masuzawa 2005), and the subsequent gap between how religious studies scholars discuss religion and how available classroom resources present it. Critics of the world religions model have raised a number of concerns ranging from the inaccurate imposition of the concept of religion onto cultures in which it is not an emic category to the distorted and simplistic image of religions that is produced by the effort to make them into parallel and comparable entities. Those of us who find such critiques persuasive are often left to our own devices to re-tool our courses so that what we teach our students reflects the current thinking in the field. Some departments of religious studies have altered their curriculum to remove world religions courses, instead offering more in-depth surveys of one or two religions at a time that allow the instructors to cover the historical and geographical diversity of practices and world-concepts within those religions. Others have changed their gateway, introductory course to focus more on theories about religion. Some textbooks have caught up with these changes. In comparative thematic courses, however, such as courses on religion and the body or religion and sexuality, the temptation to return to a world religions model can be quite strong simply because it is such an easy one with which to work, and because students still enter our classrooms expecting it. The limitations of the model remain the same in these courses; however, the alternative is a complete syllabus redesign, one often not supported by correspondingly redesigned textbooks. Except in cases where the instructor has the time to put together a hefty course reader, or cases where the students are advanced enough to read a series of monographs, the challenges faced by those teaching thematic courses can make it difficult to break away from the world religions paradigm.

We, too, have faced these challenges. In fact, when one of us introduced a new course on critical heterosexuality studies in religion, she began by designing the syllabus she ideally wanted to teach but then realized that there were no corresponding books on which to base such a syllabus. Although her syllabus at the time was forced to change, becoming structured around a series of monographs instead, the "fantasy syllabus" became the backbone for the thematic design we use here.

In addition to avoiding the simplistic overviews of a world religions focus in a sexuality textbook, our thematic design allows students to approach each religion from a place of specificity rather than generalization and to recognize that many religious perspectives more closely resemble those from similarly conservative or liberal branches of other religions than they do the perspectives of other branches of the same religion. When it comes to sexuality and the body and indeed to many other topics, for instance, a Hasidic Jew may prove to have much more in common with a socially conservative Muslim or a conservative evangelical Christian than with a Reform Jew. Likewise, a same sex attracted Thai Buddhist in Bangkok may have experiences of acceptance and rejection that resemble far more closely those of an Indonesian Muslim in Jakarta or a Filipinx Catholic in Manila than those of a white Buddhist in Los Angeles. A thematic approach makes such discoveries possible for students. It underscores the importance of transnationalism and globalization in the study of religions, bodies, and sexualities, and it gives students tools to think in more complex ways about the interactions between religions, bodies, and sex in the worlds around them.

We have found that one challenge of teaching a thematic model arises because the world religions model is woven throughout the cultural discourse of many regions of the world in the twenty-first century. Thus, although an instructor may set out to disrupt the world religions narrative, students put an equal amount of effort into reinstating it. While we believe that these dynamics offer an important opportunity to intervene in simplistic cultural narratives, such intervention is at times easier said than done. Students may express frustration, for instance, at reading about same-sex attracted Muslims without first knowing "more about Islam." This "more" is often a request for the basic and limited overview with which so many of us are familiar (indeed, which many of us can give in our sleep): the history of the Prophet Muhammad and the revelation of the Qur'an; the division into Shi'a and Sunni, with perhaps a brief nod to Sufism; the Five Pillars; and a quick rundown of "what Islam teaches." In addition to being of necessity overly simplified and suggesting to students that Islam "belongs" in the Middle East and specifically among Arabs, where all of the action in this version of the story takes place, such an overview arguably offers students very little information that can help them understand the lives and experiences of same sex attracted Muslims. Yet many will express significant discomfort with learning the specifics without the generalities.

In this book, we have attempted to anticipate such concerns in two ways. First, in the Introduction we discuss the problems with the world religions model and explain why we take a thematic approach instead and why students stand to learn more, and more accurately, about religions through this approach. Second, we offer relevant background when a new religious topic comes up, and we offer suggestions to students for further reading about the religions addressed in each chapter. Instructors who wish to add their own resources might consider an assignment that encourages students to explore the diversity within a religion of their choice, perhaps one with which they are unfamiliar. Another option is to offer students additional resources for learning more about any religion; by recommending certain resources, perhaps the *Encyclopedia of Religion* or reliable online sources, instructors can encourage students who are seeking deeper understanding toward sources that will actually provide such an understanding rather than mislead the student or confirm existing biases. Other instructors may wish to pair this book with a standard introductory world religions textbook, using each to inform and critique the other, or to pair it with a newer-format introductory textbook that shares this book's resistance to the world religions model but also offers students additional grounding in the study of religion as a field. We have found that introducing a thematic approach to the study of religion works best when the instructor explains the reasoning behind the approach and provides resources to address some of the frustrations that inevitably arise when the world religions narrative is circumvented.

Teaching tools

Case studies

Each thematic chapter of the book begins with two case studies. Rather than choose obvious and often well-rehearsed examples of the intersections between religion, bodies, and sexualities – such as the French ban on Muslim women's head coverings or the movement among conservative evangelicals in the U.S. to declare discrimination against LGBTIQ+ people a religious right – we have attempted to select case studies that will be less familiar to students. Our hope is that by approaching these case studies without prior knowledge of them, students will be better able to discern their key themes and to derive broader meaning from them about the interactions of religions, sexualities, and bodies. We also hope to move the conversation in the classroom beyond a debate over whether the state or religion is the agent of repression to a more complex consideration of religion, representation, and social power. We have attempted in our selection of case studies to be broadly representative of a wide range of religions, including indigenous religions and smaller or new religious movements, of regions of the globe, and of time periods. We use the case studies to draw students into a particular theme, to ground their ideas about the theme in actual histories and contemporary events, and to encourage them to reason inductively from these cases in order to begin discerning the various ways in which the theme of that chapter relates to sexualities, bodies, and religions. Between them, the two case studies in each chapter illustrate many, and in some cases most, of the topics in the chapter. As an instructor, you might consider asking students to generate their own topics from the case studies, or to find the topics that are addressed in the chapter within the case studies. We make a similar suggestion to readers in the Introduction.

Resources at the ends of chapters

The "Applications and reflections" questions that appear at the end of each chapter are not review questions but rather are designed to encourage students to engage with and apply the material they have learned in the chapter. Many have no right answer. These could be used in the classroom as preparation questions to be completed before the start of class, as in-class discussion questions (indeed, some are designed to be discussed in a group), or as paper or exam topics.

Each thematic chapter closes with a set of recommended readings and films, listed under "Resources for further study." The films may be useful for in-class screenings or movie nights; some of the readings are article-length and could be assigned to supplement the chapter. Recommended readings and films can also be used in assignments.

End matter: glossary and teaching resources

Please be aware, and help your students to be aware, of the glossary at the end of the book. Words in the text that are included in the glossary are printed in boldface and are defined in the text when they are initially used. Also included in the back of the book is a list of additional teaching resources, including primary source material such as films and websites that we have found to be useful in the classroom. Some of these primary materials are best presented in a setting where they can be contextualized and discussed; for this reason we have listed these resources separately from the resources for further study at the end of each chapter.

Happy teaching!

Nina Hoel, Melissa Wilcox, and Liz Wilson

Introduction

The thirteenth-century Flemish writer Hadewijch was a Christian **mystic**, someone who has religious experiences that transcend human understanding. Hadewijch experienced a love for Jesus Christ that was simultaneously ecstatic and agonizing: ecstatic when she felt oneness with him, agonizing because that merging would never be final while she still lived in a human body on earth. Like many medieval Christian mystics, especially women, Hadewijch had visions that were intensely physical and she understood Christ in physical terms as well. Historian Caroline Walker Bynum tells us that Hadewijch described one of her visions of Christ this way: "He came himself to me, took me entirely in his arms, and pressed me to him; and all my members felt his in full felicity, in accordance with the desire of my heart and my humanity. So I was outwardly satisfied and fully transported" (Bynum 1988, 156).

Around a century later, a Christian writer and mystic in Italy named Catherine of Siena wrote that when Christ had married her, he did so not with a ring of precious metals and gemstones but with one of flesh – the foreskin of his penis that was removed when he was circumcised as an infant Jewish boy. Interestingly, the men who later wrote her life story ignored Catherine's testimony and insisted that she had married Jesus with a beautiful ring of gold and gems (Bynum 1988, 174–175).

These stories about Christian women mystics in medieval Europe challenge the assumptions that many people have about the relationship between Christianity, sexuality, and the human body. Even more, they challenge many people's ideas about the bodies of sacred beings, the bodies of **renunciants** (people who renounce the pleasures and comforts of everyday life, usually for religious purposes) and especially of women renunciants, and the proper ways in which the divine and the human should relate. Many people living in the twenty-first century find these stories shocking, but many medieval Christians found them sacred.

The shock and discomfort that some people experience when they think of religion being expressed through bodily embraces and sexual organs shows us an idea of the sacred, or at least of sacred beings, as separate from sexuality. For some people, human sexuality is a part of the mundane, everyday world whereas the sacred is special, set apart, and separated from other events and activities. From this perspective, bringing the two together violates the separation between the mundane world and the sacred one; rather than elevate the former, it debases the latter. But not even all religions that have an important role for **celibate** (sexually inactive) practitioners do so because they see sexuality as **profane**, as the opposite of the sacred. Some religious texts suggest that sexuality is extremely powerful, and that if one refrains from expending that power sexually it can instead be harnessed as spiritual power. Others find the effects of sexual interaction to be harmful to spiritual progress not because sex is profane but because it creates attachment to other human beings or to this world. Even among religions whose most advanced practitioners live celibate lives, understandings of the relationship between religion and sexuality differ. How much more must these understandings vary when we consider the many religious practitioners who are not celibate, and the religions that frown on or even forbid celibacy?

This book is about the rich and varied connections, across human history and around the globe, between religions, bodies, and sexualities. Since that's too big a story for even a huge encyclopedia to tell, much less one textbook, our version here is a kind of sampler platter, arranged into topics and themes. Rather than discuss one religion at a time, trying in vain to cover everything about sexualities and bodies in that religion's past and present manifestations, and then starting over again with the next religion in the next chapter, we think there's a lot more to learn by looking at the interesting similarities and divergences in specific themes across different religions, time periods, and regions of the globe. This is a deeply comparative approach to religious studies, and we think you'll find resonances in each chapter with religious practices, beliefs, and traditions that you know about from your own traditions, those of your friends, and those in the world around you.

Studying the connections between religions, sexualities, and bodies requires that we use the tools of several different academic fields at once; using any one set of tools would give us an incomplete picture, kind of like trying to paint a beautiful sunset using only black pigment on a white background. In this chapter we'll introduce you to these different fields and to some of their most important theories and methods. Once you have those tools in your toolkit, we'll tell you a little about how to use the book. Then you'll be ready to dive in! Let's start with the study of religion.

Religious Studies: the study of religion as a human phenomenon

People study religion in lots of different ways and for lots of different reasons. *Why* they study it often determines *how* they study it. Many people, from children to elders, scholars and religious leaders to non-specialists, study their own religions in order to become better practitioners or to help make their religion better in some way. They may learn sacred stories or songs from an elder, study sacred texts, read ancient and revered interpretations of those texts, work with an elder or other teacher to learn specialized practices, or create new stories, practices, songs, and interpretations. Scholars who engage professionally in these sorts of activities do so both in religious settings such as rabbinical schools, madrasas, gurdwaras, temples, and seminaries, and in some secular schools.

While what you learn from this book might end up affecting your own religious practices and beliefs, that's not the purpose of this kind of study of religion. Some people call the approach that this book takes the "academic study of religion" or "religious studies." But scholars who study their own religion in order to engage in and improve it are also academics, and they're certainly doing a form of study. So for clarity, we'll use the terms "non-confessional" and "descriptive-analytical" interchangeably to specify the kind of religious studies you'll encounter in this book. One way to think about this approach to studying religion is that it's the study of religion as a human phenomenon.

Religious studies in this sense is an interdisciplinary (connecting or bridging between disciplines) or even transdisciplinary (combining across disciplines) field. Although it has specific ideas about how religion itself should be studied, it draws widely from many different academic fields, or disciplines, for the methods it uses to do so. Scholars in this area of religious studies may engage in sociological or anthropological methods, use cultural and media analysis or postcolonial theory, practice history or archaeology or philosophy or linguistics, work in art history or ethnomusicology, or even focus their work on psychology and neuroscience. Many combine different methods in innovative and insightful ways. The overarching goal in this field is not to study a specific aspect of religion – religion in popular culture, say, or the neurology of religious visions – although most scholars have such a specialty, but instead to study religion from many different angles and perspectives as a human phenomenon.

In order to approach religion in this way, we need to begin with a thorough understanding of the religious practices, perspectives, and **world-concepts** – ways of understanding the world around us – of the people, texts, stories, architecture, or other phenomena we're trying to study. The early twentieth-century Dutch philosopher Gerardus van der Leeuw (1967) called this approach "empathetic understanding"; we might think of it as understanding someone's religious experiences from inside their head or inside their culture. Van der Leeuw suggested that the best way to attain such empathy was through what he called *epoché*, or "suspension." By this, he meant suspension of one's own world-concept while trying to develop empathy with another's. This doesn't mean that someone doing descriptive-analytical studies of religion has to give up their religion or adopt the religion they're studying. Instead, think about the problem this way:

- Imagine that you're studying a religious group that believes there is a race of more advanced beings living on other planets, who sometimes pass by Earth in spaceships that we can't detect. If you want to comprehend the actions chosen by members of this group, you need to develop an empathetic understanding of what it's like to live in a reality where such beings exist. This is easy if you share those beliefs, but if you don't, then your incredulity can get in your way. How can you deeply understand members of this religious group if your thoughts keep focusing on how ridiculous you think their ideas are? Practicing *epoché* in your studies of this group, as a non-believer, means suspending or setting aside your doubts, not so that you can come to share their beliefs but so that you can imagine what it might be like to do so. (By the way, the most famous group with the beliefs described here is called Heaven's Gate; many of their members left their earthly bodies behind back in the 1990s in an attempt to get to one of those spaceships.)

If you haven't tried this approach before, you might be surprised by how logical certain actions appear once you gain an empathetic understanding of the world-concept on which they were based. In the case of Heaven's Gate, you might start to understand that what media accounts called "mass suicide" was, for the movement's members, a logical attempt to leave a spiritually underdeveloped plane of existence and advance to a more highly evolved one. As sociologist Meredith McGuire writes, "a mode of action is not irrational if a person perceives it to work" (McGuire 2008, 33).

Once you've developed an empathetic understanding of the world-concept that underlies the practices, texts, artifacts, people, or groups you're studying, what next? Here, scholars differ in their perspectives. Some, mostly older, opinions suggest that we should stop at description and perhaps categorization. Scholars who use this approach believe that once you've understood, and described your understanding, your job is done. Others suggest that instead scholars should be analyzing what they find in light of other scholarship in religious studies: in what ways do your findings align with current scholarly understandings of the group or religion you're studying? In what ways do they align with current understandings of religion as a whole? In what ways do they differ from those understandings? Do the differences perhaps require us to re-think our ideas about religion? Many of those who promote such an approach believe that scholars should keep their analysis strictly academic, focused on advancing scholarly knowledge. Some frame this perspective through the value of objectivity, the idea that the role of the scholar is to observe and describe the world around us as dispassionately as possible and that such dispassion brings us closer to the truth, to an accurate description of reality.

Others, though, disagree with this perspective on objectivity. They say that we all have a perspective, a specific angle from which we think about and perceive the topics of our study, and that by claiming to be dispassionate and detached we simply end up hiding the impact that our passions and commitments actually have on the knowledge we produce as scholars. This approach, often supported by scholars who work in areas closely related to social justice concerns, also raises questions about the ethics of dispassionate description in an unjust world. Is it ethical, they ask, for a scholar to dispassionately describe the perspectives of certain Christians who believe that white people are the true Israel, that people of color and white people should not intermarry, and that same-sex eroticism should be punished by death? Is it ethical to dispassionately describe the perspectives of the small group of such Christians who believe they are called by God to assassinate interracial couples, Jews, and LGBTIQ+ people? No, they answer, and they argue that those who have the skills and the expertise to produce knowledge about religion also have the responsibility to use those skills and that expertise to make the world a more just and equitable place. But, in keeping with the principle of *epoché*, scholars who hold these perspectives and work within non-confessional religious studies don't think that they should make claims that the Christians mentioned above aren't "real Christians"; nor do these scholars think it's their job to argue for anti-racist, anti-homophobic, anti-transphobic, and pacifist interpretations of Christianity as the "true religion." However, their critiques often entail demonstrating the connections between, for instance, colonial forms of religion and the larger oppressive project of colonialism, or the resonances between self-avowedly racist, violent forms of Christianity in the present day and the attitudes toward race expressed in seventeenth-century white Christians' sermons.

These tools of *epoché* and empathetic understanding, along with a consideration of whose perspective you agree with when it comes to the next steps after you use these tools, will be invaluable as you move into the study of religion in this book. You're likely to encounter connections between sexuality, bodies, and religion that will surprise you; when this happens, practice using these tools to suspend the assumptions that led to your surprise, and work instead to understand the perspectives that make these connections logical, even obvious, to those who hold to them. But thinking about religion, bodies, and sexualities raises another question: What exactly *is* religion?

A U.S. Supreme Court justice once famously claimed to know pornography when he saw it; he made this claim instead of giving a specific legal definition of pornography. Many people in cultures where the word "religion" is recognized take the same approach: we think we know religion when we see it. But do we? Here's an interesting exercise to test that theory.

- Set your reading down, and in no more than sixty seconds, write a definition of religion.
- Was that easy? Hard? Why?

Now read over your definition, and consider whether there are exceptions to it. Many people, for instance, focus their definitions on belief. But there are religions where belief isn't particularly central. The defining aspect of the religion isn't what you believe, but what you do. For many Hindus, for example, reciting a set of **creeds**, or statements of belief, is fairly irrelevant to their religious lives, even if they're devout practitioners who regularly honor and make offerings to the gods. So belief can't be a definitive part of religion. Did your definition include God, or deities? Some branches of Buddhism have no deities; in other branches there are gods but they're simply a particularly comfortable form of reincarnation. They don't suffer much, if at all, but they do die – and the reincarnation that follows such luxury is held to be quite unpleasant. So gods also aren't a definitive part of religion, which means that worship isn't, either. Now what?

To solve this problem, it may help to understand why the problem is there to begin with. The concept of religion as a universal human societal institution is an invented concept, what some scholars call a **social construct**. As scholars like anthropologist Talal Asad (1993), sociologist Meredith McGuire (2008), and historian of religions Tomoko Masuzawa (2005) have explained, this meaning of religion came about in the aftermath of bloody wars that wracked Europe in the sixteenth and seventeenth centuries, after Protestant Christianity split apart from Roman Catholic Christianity. Desperate for the bloodshed to stop and to find a way for Christians of different denominations to live together, some philosophers began to look for the similarities between Protestantism and Catholicism. They suggested that maybe the two groups could accept each other's differences and agree that religion was a social good no matter whether it was Protestant or Catholic.

Astute readers will have noticed that these philosophers were (so far) just using their new understanding of religion to argue that two different kinds of Christianity were both good for society. Not only did they leave out other Christians, like Eastern Orthodox Christians and Coptic Christians, but other religions that were also present in Europe at the time – most notably Judaism – played no role in this new concept. They didn't yet fall under the rubric of "religion." Over the years, though, that changed. For a while, religion retained its connotation of "good," and scholars suggested various qualities that made cultural beliefs and practices "religion" (good) rather than "superstition" or "magic" (bad). These qualities were often based on assumptions about reason; beliefs and practices that these philosophers deemed rational counted as religion, while those they deemed irrational were relegated to the realm of superstition. By stressing belief, textual study, and prayer over practices such as following kosher dietary laws (*kashrut*) or placing a small sacred scroll (a *mezuzah*) on one's doorpost, some Jewish philosophers managed to create a space for Judaism within this slowly expanding perspective on religion; this process was an important part of the origins of the Jewish Reform movement and later the Conservative movement, which accepted some of the changes instituted by Reform Judaism but refused others. Now some branches of both Christianity and Judaism were religions, according to these European scholars; everything else was still defined as superstition, magic, or **heresy** (false belief).

Because these early framings of religion focused on beliefs, texts, and teachings, they also focused on aspects of religion that were most easily accessible to men and to economic elites. In order for a person's religious practice to focus on reasoning through a sacred text, that person must have had access to education. They must have been able to read complex texts, often in a different language from the one they spoke in everyday life, and they must have been taught the principles of reason that European philosophers promoted. In other words, in order to practice in a way that would be understood as "religious" in this context, they had to have had access to an elite European education and a religious education. Very few women had such access, and few men whose families were not financially well off had such access either. Furthermore, both Christianity and Judaism in Europe at the time had important ritual roles for women that focused largely on aspects of home life. These shifting definitions of religion redefined women's practices and poor people's practices as "superstition" and "magic," not religion.

As the concept of religion was developing in Europe, the reach of European colonization was also expanding, and it brought the conversation about defining religion along with it. Weighed against European Christian principles of reason, belief, and the centrality of texts in representing the sacred, tradition after tradition was dismissed as superstition by European colonizers. Oral cultures, their histories and sacred stories preserved for millennia through oral tradition as carefully as medieval European scholars had copied the Jewish Torah or the Christian Gospels, found themselves brushed aside as ignorant because their cultural knowledge was recorded in speech rather than in writing. Asian and North African cultures, in line with a rising European **Orientalist** perspective, saw their contemporary practices derided as corrupted versions of long-lost, once-great teachings. Significantly, though, Orientalist scholars began to deem those ancient teachings, and the texts in which they were found, religious. Even more strikingly, these European scholars suggested, in theories that have since been disproven, that they and not contemporary Asians were the descendants of the people who wrote the ancient texts, and therefore were the inheritors of Asian traditions they were now willing to deem "religions." This was the case especially with European Orientalists' understanding of the history of India, where both Hinduism and Buddhism began. Since these scholars thought that they and other Europeans, not contemporary South Asians, were the descendants of the authors of early Hindu and Buddhist texts, it's perhaps not surprising that they were willing to consider at least *ancient* Hindu and Buddhist *texts* as religions.

So now there were four religions: Christianity, Judaism, Hinduism, and Buddhism. The tale of the "world religions" was beginning to emerge. Over time, Islam would be added to constitute the group that some religious studies scholars jokingly call the "Big Five." Some systems add religions like Sikhism and Jainism to the list; some add Taoism or Confucianism, although there's ongoing debate over whether Confucianism is a religion or a philosophy. As you can guess by now, the answer to that question depends on how you define religion! Other scholars have grappled with how to include indigenous lifeways and traditions, and still others have pushed for the inclusion of new religious movements that are unrelated to the "Big Five" (or Seven, or Eight). These moves toward inclusion clearly indicate a development that took place roughly around the start of the twentieth century toward defining religion as a universally shared aspect of human life. By this time, people who studied religion knew it when they saw it, even if they struggled to define exactly what "it" was.

So now we had "world religions." To some extent the narratives of superstition and magic continued alongside this conversation about world religions throughout the twentieth century and into the twenty-first; in some ways discussions of "good" and "bad" religion replaced the divide between "religion" and "superstition." With "religion" now considered to be something every human culture had, there was no way to retain the equation between "religion" and "socially beneficial"; instead, religions had to be judged and labeled as socially beneficial or socially destructive. This divide between "good religion" and "bad religion" is still with us in many cultures today; in some regions, "good religion" is now called "spirituality" by many people in the culture. In other places, the meaning of "spirituality" is closer to "bad religion" because people understand the word "spirituality" to refer to what they consider an irresponsible, shallow, and self-serving practice. Scholars who work in the descriptive-analytical aspect of religious studies, however, generally try to avoid making such distinctions.

There are other complications, too, to the usage and definition of the word "religion." Cultures that believe they "know religion when they see it" often apply the word to all other cultures, yet many cultures don't have an indigenous term that means "religion." If so many cultures don't have a word for religion, can it really be accurate to claim that religion exists in all cultures? The world religions story also imposes overarching groupings where they didn't exist before. The classic example of this phenomenon is Hinduism, which many historians tell us was invented by the British when they colonized India. Prior to British colonization, people in South Asia followed many different beliefs and practices. Buddhists had largely left the subcontinent, but Sikhs were there, and Jains, and Christians, Muslims, and Jews. There were also – and often interwoven with other practices – a wide range of sacred stories and ritual practices centered on both local and more widely-known deities. How one engaged in these practices varied depending on region, caste, and family tradition. The language of practice varied depending on region and caste, as did the deities with whom one typically interacted. While these varied practices had shared features, as indigenous traditions from neighboring regions tend to do the world over, they did not constitute a singular tradition. But Orientalist scholars and British colonials, looking for the "Indian religion," created it by naming it (like India itself) after the Indus River. Thus: "Hinduism." A similar colonial misperception led to the ongoing, inaccurate categorization of indigenous North American lifeways as "Native American religion" or, in keeping with the newer "good religion-bad religion" language and the current popularity of all things Native American among many non-Native people, "Native American spirituality."

These histories make it clear that the concept of religion is a cultural construct, and that it also has often been a political tool. So what do we do? Should we give up studying religion altogether? Should we just study cultures, avoid attempts at comparison, and use only concepts that are what anthropologists call **emic** – that is, stemming from within the cultures themselves? Maybe not. Because to make things even more complicated, social constructs have a way of taking on a life of their own. As critical race theorist Kimberlé Crenshaw (1991), among many others, has reminded us, the fact that something is socially constructed doesn't mean it isn't real.

Take Hinduism, for example. The British may have invented Hinduism as "the religion of India" out of a group of related sacred stories and practices (disregarding all of the other religions present in that deeply pluralist region), but as Indians intensified the fight to regain control of their society and to push the colonizers out, many of them rested their nationalist movement on a commitment to Hinduism. The partition of India and Pakistan in 1947, part of the British colonial retreat, relied on a definition of India as Hindu and Pakistan as Muslim. And today's Bharatiya Janata Party (BJP) in India promotes Hindutva, or Hindu nationalism, as a way of unifying the country, downplaying as the British did the religious pluralism that characterizes the Indian past and present.

The word "religion," even if as a borrowed word, is widely recognized around the world. Some groups have used legal arguments that their lifeways constitute a religion to gain much-needed rights from their government, even when they have no word in their own language to translate the word "religion." As historian Tisa Wenger has demonstrated (2009) in the context of Native American religious rights in the U.S., taking ownership of this constructed and political term as an activist strategy is not without its disadvantages. Like most political strategies used by disempowered groups, squeezing one's traditions into a government's definition of religion is a compromise in which the group may lose out in some areas but hopes overall to gain more than it loses.

As scholars and students of religion, we too may have to compromise. By acknowledging that the concept of religion is socially constructed, we release ourselves from the impossible task of trying to create a universally applicable definition of religion. Instead, we might take the advice of the late sociologist Peter Berger (1967), who recommended that scholars should define religion in whatever way would best help them to learn what they needed to learn in any given study. From this perspective, we can define religion one way when we're seeking to learn about people who call themselves "very religious," and another way when we're curious about the ways in which deeply committed nationalism functions like deeply committed religion. Is nationalism a religion? Are sports a religion? What about the Pastafarians, followers of the Church of the Flying Spaghetti Monster? Are they religious? Maybe that's not the right question to ask; maybe the right question is what we might learn about this complex set of human ideas and behaviors that we group under the made-up word "religion" when we study each phenomenon.

In this book, following Berger's advice, we'll define religion in the way that best helps us to learn about the connections between religions, bodies, and sexualities. We'll primarily be considering more-or-less organized movements that focus, seriously and sometimes parodically, on a reality beyond the human. Often, but not always, this reality includes superhuman beings like deities, demons, spirits, ancestors, ghosts, and the like. Often, but not always, such movements include a fairly standard set of practices and/or beliefs. They always include a world-concept, because all humans have a world-concept; it's simply our way of perceiving and comprehending the world around us. Not all world-concepts are religious – or are they? In this book we won't spend much time pondering where the boundaries of religion lie, but we *will* be exploring boundaries when it comes to bodies and sexualities. For that endeavor, we need the next set of tools: those of gender studies and transgender studies.

Gender studies and transgender studies

At a time when "gender reveal parties" are all the rage for expectant parents, let's get one thing clear right from the start: neither genetic testing nor an ultrasound can reveal a fetus' gender. Certainly the over-the-counter "gender testing kits" can't. Hormones, chromosomes, and external sexual organs are part of what defines sex, not gender. And just like religion, sex and gender are socially constructed. Like all constructs, they're also very real in their effects. But we're getting ahead of ourselves – let's back up and talk about the difference between sex and gender.

As a description rather than an action, "sex" refers to embodiment. When biologists say that a species exhibits sexual variation, they don't mean that the species has sex in lots of different ways; they mean that one of the ways in which the species varies within itself, both anatomically and physiologically, is connected with how it reproduces. Most species have a fair amount of anatomical variation, some of it common and some of it rare. Sometimes we call identifiable sets of variations "breeds," like with dogs or cats or chickens or horses. Some variations are simply part of a normal range of physical variation, such as differences in height or coloration. And sometimes they're connected to reproduction.

Not all species reproduce through the combination of two different elements such as egg and sperm, pollen and ovule, and so on. Some reproduce asexually — literally, without (differing) sexes – and some transition from one sex to another in order to reproduce. While humans do reproduce through the combination of two specific elements, we also come in more than two sexes. That is, the variation in the aspects of our bodies that scientists and others use to determine sex – our chromosomes, hormones, external and internal sex organs, and secondary sex characteristics such as breast development or beard growth – is far more complex than the binary categories of "male" and "female" would suggest. Historically, many cultures have recognized this complexity. The ancient Greeks named people with ambiguous genitalia "hermaphrodites" after Hermaphroditos, the child of the god Hermes and the goddess Aphrodite, and the ancient Jewish rabbis devoted a few of their writings to determining how such a person (whom they termed an *androgynos*) should best follow religious laws that pertained to women only and to men only. Today, many cultures recognize both variations in sex that arise during the body's development and those that are medically created. The most widely accepted respectful term in English today for the former is **intersex**; for the latter, many people today use the term **transsexual**. Some transsexual people do not see themselves as a third (or more) sex, but rather as the sex to which they have transitioned: male or female. Some see themselves as both a third sex and as male or female, and some intersex people are also transsexual. Already it's evident that how we name and categorize these specific forms of variation in human embodiment has at least as much, if not more, to do with culture as with biology.

This is what we mean by **social construction**: it's the process by which a culture determines that certain aspects or traits of human beings have meaning while others don't, and the process by which the culture then decides what that meaning is. European cultures, for example, have long believed that how people interact with the sacred is a meaningful aspect of human variation; those philosophers who were worried about wars between Protestant Christians and Roman Catholic Christians named that variation "religion" and chose a specific meaning for it. Over the following centuries, scholars, activists, colonizers, nationalists, and lots of other people have challenged and altered that meaning. In the context of human anatomies and physiologies, when we say that sex is socially constructed we aren't saying that some society invented the fact that some people have penises and beards, some people have vaginas and breasts, and some people have various combinations of these traits. Instead, we're saying that the process by which these particular traits come to be important in distinguishing humans from one another is a fundamentally social process, and the meanings assigned to each kind of trait are chosen by the cultures as well. We call those meanings gender – more on that below. But if you're still puzzling over the idea that sex is socially constructed, consider all of the other human variations that aren't assigned the same importance and meaning as sex. All humans, for instance, have either a concave (innie) or a convex (outie) navel, yet cultures generally do not divide humans into "innies" and "outies," preventing them from swimming in the same pool or allowing only outies to work at certain professions. While people are often treated differently based on their height, we don't usually give different toys to children who are expected to be tall than we give to children who are expected to be short. Differing heights, which result in differing abilities to complete certain tasks, have traditionally led to some differences in social roles; differing belly buttons produce differences in appearance. Yet most cultures don't focus on these traits as the source of significant meaning about a person or that person's role in the world – certainly not to the extent that they focus on the meaning of sex.

Many biological and medical textbooks today still present human sexual variation as binary – female and male – and reduce all other variations to "abnormalities" in maleness and femaleness. As you should be able to see by now, this type of categorization is an intentional (and, many people feel, a demeaning) choice. It also has a fairly short history; as feminist scientist Anne Fausto-Sterling (2000) explains, intersex bodies began to be medically scrutinized, classified, and reduced to "flawed" versions of femaleness and maleness only during the nineteenth century, and then only in Europe and its settler colonies such as the U.S., Canada, and Australia. While most if not all human cultures differentiate between male and female bodies, then, differentiating them on a strict binary with no room for less common variants is a new development, and is relatively rare in human history. Certainly intersex bodies have not always been regarded neutrally by human cultures; some have revered intersex people and others have reviled them. Contemporary medical science, though, is the first to designate intersex people as flawed males or females and to attempt to "repair" the flaw through extensive childhood medical treatment. Since the late twentieth century, intersex rights activists have been protesting such non-consensual treatment, which often leaves extensive physical and emotional scars, and advocating for a return to a culture that appreciates rather than pathologizes the rich variety of human anatomies and physiologies.

Whereas sex is a biological term, referring to a varying set of anatomical, genetic, and physiological traits, **gender** refers to the roles someone plays, is expected to play, or desires to play in society. Some people say that gender is the identity and sex is the biology, but that's not quite true since people identify with particular sexes as well. For some males, maleness is an important part of their identity regardless of how they identify in terms of gender; the same is true for females, and it's even more true for intersex and transsexual people who often have to insist on their right to identify with a particular sex. But many (not all) societies assign a specific set of tasks to males and another set of tasks to females. These tasks are called gender roles. When combined with widespread social ideas about what males and females are generally like, these gender roles become part of a set of gendered categories that offer people a shortcut for making assumptions about others. In societies that are structured heavily around gender, "women" and "men" are usually the main two available genders. "Femininity" refers to the gender roles, traits, and appearances associated with women, and "masculinity" refers to those associated with men. Remember, "man" and "woman" are gender terms; they're not the same as "female" and "male," which are sex terms. In many cultures it's possible to be a female man or a male woman, or (put in other terms) a masculine female and a feminine male.

Try this exercise to explore what you already know about gender in the world around you:

- Pick a common gender that's widely accepted in your culture. In most cultures, "woman" and "man" are both good choices.
- Write down a list of positive traits that your culture commonly associates with that gender specifically, such as strength, nurturance, courage, or kindness.
- Write down a list of negative traits that your culture commonly associates with that gender specifically, such as greed, violence, or vanity.
- Write down a list of roles that your culture commonly associates with that gender specifically, such as political leadership, parenting, growing crops, or getting an advanced education.
- Write down a list of roles that people of that gender hardly ever play in your culture, and the reasons why your culture says people of that gender can't play those roles. Are any of these reasons connected to the traits you wrote down above?
- Think about people you know who consider themselves to be that gender. In what ways do they match the traits and roles you wrote down? In what ways do they not match?

Probably the people you know match these traits in some ways and differ from them in others. That's because gender is socially constructed, and as a social construct it has very real effects in the world. Societies and their individual members play an important role in perpetuating the reality of this social construction by helping new members of the society to learn their assigned roles, to understand them as natural, and at times, to learn how and when to deviate from or resist those roles. But how are people assigned to a gender? Well, that depends on the society and on how many genders exist within it.

In many societies, gender is assigned at or before birth and is based on sex. Fetuses and newborn babies who are designated as female are assigned the gender "girl" and are subsequently taught a culturally acceptable version of femininity; those who are designated as male are assigned the gender "boy" and taught a culturally acceptable version of masculinity. There are many different culturally acceptable forms of gender. For instance, some girls learn to be sweet and generous, and to value and cultivate their beauty over all else; others learn to be outgoing, smart, and sexy; still others learn to be athletic, outdoorsy, and self-reliant. Many girls combine these traits in other ways, and with additional traits. As a result, what it is to be a girl or a woman, a boy or a man, can vary quite a bit and still remain within culturally accepted boundaries.

Developmental psychologists tell us that children understand gender earlier than they understand sex, and that this capacity usually develops between two and three years of age in cultures that distinguish people in significant ways based on gender. When this understanding first develops, a child can tell from appearance whether a traditionally-gendered doll or person is a boy or a girl but cannot make the same distinction when the figure is naked, even if it's anatomically detailed. In cultures that tie gender closely to sex, it's within the following year that children develop the ability to understand sex and its cultural relationship to gender. But before this point, when they start to distinguish genders, some children become very clear that they are not the gender to which they have been assigned. While in many Western countries in the twenty-first century these children are identified as **transgender** and are supported in that identity to greater or lesser degrees by their parents, communities, and medical providers, other cultures in both the past and the present have had other ways of approaching children's genders.

Many Native North American and First Nations cultures, for instance, encompass multiple understandings of gender, ranging from three genders to as many as five in traditional Navajo (Diné) culture. In such cultures, people who follow traditional practices often attribute gendered meaning to the toys and activities each child prefers. As consistent patterns develop in regard to gendered toys and activities, traditionalist adults will encourage children to further explore their chosen roles and will begin to teach them to perform those roles well. Such cultures often have gender terms for females who perform what are traditionally women's tasks, males who perform traditional men's tasks, females who perform men's tasks, and males who perform women's tasks. Sometimes the latter two are the same gender. Navajo tradition adds intersex people as a separate gender, for a total of five. With the wide range of languages spoken, and being actively reclaimed, among Native peoples, every culture that recognizes roles beyond male man and female woman has different terms for these roles. Since 1990, however, some gender-variant and same-sex attracted Native people in North America, including people who identify as lesbian, gay, bisexual, transgender, intersex, or queer+ (LGBTIQ+), have organized together under the English-language translation of the Ojibwe term *niizh manidoowag*: Two Spirit.

People who do not consider their own gender to match closely to the gender they were assigned at birth use a number of different words to describe themselves. Particularly in Western countries, the word transgender is especially common. Depending on the person using the term, "transgender" can sometimes refer solely to people who identify with the gender that is "opposite" to their assigned gender in a binary system: to people assigned male, and therefore as boys, at birth who identify as women, and to people assigned female, and therefore as girls, at birth who identify as men. At the other end of the spectrum of this word's usage, "transgender" is used as an overarching term for all people who are not **cisgender** – that is, who do not identify with the gender they were assigned at birth. In this usage, "transgender" may include other identities such as genderqueer, gender fluid, agender, and nonbinary, all of which name various ways of identifying neither with "man" nor with "woman" as forms of gender.

Many cultures around the world, both past and present and on every continent, have traditional gender-variant roles. Some are reserved for people born male; fewer are reserved for people born female. Some are reserved for intersex people, while others encompass all sexual and gender variance beyond the statistically more common masculine man and feminine woman. But in keeping with gender being socially constructed, these gender-variant roles differ across cultures not only in how they are named but in how they are understood and lived out. "Transgender" is a term chosen by many gender-variant people in European and European-derived cultures to describe themselves; applying the term internationally and trans-historically can produce many of the same problems as applying the term "religion" across these cultural and historical divides. People who identify with traditional, indigenous, gender variant roles may choose (or feel it necessary) to use the term "transgender" in order to make themselves and their organizations comprehensible to foreign agencies and funding sources. They may also find the term strategically useful for organizing solidarity movements across cultural boundaries. But because the term "transgender" was developed in the West, some people see it as a Western imposition. It carries meanings that may not match those of indigenous gender-variant roles, and it can create opposition in colonized or postcolonial countries where people may be willing (even if reluctantly) to tolerate traditional gender variance but may see a "transgender rights" movement as a colonial imposition. Because of these complexities, while recognizing that people around the world make strategic use of the term "transgender," we will use "gender variant" rather than "transgender" as a general, comparative descriptor and will use indigenous terms when speaking about specific cultural traditions. Of course, this includes using the term "transgender" to describe organizations and people who understand themselves that way.

The topics we've covered in this section – the social construction of sex and gender, the meanings that different cultures assign to specific sexes and genders, the roles assigned to intersex and gender-variant people, and the portrayals of various genders in cultures over time – fall within two closely related academic fields: gender studies and transgender studies. Although gender studies considers all genders, along with their relationships to bodies and sexes, to be under its purview, through much of its history it has tended to focus primarily on cisgender people. When it has turned its attention to gender-variant people, this has often been in the interest of learning more about cisgender people through studying those who are not cisgender. For these reasons, the development of transgender studies over the past several decades has been critically important. In considering the relationship between religions, bodies, and sexualities, we will draw heavily on the tools provided by both gender studies and transgender studies.

Sexuality studies and queer studies

The third set of tools we'll need in our methodological and theoretical toolkit for studying sexualities, bodies, and religions comes from sexuality studies and queer studies. In one form or another, modern sexuality studies has been around since the middle of the nineteenth century, although it's changed a lot over that time. Gay and lesbian studies branched out of feminist studies and sexuality studies in the 1970s, and queer theory developed from gay and lesbian studies in the early 1990s. As queer theory broadened its scope and methods, it incorporated much of gay, lesbian, and eventually bisexual studies to become queer studies. Its theoretical stance of investigating the social construction of desires and bodies in turn led to new developments in sexuality studies, particularly the rise of critical heterosexuality studies. Using the term "critical" in its meaning of "analysis," not in its meaning of "criticism," critical heterosexuality studies applies the tools for investigating the social construction of desires and bodies to the concept of heterosexuality and the people who identify with it.

During the nineteenth century, European and European-derived cultures were deeply interested in studying and classifying the world around them, creating grand narratives and universal theories that, to whatever extent proved possible at the time, explained everything they came across in relation to everything else. This impulse has several sources. One was the scientific revolution that began in the sixteenth century and coalesced around the development of the scientific method that is used today by scientists the world over. Another was European colonialism, which began in the fifteenth century and was widespread by the nineteenth. As they invaded lands across the world, creating massive settlements and eventually new, European-based cultures and governments in some and controlling others with smaller forces in order to exploit natural, human, and cultural resources, Europeans were awed by the wide diversity of the natural and human worlds they encountered as well as by the similarities they saw to their own worlds. These similarities also worried at least some Europeans and their settler-colonial descendants in places like Canada, Australia, South Africa, and the U.S., because they had created and continued to uphold societies that were rife with social inequality even as some of the most important European philosophical developments in the eighteenth century had emphasized the fundamental equality of all human beings. That the philosophers were thinking of all humans as equals was disturbing enough to the people at the top of the hierarchies in deeply unequal societies; that their own observations also hinted at such equality was unacceptable. Convinced that social inequality must have natural causes, some dedicated themselves to applying recent scientific advances and new scientific theories to humans.

In the era that gave us Linnaean classification, which sorts all living beings into specific locations on a massive tree of life and names them sequentially by kingdom, phylum, class, order, family, genus, and species, some scientists assumed that humans were made up of different species or at least different breeds; these came to be called "races." In an era that gave us Darwin's theory of natural selection, some scientists argued that colonized cultures were destined to die out, like less well-adapted members of a species in Darwin's theory. And in a time when colonized people were being scrutinized by Europeans in order that those Europeans could learn more about themselves, European scientists turned their scrutiny as well on disempowered groups within their own "race" and culture: working-class and poor people, people with disabilities, women, intersex people, gender-variant people, and same-sex attracted people. All were considered, as non-dominant groups, to experience forms (including absences) of sexual desire and pleasure that were different from those of elite, white, straight, fully-abled, cisgender men. Since the desires and pleasures of the latter were considered normal, all others were considered deviant. Though there was some debate on the naturalness of such "deviance," the dominant perspective was that "deviants" could, and should, be cured. And in order to cure them, they must be studied in great detail.

These assumptions on the part of scientists led many of them to engage in horrifying practices with their research subjects and patients. Working-class and poor people of all races, ages, and genders, like colonized people, were subjected to "scientific" experimentation and intrusive and disrespectful observation with little regard to their rights and selfhood. All varieties of discontent among women, including unfulfilled sexual desires, feminist objections to sexism, and interest in higher education, were diagnosed as stemming from uterine problems; all too often women patients endured public examinations of their bodies in front of rows of all-male medical students and forms of uterine "healing" that would be considered in many cultures to be grievous sexual assault. Intersex people had their genitalia and internal sexual organs scrutinized in detail, sketched out, later photographed, and pontificated over, with the result that non-intersex people recategorized them into "true hermaphrodites" and "false" ones and set about figuring out how to "cure" the latter. In the midst of all of this consternation over people whose bodies and desires failed to match up to the elite, white, heterosexual, fully-abled, cisgender, male norm, a group of people who came to be known as sexologists became very interested in people who desired others of the same sex.

The sexologists invented various terms for same-sex attracted people; the one that stuck was **invert**. This term reflected the theory underlying it: that people who desired the same sex did so because their sense of self as a woman or a man was reversed, "inverted," from what Western cultures at the time said it should be. In today's Western terminology, the sexologists thought that everyone who was attracted to the same sex was actually transgender, and that all transgender people were attracted to the same sex.

Well, not all. If everyone with same sex attraction was an invert, it would create an unresolvable paradox. Let's take as an example two men who are attracted to each other. If everyone with same sex attraction is an invert, that makes them both inverts. Under this theory, male inverts are really women. So now we have two women attracted to each other. That makes them both inverts, and under this theory, that means they're both men. So which is it? Interestingly, by itself the inversion theory of desire and gender completely messes up the gender binary. Sexologists resolved this problem by theorizing that same sex pairings were made up of one "invert" and one so-called "normal." Why would a "normal" be attracted to someone of the same sex? For very (cis)gendered reasons. If the normal was a man, many sexologists reasoned, he might be drawn by his "naturally" powerful sexual drive. Sex with a man might seem kinky, or like the ultimate sexual conquest. If the normal was a woman, however, the answer had to be different since most nineteenth-century sexologists believed that (elite, white, cisgender) women had little to no sexual desire at all. Instead, they were the victims of the masculine female invert, whose "unnaturally" masculine sexual drives led her to seduce innocent, "normal" women.

Another aspect of inversion theory becomes clear in this discussion of inverts and normals. Whether or not these nineteenth-century sexologists intended it, their theory relied on what poet and essayist Adrienne Rich (1980) would later come to call **compulsory heterosexuality**: the cultural expectation that all humans are naturally heterosexual. If all humans are heterosexual, then same sex desire can only be possible if one partner – and not both – is really the "opposite" sex. While these early sexologists debated whether inversion was due to nature or nurture, whether it was an illness or a benign human variation, they all relied on a fundamental presumption that women only desire sexual relations with men and vice versa.

As sexology developed through the twentieth century, such assumptions soon came undone. The most famous study that challenged the invert model and its attendant compulsory heterosexuality was published in two volumes known as the Kinsey reports, written by Alfred Kinsey and his colleagues from Indiana University. The books, *Sexual Behavior in the Human Male* and *Sexual Behavior in the Human Female*, were published in 1948 and 1953, respectively, and offered extensive data and analysis about human sexuality based on interviews with a large sample of adults in the U.S. The Kinsey reports refused to divide humans into categories based on sexual desire, such as "homosexual" and "heterosexual," and instead used a seven-point scale to indicate the frequency with which participants had experienced desire for men and desire for women over the course of their lives.

The Kinsey reports played an important role in opening up space for further studies of same sex desire that resisted classifying it as a disease. Early books on gay and lesbian communities began to appear in the 1950s, and a small but growing number of books and articles, increasingly sympathetic and more frequently also written by lesbian and gay authors, were published in the 1960s. In the wake of widespread uprisings in gay and lesbian communities during the 1960s, especially in the U.S., and of the removal of same sex desire from the American Psychiatric Association's list of mental illnesses that was published in 1974, gay and lesbian studies began to flourish. Moving away from sexology, this field focused on gays and lesbians as types of people, same sex attracted and perhaps possessed of related characteristics as well, as they appeared in history, literature, anthropology, music, art – and even religion.

The legacy of the invert lingered during this time in at least two ways. First, much of gay and lesbian studies in this period tended to represent gay men in ways that included feminine men, even as it also acknowledged the presence of masculine gay men in a way that classic inversion theory was unable to do. Likewise, lesbians often thought of themselves and their forebears in ways that evoked images of strength, courage, and power – all masculine images – even as lesbian studies and lesbian politics of the time regarded women who were too masculine as suspicious and "male-identified." As transgender people became increasingly outspoken and organized between the 1960s and the 1990s, many who experienced desire for people of the same birth sex described being confused or encountering others who were confused about whether their gender variance was simply a part of their same sex desire. Again, these experiences are part of the lingering legacy of the invert, as are ongoing stereotypes of gay men as feminine and lesbians as masculine.

Transgender studies was in nascent form by the 1980s, and both it and the transgender rights movement gained increasing strength and prominence during the 1990s and into the 2000s due to the tireless work of transgender scholars, activists, and scholar-activists. In the meantime, in 1990, the University of California at Santa Cruz hosted a conference that aimed to develop a new, more intersectional approach to gay and lesbian studies. The concept of **intersectionality** (Crenshaw 1991) is one way of addressing the fact that any area of social power (some people call these areas *axes* of power, like an x-axis or a y-axis on a graph) is inevitably affected by other areas. The different axes of power intersect, but unlike the axes of a graph they don't intersect at a single point, they don't intersect neatly, and they change each other when they intersect. For instance, we might want to find out the experience that Christians in the U.S. today have with sexuality. But the axis of power along which religion lies – in which Christianity has a great deal of power in general, in a culturally Christian country like the U.S. – intersects with lots of other axes. There are different Christian denominations, some of which have very different levels of power. Religion intersects with race, with class, with region of the country and urban/suburban/rural locations, with gender, with sexual orientation, with age, and more – and all of these intersect with each other as well. So we can't even ask our question well, much less answer it thoroughly and accurately, without thinking about how Black Christians' experiences with sexuality may be different from and similar to those of Latinx Christians, which in turn may differ from those of Asian Christians, Arab Christians, Native American Christians, white Christians, and so on. In turn, Black Christian women will have different experiences from, and similar experiences to, Black Christian men and likewise Black Christian girls. Black Christian lesbian women will have different, and some similar, experiences when compared to Black Christian straight women. And the list goes on.

The people who convened the UC Santa Cruz conference thought that gay and lesbian studies scholars weren't paying enough attention in particular to gender and to race. They wanted a more intersectional approach to their subject, although they didn't use that specific word. Drawing from the growing reclamation of a pejorative epithet for gays and lesbians, they proposed the term "queer theory" for their new approach. Although it took almost a decade for the intersectional part of their vision to catch on – so long that the person who initially coined the term, literature scholar Teresa de Lauretis, gave up on queer theory and publicly repudiated it (de Lauretis 1991, 1994) – the term itself stuck.

Queer theory means many things; indeed, as a field it sometimes takes pride in being difficult to define. But it draws heavily on older meanings of the word "queer" as both a noun and a verb: meanings like "odd," "out of place," and "to disrupt." Queer theory examines and analyzes that which appears or is designated as odd and out of place, especially with respect to desire and gender, and it attempts to disrupt habitual and taken-for-granted perspectives on gender, sexuality, and desire. Initially focused quite strongly on literary theory, likely because this was its place of origin, queer theory broadened by the late 1990s to include cultural studies and eventually came to impact a wide range of academic and political arenas. As it broadened and came into wider conversation with other forms of theory and analysis that focus on social power – critical race theory, feminist theory, postcolonial theory, disability theory, and the like queer theory increasingly came to be called queer studies as a reflection of this breadth in the methods it uses and the topics it addresses. At the intersection of this queer theoretical and methodological approach with newer forms of sexology is critical heterosexuality studies, which applies to the analysis of different-sex desire and heterosexual cultures and communities the theoretical tools of queer studies and the other bodies of theory with which the latter engages.

It probably won't surprise you by now to learn that desire, too, is socially constructed. Like with religion, sex, and gender, to say that desire is socially constructed is not to say that it isn't real; it's not even to say that it isn't physiological. No constructivist would deny that something is happening in a person's body when they see or even think about someone they find attractive. Hormones shift, one's face may flush, one's stomach and chest may flutter, one's sexual organs may become aroused – these are all clearly physiological signs of sexual arousal and commonly of desire. But what makes us desire certain people and not others, and why? A complete answer to this question may well be out of our reach, and it's certainly possible that there may be deep-seated factors. Psychologists tell us that people who do not desire a particular group or type of people cannot learn to desire that group or type, and that efforts to force such a redirection of sexual desire (such as conversion therapy, which claims to be able to eradicate same sex desire and install different sex desire in its place) are not only ineffective but deeply psychologically damaging. But there are also important cultural factors. Here's a quick thought experiment to explore those cultural factors and the social construction of desire.

- Think back to your childhood and your adolescence. While you may or may not have been experiencing forms of desire that were condoned by your family and/or your culture, you also were learning what is supposed to be sexually desirable and what is not. Consider these questions:

  a   How did you learn what human beauty looks like?
  b   How did you learn who is "sexy" and who isn't?
  c   Whatever your own desires were, how did you learn what kinds of people and bodies you were supposed to desire?
  d   How did you learn to make yourself desirable?

- If there are children in your life right now – your own, or your grandchildren, or younger siblings, or the children of close friends or relatives – how are they learning about desire? Are they learning different things about desire than you did, or the same things? How?

Different cultures, and different subcultures within them, define what's desirable differently. In the context of women's bodies – often the ones defined by cultures as the most sexualized, and therefore the most carefully scrutinized when it comes to desire – some cultures focus attention on women's breasts as the most sexualized, desirable parts of their bodies. Some cultures focus on legs, others on hair, others on lips, and so on. In male-dominated cultures, where women's desirability receives attention both through efforts to hide it and through efforts to hint at or reveal it, one can easily see these different bodily areas of desire. What parts of a woman's body are required by law to be covered? What parts of a woman's body are most commonly uncovered, or nearly revealed, in sensual performances? What body parts is women's clothing designed to cover, to reveal, to hint at? Most importantly, how do the answers to these questions differ from culture to culture? Some cultures casually bare what other cultures insistently cover, and those who desire women and have been raised within these cultures will often find their bodies reacting to exactly those aspects of a woman's body that the culture deems the most desirable and sexualized. Sexual desire clearly has a physiological component, but when and how that physiological reaction occurs is heavily shaped by cultural context.

Desire is also socially constructed in another way. Not only is it shaped by sociocultural values, but like other aspects of human experience that are socially constructed, desire is culturally identified as a human trait that carries meaning, and the meaning it carries is socially determined. In mid-nineteenth-century Europe, at least to certain scientists, the meaning of exclusive same sex desire had to do with gender: it indicated that you were an invert. In psychology for the first three-quarters of the twentieth century, the meaning of same sex desire had to do with mental illness: it indicated that you had a neurosis. In some socially conservative religious circles around the world today, the meaning of same sex desire is theological: it means that God is calling you to celibacy. In other religious circles, the meaning is differently theological: it means that God is calling you to a lifetime of joy with a same-sex partner. In past and present cultures, same sex desire may indicate virility in men, sexual openness in women, special talents in both. Different sex desire also carries meanings. Depending on the context, those meanings may range from normalcy through neutrality to perversion and even sinfulness. In short, the meanings of desire are determined by the sociocultural contexts in which it occurs and in which the desiring people and those around them have lived. Moreover, the very fact that desire has such broader meanings at all is also determined by sociocultural context. Desire is socially constructed.

Each of the fields we've covered above – gender studies, transgender studies, sexuality studies (including critical heterosexuality studies), and queer studies – has been incorporated into the study of religion on both the constructive or confessional side of the field and the descriptive-analytical or non-confessional side. While the incorporation has at times been slow and is certainly incomplete, and while the gender and sexuality fields we've discussed are often reluctant to include religion in their analyses, at the intersection of these fields that study religions, sexualities, bodies, and genders is a fascinating and intensely rich area of study. With these tools now gathered in your toolkit, you're ready to accompany us into this area. Let's consider how the book is organized before we move on to the next chapter.

Using this book

Part of the problem with the idea of "world religions" is that it implies that there are separate entities that can be clearly identified as discrete "religions," and that each is monolithic, taking one or a few closely related forms. Another part of the problem, as we discussed above, is that this idea also tends to focus on beliefs. If things were so simple, we'd be able to tell you in ten or twenty pages what each of the "Big Five" (or Seven or Eight) religions "believes" about sexuality, and we'd be done. But things aren't that simple. If you practice a religion, or if you know someone who does, then you've already seen the evidence for this complexity. How many times have you seen people from the same religion disagree over whether a particular action is religiously acceptable, or over the correct interpretation of a passage in a sacred text? In many cases these disagreements get framed as debates over who's "right," but each person thinks their perspective is correct – otherwise they wouldn't be arguing in the first place! From a religious studies perspective, such disagreements take place between people with differing interpretations of the religion, not between people who have it right and those who have it wrong. That means there's more than one approach to the issue within that religion, because religion isn't monolithic.

In fact, sometimes people from different religions share more perspectives with each other than they do with their **co-religionists** – the people from their own religion. On the topic of sexual activity before marriage, for instance, a socially conservative evangelical Christian may agree more with an Orthodox Jew or a conservative Muslim or Hindu than with a liberal Christian. So in order to offer you an accurate and adequately comprehensive discussion of the intersections between bodies, sexualities, and religions, we've designed this book around a number of topics, and specific themes within those topics, that appear in various religions' interactions with sexuality. We begin with two topics that many people expect from religion and sexuality: celibacy and regulation. We then move on to less-expected topics that will still be unsurprising to many people: controversy and violence. The final three topics explore areas of religion and sexuality that are less familiar to many: innovation, or the challenging of social and religious norms around sexuality, either in more restrictive or more liberal ways; instrumentalization, or the use of sexuality as a religious instrument or tool; and ecstasy, in which we explore the inter-relationship between sexual ecstasy and religious ecstasy, including among celibate religious specialists like the Flemish mystic Hadewijch whose sensual experience of Christ we described at the beginning of this chapter. Within each chapter, we discuss several themes that commonly characterize the relationships between religions, sexualities, and bodies. None of this coverage is exhaustive, because it simply couldn't be: there's far too much complexity and diversity in the connections between sexuality and religion for us to fit it all into one book. Each chapter, therefore, highlights relevant and varied examples in an effort to give you a comprehensive, albeit not exhaustive, overview.

Throughout the book, we take what is often called a **lived religion** approach that's consistent with the empathetic understanding we described earlier. This approach focuses less on official pronouncements and sacred texts than on what everyday people do with those pronouncements and texts. Roman Catholic leaders may have been disturbed by Catherine of Siena's insistence that Christ had married her with his foreskin as a ring, but Catherine insisted that this was true. A lived religion approach accepts Catherine's words, not to make a theological statement about what Christ actually did (we can't know this through non-confessional methods, nor does this question matter in the descriptive-analytical study of religion) but to affirm that Catherine was quite insistent that this was her experience.

In order to help you to practice this descriptive-analytical, lived religion approach, and in order to ground each topic and its themes in concrete examples right from the start, we open each chapter with two case studies. We've generally selected case studies that are less commonly known, for two reasons. First, we want you to be able to approach the case studies with a fresh eye, not as something you've already analyzed. When you have pre-existing experience with a story, it can be harder to interpret it in new ways. Second, we want to challenge you to think beyond those established and common stories. For instance, religious celibacy is often in the news in the twenty-first century, usually either because of scandals surrounding celibate men who break their vows of celibacy in violent and awful ways or because of the reverence that many cultures continue to hold for celibate religious specialists such as nuns and monks. So we've chosen other, lesser-known case studies of religious celibacy.

When you approach the case studies, read each one like a researcher. Practice suspending your own world-concept and imagining what it might be like to be a part of the world-concept(s) described in the case study. Consider what you can learn from the case study about the relationships between religions, sexualities, and bodies. The chapter's topic can be one guide for you, but also ask deeper questions and look for themes that we might discuss in the chapter. If you're reading the case studies in the chapter on innovation, for example, consider *how* innovation is a part of the story. What kinds of innovation do you see in each case study? What are these people innovating with? What's so innovative about what they're doing anyway? Do *they* see it as innovative? Why or why not? How are the innovations in the two case studies different? How are they alike? What can we learn from each one? What can we learn from comparing them? These are just a sample of the wide variety of possible questions you could ask in this regard.

You should also be asking what other topics and themes – those from other chapters, or even those we don't address in this book – are present in the case studies. Our topics and themes are **ideal types**, categories that are designed to help with comparison but that are not a perfect, exact match for everything that falls within them. When we offer a case study within a particular chapter, we're not trying to say that this case study relates only to the topic in that chapter. Let's go back again to Hadewijch's story, for example. Since Hadewijch was celibate, her story could be considered an example of the topic of celibacy. But it's clearly also about ecstasy. As many Christians have become more uncomfortable with the idea of connecting sensuality to the divine, visions like the one Hadewijch describes might be a good example of the topic of controversy. We could make a case for other topics and themes, too. So as you read the case studies and the chapters themselves, stay alert for how the different topics and themes intertwine.

There are other tools for study in the book as well. You may have noticed that a number of words in this chapter have been printed in boldface when they first appear. These words are included in the glossary at the end of the book. At the end of each chapter you'll find suggestions for further reading and, when available, other resources such as films and websites. You'll also find an outline of the chapter and a set of questions for further thought called "Applications and reflections." These questions will help you to review and to solidify your learning, not by asking you to look up or recall facts discussed in the chapter but by asking you to apply the concepts you've learned. If you're reading this book for a class, your teacher might use these questions in class; if that doesn't happen, or you're reading this for your own learning, you might enjoy thinking through the questions on your own.

We hope you'll appreciate learning about this field of study that all three of us find so fascinating. We hope you discover new perspectives and new forms of analysis, and that you come to see the richness and complexity at the intersections of bodies, religions, and sexualities that drew each of us to make this field our life's work.

Review: chapter highlights

- Religious studies;

  a   The study of religion as a human phenomenon;
  b   Descriptive-analytical or non-confessional;
  c   Empathetic understanding and *Epoché*;
  d   Defining religion;
  e   Religion as a social construct;
  f   Problems with defining religion.

- Gender studies and transgender studies;

  a   What is sex?
  b   Sex variations: intersex and transsexual people;
  c   The social construction of sex;
  d   What is gender?
  e   The social construction of gender;
  f   Transgender and Two Spirit people;
  g   The global politics of gender identity;
  h   Transgender studies and gender studies.

- Sexuality studies and queer studies;

  a   Nineteenth-century European sexologists and the invert;
  b   Twentieth-century sexology and the Kinsey reports;
  c   The rise of gay and lesbian studies;
  d   The rise of queer theory;
  e   Queer studies and critical heterosexuality studies;
  f   Social construction of desire;

- About the book.

Applications and reflections

1   Try practicing *epoché*. Do you ever talk to a person, or read about a group, and wonder, "Why would they think/say/do something like that?" Pick an example like this that has to do with religion – maybe a religious group whose members do something you don't understand, or a friend who believes something you don't understand. Suspend any disagreement you may have with their perspective, and learn what you can about their world-concept. Remember Meredith McGuire's point that "a mode of action is not irrational if a person perceives it to work"; can you figure out why the practice or belief you're focusing on makes sense within this world-concept?
2   What's your opinion about the scholarly debate over methods in the non-confessional study of religion? Should people who study religion this way simply describe

and categorize what we find, and leave the analysis to religious practitioners? Should we use description and categorization to analyze our findings objectively? Or should we accept the argument that objectivity isn't really possible, and instead use our findings to create greater justice and equity in the world? Make a case for your opinion: why is yours the best way to approach the study of religion? Why are the other ways not the best approach?

3   What does the social construction of gender look like in the world around you? How were you taught your assigned gender? What cultural resources, ranging from traditional stories to contemporary toys, children's shows, and music, teach children and teenagers about their assigned gender? What cultural and legal forces are in place to enforce gender norms among adults? When people resist gender norms, in what ways to they do so? What support do they have? What roles does religion play in creating, enforcing, and resisting these norms?

4   The European sexologists' ideas about inversion had a deep and widespread impact. Does the culture (or do the cultures) you live in right now have an invert model for same sex desire and gender variance? If so, what is that model, and how do you know? Are there other models, other ways of understanding same sex desire and gender variance, that exist alongside this model – or instead of it, in cultures without an invert model?

5   How do people resist the social construction of desire? Think of people or movements you know of that speak out about cultural norms of sexuality and desire, for instance by showing that bodies declared undesirable by the culture (those whose size or skin color, for instance, don't match cultural beauty standards) are in fact sexy and desirable. How do people counter the cultural messages around them when it comes to bodies and sexualities? How does religion change – or not – the answers to these questions? Do specific religious groups challenge social norms when it comes to sexuality?

Resources for further study

Asad, Talal. *Genealogies of Religion: Discipline and Reasons of Power in Christianity and Islam*. Baltimore, MA: Johns Hopkins University Press, 1993.

Fausto-Sterling, Anne. *Sexing the Body: Gender Politics and the Construction of Sexuality*. New York, NY: Basic Books, 2000.

Fine, Cordelia. *Delusions of Gender: How Our Minds, Society, and Neurosexism Create Difference*. New York, NY: Norton, 2011.

Hall, Donald E., and Annamarie Jagose with Andrea Bebell and Susan Potter (eds.). *The Routledge Queer Studies Reader*. New York, NY: Routledge, 2013.

Masuzawa, Tomoko. *The Invention of World Religions, or, How European Universalism was Preserved in the Language of Pluralism*. Chicago, IL: University of Chicago Press, 2005.

McGuire, Meredith B. *Lived Religion: Faith and Practice in Everyday Life*. New York, NY: Oxford University Press, 2008.

Stryker, Susan, and Stephen Whittle. *The Transgender Studies Reader*. New York, NY: Routledge, 2006. See especially Susan Stryker, "(De)Subjugated Knowledges: An Introduction to Transgender Studies," 1–17.

Stryker, Susan, and Aren Z. Aizura (eds.). *The Transgender Studies Reader 2*. New York, NY: Routledge, 2013. See especially Susan Stryker and Aren Z. Aizura, "Introduction: Transgender Studies 2.0," 1–12.

1 Celibacy

Case study 1

Our first case study is the Buddha. The founder of Buddhism was born in present-day Nepal and lived most of his life in the sixth century B.C.E. He discovered what is known as the middle path between the extremes of self-denial and self-indulgence. He taught that life is subject to constant change, that what appears to be permanent is in fact ephemeral. The Buddha used contemplative techniques to focus the mind on reality as it really is and allow the mind to divest itself of the expectations that we typically place on objects and persons. In this way, the Buddha taught, we are able to avoid the dissatisfaction that comes with misperceiving the nature of things and experience **nirvana**: the satisfying state of freedom from ignorance and attachment.

The Buddha first came to realize the pain of how life fails to meet our naïve expectations of permanence and pleasure in a dramatic way. He had led a sheltered life as a prince, protected from the realities of old age, disease, and death. His father had heard a prediction about the boy becoming a religious teacher. To prevent that outcome, the Buddha's father attempted to shield the child from the painful realities of life. One day, however, the young prince took an excursion on a chariot in the countryside, far away from the palace where he'd been living in great ignorance. He saw an old man and asked his charioteer what manner of thing stood on the road in front of him. Shocked to hear that this was a human being and that what the man experienced would also be his own fate, the young prince asked to return home. He went out the next day and saw a sick man with similar results. On another occasion, he encountered a dead man. He nearly fainted from the emotions the sight of this corpse engendered in him. Later he encountered a man who lived a very simple existence with one set of clothes, who wandered from place to place and spent his days in yoga and meditation in search of a deathless state. The renunciant lifestyle of that man attracted the young prince. He made plans to leave the palace and follow the example of the renouncer. But it was not an easy thing to leave the palace. The youthful Buddha was married and had already established a family life. He had a chief wife along with a large harem of lower-ranking wives and female consorts, as was appropriate for men of the warrior caste in the Buddha's time. Moreover, his chief wife had given birth to a son (in some versions of the story, the child was not yet on the scene but rather was conceived the night that the Buddha fled from the palace). The Buddha chose to leave in the dead of night, while his family slept, and flee quietly into the wilderness. Living a peripatetic lifestyle, the Buddha eventually gathered a band of monastic followers who emulated his celibate lifestyle. Others joined the religion as married householders who provided support for the celibate women and men who walked with the Buddha.

Scriptures attributed to the Buddha praise the celibate life as one that affords unique opportunities for focusing the mind and emotions without the complications and aggravations of family life. One might compare Buddhist nuns and monks to people in secular communities who are resolutely single as a way of focusing on personal exploration or career achievement. Steven Collins (Collins 1988) analyzes scriptural metaphors about monastic life that others have interpreted as being about solitude and suggests that what Buddhist texts really value is a state of companionate singleness. To be single, to separate oneself from the social world of the Buddha's day that was defined by a thick web of family and vocational obligations: that is the freedom that Buddhist monastic life offered women and men, according to texts that praise it. To be in a sorority or fraternity of like-minded single people offered the highest levels of freedom available in ancient India. Sayings attributed to the Buddha praise celibate renouncers, people who have opted out of the social world, the world of production and reproduction by renouncing vocation and family, as single-minded and single in social status. They wander the land or reside in monasteries in such a way as to be available to all beings but attached to none. In this, such people operate socially as a singular presence. They are a unit of one. Metaphorically speaking, they are like the mighty rhinoceros, a forest creature with a single horn. The Buddha was born in a tropical region on the border between India and Nepal (today's Chitwan National Park) that has known rhinos for a long time. No doubt the Buddha, or those who attributed this metaphor to him, would have been familiar with the ways of this powerful animal. Weighing up to a ton, the rhinoceros is a large herbivore that has no predators other than humans and can wander freely. Its only need is to fuel a body that is tough, composed of a horn that is mostly cartilage and protective skin that is formed from layers of collagen. Metaphors in Buddhist texts suggest that the Buddhist nun or monk who chooses celibacy wears an armor formed by self-control. The teeth and claws of most animals are ineffective in tearing into the hide of a large formidable rhinoceros. Likewise, changing fortunes in day-to-life do not readily penetrate the consciousness of one who practices a celibate path. The arrows of sexual attraction and the attendant highs and lows that sexually active people experience in romantic life and in the fickle, sometimes dangerous business of reproduction, are likewise ridiculously impotent when it comes to penetrating the hide of a committed celibate.

According to early teachings attributed to him, the Buddha explained his choice to be celibate by situating sexual desire within the larger doctrinal framework that holds desire or craving for pleasures of the senses responsible for continual rebirth and endless suffering. He taught the value of self-awareness and control of craving in the first teaching he gave after his enlightenment, offering four propositions about the nature of existence known as the four noble truths. The four noble truths of Buddhism are: suffering, the origin of suffering, the end of suffering which is the state of nirvana, and the path that leads to nirvana. The four truths have often been compared to a medical diagnosis. According to this analogy, suffering is the illness or problem condition that Buddhism cures. Craving is the cause of this suffering. Hearing the Buddha explain that our unreasonable craving or thirst for pleasure in the face of short-lived phenomena that will not endure long enough to sustain pleasure is equivalent to going to visit a doctor and having her explain that the symptoms one suffers are caused by behaviors that one can control. Thus the second noble truth is essentially a diagnosis that shows how to achieve health. The abolition of craving is the cure for suffering. The Buddha taught an Eight-fold Path to cure us. It is the treatment plan that leads to the alleviation of suffering.

In his work as a teacher of the path to alleviate suffering and transcend death, the Buddha is reported to have had many frank conversations with followers about sexual impulses and actions. In the Buddhist context, sexuality must be seen not as a sin but as a signifier – namely, the sign of an untamed mind that is greedy for sensual gratification because it is unaware of the ills to which all flesh is heir. Because it is associated with ignorance, sexual desire has its locus in the head or the heart (the word *citta*, identical in Sanskrit and Pali, denotes both) as much as the genitals. What Peter Brown suggests of the Desert Fathers tradition, which also emphasizes the renunciation of familial bonds, applies here as well: sexual desire is seen as an indication of one's mental state, a "seismograph" that tells what is going on deep inside a person (Brown's insights are summarized in an essay by Michel Foucault and Richard Sennett in the *London Review of Books*, Foucault and Sennett, 1981). A person who has rooted out sexual desire is free from the psychic and social forces that cause suffering.

The Buddha often recommended specific types of meditative practice to counter the lustful impulses of his followers. For love-smitten monks considering leaving the monastic order and returning to lay life on account of their romantic and sexual feelings, the Buddha is reported to have sent the men to the charnel fields of cremation grounds, where the bodies of paupers were abandoned to rot (cremation can be expensive in areas where trees are scarce, and burial was not a culturally accepted practice). Commentators develop this theme. Buddhaghosa, a writer of commentaries on the Buddha's words and compendia of the Buddhist path who lived in the fifth century of the Common Era, explained that there are ten types of corpses that a lust-filled monk may select to examine in a cremation ground, each one serving as an antidote to one of ten different types of attraction to physical form (Rhys Davids 1920, vol. 1, 193–94). The ten types of corpse differ according to circumstance: there is the bloated corpse that is filled with the gases of putrefaction, the livid corpse that is discolored by all the chemical activity within, the festering corpse that is erupting with all manner of nasty things, the cut up corpse that has been dismembered by accidents or animals, the gnawed corpse that has been a meal or a snack for animals, the scattered corpse that has had parts removed, the hacked and scattered corpse that has been subject to much disruption, the bleeding corpse that has been cut, the worm-infested corpse that is host to parasitic worms and other creatures, and the skeletal corpse that is desiccated. Buddhaghosa followed the Buddha's example in dealing with sexual desire. He trained lustful men to look for signs of decay and cultivate a feeling of disgust toward female bodies (Wilson 1996). According to legends about the Buddha's teaching methods, he occasionally arranged elaborate scenarios whereby horny monks ended up in cremation grounds looking for trysts with their beloved, only to find that the objects of their affections had died and become pus-filled corpses or skeletons.

There are many ways that a corpse can be hideous; a vulture-inviting stench that is ideal for deflating one man's arousal may not be effective for another man. Buddhist meditation manuals recognize that just as there are different strokes for different folks, there are different corpses that serve as good remedies for different types of sexual desire. Each one of the ten different corpses that Buddhaghosa describes has something to say to those troubled by specific types of sexual desire. The discolored corpse speaks to those who love a creamy skin-tone; the bloated corpse instructs those who desire voluptuous curves by showing them precisely what will become of a shapely body. This contemplative practice, known as *aśubha-bhāvanā* in Sanskrit and *asubha-bhāvanā* in Pali, still goes on today in Buddhist countries such as Sri Lanka in the absence of charnel fields. In contemporary Buddhist countries, the autopsy room where bodies are dissected today provides the occasion to observe how death ravages sexy bodies (Boisvert 1996, 47).

The Buddha not only recommended that horny monks do meditation in charnel fields. He also, as indicated above, arranged elaborate scenarios whereby monks hell-bent on romance and sex learned the folly of their ways. According to one legend, a monk was in love with a beautiful courtesan named Sirimā. Thanks to orchestration by the Buddha behind the scenes, this monk ended up in a cremation ground thinking he was going to see Sirimā (due to their privacy, cremation grounds were often used in ancient India as places where lovers would meet). But the lovely courtesan had died and her body had been rotting for days. The Buddha had calculated the amount of putrefaction Sirimā's body would undergo and arranged for the naïve, love-smitten monk to arrive at the charnel field just as the courtesan's body was exploding with maggots. To drive the point home in a way that even a foolish young man would get it, the Buddha held an auction of sorts. The Buddha offered a night of pleasure with Sirimā to anyone who would pay a thousand copper coins. This macabre auction and the harrowing evidence of how quickly beauty fades quickly cured the young monk of his ignorance.

Celibacy is clearly a hallmark of Buddhist practice for many monks and nuns. It was central to the identity of the Buddha as a single man who left family behind to roam the countryside in search of teachers and contemplative practices that would free him from the cycle of birth and death and give him access to a deathless condition. In order to engage in contemplative practices, the Buddha had to disengage from his role as a family man and a representative of his warrior clan. Others followed in the Buddha's footsteps, adopting a celibate lifestyle to facilitate the process of disengaging from the world of production and reproduction. Many men sought ordination as monks. Women also wished to join the religious order the Buddha had founded. Five years after the Buddha established an order of monks, his foster mother Mahāprajāpatī Gautamī went to him and requested that women, also, be allowed to "go forth from the home to the homeless life" (as many Buddhist scriptures and ritual formulas put it) and be ordained as Buddhist nuns. Permanent voluntary female celibacy was unusual in ancient India, although the Jains accepted women as nuns. According to some accounts, the Buddha initially refused to grant his foster mother's request. He was likely to have been worried about the loss of financial support from the lay community. Laity may have been scandalized by the pro-spect that women and men would mix in remote forest settings. But the Buddha was eventually convinced to allow women to enter the order. He allowed his foster mother and her companions to take ordination, but he established eight special rules to guide the lives of nuns. These rules ensured that the women of the Buddhist monastic community would not be perceived as breaking away from male social control. One rule, for example, mandates that within the monastic order women display a high level of respect and bow to a man in robes no matter how long the man had been a monk and no matter what the man's level of achievement. This rule states that any nun, no matter how long she had been in the order, must treat any monk, even the rudest novice, as if he were her senior. Other rules subordinate the women's order to the men's in matters such as setting penances for nuns.

Despite these restrictions, women were attracted to the prospect of living as Buddhist nuns. For some, ordination as nuns meant escaping from unsatisfactory marriages. The nun Muttā, for example, was married to a hunchbacked husband. She convinced him to let her take ordination and she eventually achieved the deathless state of nirvana through Buddhist practice. Muttā left behind this verse (my translation of verse 11 in Pruitt 1998, 15) celebrating her enlightenment:

Free am I, so deliciously free
Free from three mundane things—
From mortar, from pestle and from my hunchbacked lord,
Freed from rebirth and death I am,
And all that has held me down is tossed aside.

Sumangala was another nun whose poetry records her life story. She was born into poverty and married a basket-maker. Her son became a monk and she eventually took ordination as a nun. In her enlightenment verse (my translation of verse 23 in Pruitt 1998, 27–28), she exalts in the freedom to meditate, far away from the dreary kitchen that was once her world:

Free, I am free
How delighted I am to be free of my kitchen things
My cooking pot seems absurd,
So too my unpleasant husband & his workshop.
Aversion & desire are gone, eliminated. I live foot of a tree, meditating, at ease: "What bliss!"

Wives who left their husbands for life in Buddhist monasteries had legal protections in doing so. When former husbands sought the return of their wives, we know from the historical record that such men were thwarted in their efforts to recover their wives. Ordination as a Buddhist nun effectively dissolved the marital bonds between a man and a woman. Unmarried women evidently also felt the allure of monastic life. For them, celibacy seemed a smart choice in a world in which bodily decline and economic uncertainty was inevitable. Better to train the mind and gain perspective on the nature of reality than to invest in rickety supports for happiness like beauty and wealth. In the *Therīgāthā* poetry collection, the last entry is that of Sumedhā, who made an eloquent plea to be allowed to become a nun rather than marry the man her parents had chosen for her. Sumedhā had been taking instruction from the nuns as a lay disciple for many years and, as a young woman of marriageable age, had decided not to marry but to join the nuns order. When she learned that her parents had promised her in marriage to King Anikaratta, Sumedhā retired to her room and defiantly cut off all her hair in imitation of the tonsure ceremony that heralds entry into monastic life. While getting their heads shaved, novice nuns and monks are given a lock of tonsured hair as an aid to meditation on impermanence; Sumedhā, recreating the ordination ritual in her own home, likewise focused her mind on impermanence while contemplating her shorn hair. In doing this meditation, she entered a trance state and was absorbed in contemplation when her parents entered her room to prepare her for marriage. Sumedhā was a very persuasive speaker, and in the end she not only convinced her parents to let her join the monastic order, but she also made Buddhists out of her family and household staff as well as her bridegroom and his retinue. Not only does Sumedhā speak most eloquently to her parents and bridegroom about the folly of sensual pleasure – she also shows a certain dramatic flair in using her symbolically laden tresses as a stage prop. Interrupted from her hair-induced meditation, Sumedhā holds her dark tresses in her hands while admonishing her audience with images such as this (my translation of verse 466–471 in Pruitt 1998, 258–259):

What is this foul, impure thing smelling of its own emissions, a horrible bag of skin filled with corpses, always flowing, full of impurities?

What do I know it to be like? The body is repulsive, smeared with flesh and blood, food for worms and birds. How can it be given away [in marriage]?

Before too long the insensate body is carried off to the charnel field and disgusted relatives throw it out like a piece of wood.

When they have thrown it out in the charnel field as food for others, even one's own mother and father are disgusted and wash themselves; how much more so people in general?

People are attached to a body that has no essence: an aggregate of bones and sinews that's full of saliva, tears, excrement, and urine – a putrid thing.

If it should be turned inside out while being dissected, even one's own mother would be disgusted, being unable to bear the smell of it.

After thirty such verses, Sumedhā concludes by tossing her hair on the floor in a final dramatic gesture of repudiation. At this point, the suitor rises to his fiancée's defense. King Anikaratta convinces Sumedhā's parents to allow the young woman to pursue her chosen path.

Clearly, the celibate life held allure for women in ancient India. Buddhists (along with the Jains) broke new ground for girls and women in Asia. The opportunity to meditate, to travel in search of teachers and as teachers, and to engage in scholarship and leadership of all-female communities gave (and continues to give) women a sense of certainty in a world where one cannot count on lasting health, wealth, or happiness. Even at the price of following additional rules that monks were not required to follow, rules that made women the subordinates of men in robes, women in premodern South Asia found refuge and meaning as celibate individuals supporting each other in monastic life. Perhaps the attractiveness of this religion to girls and women helps explain why Buddhism became the first global religion: that is to say, it spread rapidly beyond its place of origin on the border of today's India and Nepal and soon had reached all of Asia and parts of Europe within just a few centuries of the Buddha's life. Girls and women continue to enjoy opportunities for education, meditation, and leadership as ordained nuns in Asian and East Asian countries, such as China, where the women's monastic order still thrives today, as well as Europe, North and South America, and other regions. Within Asia, even in places where the female monastic order died out, the women's order persisted in the form of what some scholars call "lay nuns" or "precept nuns." And in parts of South Asia where the female monastic order died out centuries ago (such as Sri Lanka), it has been revived.

Case study 2

Our second case study illustrates how sexual renunciation can operate within marriage and family life as a way of avoiding the limitations of one's social location. Mirabai, a sixteenth-century Hindu saint also known affectionately as "Mira," practiced celibacy within marriage. Her love for the god **Kṛṣṇa** aligned her with a tradition known as **bhakti**, a Hindu tradition of passionate devotion to a personal god. Kṛṣṇa (pronounced "Krish-nuh"), is believed to dwell in a transcendent realm but also to be present within icons and human incarnations. A protective deity who is said to take form on earth in response to the needs of those devoted to him, Kṛṣṇa is depicted in iconic and legendary form as an adorable child, a sexy young man, and a mature warrior. Her love for Kṛṣṇa was so strong that it led her to forge her own unique marital path, to compose a corpus of poetry, and to eventually form a large following at a time and a place where few women saints were so recognized. Where the Buddha's celibacy enabled him to avoid the blazing fire of sexual desire and the hardships of family life, the Hindu saint Mirabai's celibacy allowed her to avoid the disappointments of an incompatible, abusive set of in-laws and to enjoy the blissful company of her beloved god-mate, Kṛṣṇa. Arranged marriage was the rule in Mirabai's day and her marriage was in line with the norm. Mirabai was wed as an eighteen-year-old bride to a man named Bhoraj, heir of one of the most powerful North Indian dynasties of her day. Her marriage to Bhoraj was a political alliance that Mirabai was opposed to from the start. Legend says (Kinsley 1980, 88) that where she should have circumambulated her husband at the wedding as the ritual calls for, she circumambulated an image of her spiritual lover, Kṛṣṇa. When it came time to depart for her new home with her in-laws, Mira had no interest in taking along a dowry. She wanted only one thing: an image of her beloved Kṛṣṇa. Once she arrived at the home of her new husband, Mira would not consummate the marriage on the grounds that she was properly married to Kṛṣṇa: having sex with Bhoraj would be adultery.

As one might imagine, conflicts between Mirabai and her husband's family surfaced immediately. In North India, when a Hindu bride moved in with the family of her husband, she was to revere the deities of the new household. Mirabai would not reject Kṛṣṇa and adopt Durgā, the family's deity, as the focus of her devotion, and the women of her husband's family treated her savagely because of her refusal to honor their chosen deity. Bhoraj died of battle wounds not long after the couple were wed. Her husband's death led to further conflict with her in-laws, some of whom felt that Mirabai should have followed her husband into death by performing the ritual of self-immolation on the funeral pyre of her husband. This ritual, known as *sati*, was once common among the warrior caste of North India's Hindus in medieval and early modern time periods. Another option for women whose husbands predeceased them was to lead a nun-like celibate existence. This option is still popular today among North Indian Hindus: widows often give up ornamentation, shave their heads, and live on very little means. This would probably have been a fine option for Mirabai. In living ascetic lives, Indian widows were and are often able to pursue religious activities. But Mirabai was not left alone to follow her chosen religious path. Her in-laws kept Mirabai under constant surveillance and found fault with everything she did.

Mira's greatest desire was to be in the company of others devoted to Kṛṣṇa. She tried to associate with a band of Kṛṣṇa-oriented saints. The women of the family did not approve of this association, deeming it shameful for a royal lady such as Mirabai to associate with wandering mendicants. Not only did comments from her mother-in-law and sisters-in-law make Mira's life hellish, but it appears that there were attempts on her life. In her devotional poems, Mirabai refers to attempts by the *rana* ("ruler") to take her life. It's not clear whom Mirabai meant by the term *rana*. It could have been her father-in-law; the same term might also have indicated her dead husband's brother. In any case, it is clear that one of the men related to her deceased husband was opposed to the leaving Mirabai alone to follow her chosen path. The rana tried to have her killed in various ways such as concealing a poisonous snake in a basket of flowers that he pretended to freely give her to offer to Kṛṣṇa.

The following poem (Nandy 1975, 18) voices in the words of the saint (but also shifting between first and third person address) how Mirabai (shortened to "Mira") irritated her family and how they reacted to her:

> Mira danced with ankle bells on her feet.
> People said Mira was mad; my mother-in-law said I ruined the family reputation.
> Rana sent me a cup of poison and Mira drank it laughing.
> I dedicated my body and soul to the feet of Hari.
> I'm thirsty for the nectar of the sight of him.
> Mira's Lord is Giridhar Nagar [mountain-lifter]; I will come for refuge to him.

After a number of devious homicidal attempts by the rana failed to take her life, Mira was able to leave the town of Mewar, her in-laws' home, and go off to the town of her uncle, where she joined a band of Kṛṣṇa devotees. One reason that Mirabai was able to relocate is that she and Bhoraj had no children. Had she been a mother of children, the freedom of movement that Mirabai enjoyed in later life might not have happened with ease. Mirabai eventually became a wandering Kṛṣṇa devotee who visited a number of places in North India that were holy to her Lord. She composed poems as she went and gathered a large following. A poem translated by Robert Bly and Jane Hirschfield (Bly, Mirabai, and Hirschfield 2004, 21) shows how the saint would have responded to people suggesting that she should return home and settle down. In it, Mirabai indicates that her role as a lover of Kṛṣṇa puts her on a different path from other women. Hers is not a traditional path, but in her view it is a superior path:

> The colors of the Dark One have penetrated Mira's body;
> All the other colors washed out.
> Making love with the Dark One and eating little,
> Those are my pearls and my carnelians.
> Meditation beads and the forehead streak,
> Those my scarves and my rings.
> Approve me or disapprove me.
> My teacher taught me this.
> I take the path that ecstatic human beings have taken
> for centuries.
> I don't steal money; I don't hit anyone. What will you
> Charge me with?
> I have felt the swaying of the elephant's shoulders;
> And now you want me to climb on a jackass?
> Try to be serious.

Vijaya Ramaswamy suggests that North Indian women saints had tighter cultural constraints than the women saints of South India (Ramaswamy 1992). It was the rare woman saint in the north who achieved the status of a founder of a movement. Mirabai was that rare religious virtuoso whose songs were on everyone's tongues. She garnered a significant following and was one of the few women who had a sect in her name in the medieval period. Hawley and Juergensmeyer (2004, 120) suggest that not only is Mirabai the best-known women saint in India, but her poems are the most quoted of any North Indian saint. Clearly, this strong-willed wife who made love as she wished while avoiding sex with her fleshly husband has left her mark on the religious landscape of India. Mira was not lauded by her immediate community. She shocked her family in the lifestyle that she chose. But through the songs that Mirabai sang while persisting on her chosen path, she won the hearts of North India's people and remains enshrined there today. The songs that Mira sang have not only thrived for over five centuries, but have given birth to hundreds of their own poetic children – poems in the style and voice of Mirabai. As a result of her persistent commitment to a higher calling, Mira helped many who puzzled over how to handle the conflicts of marriage and family life. Her work was more long-lasting than a clean diaper or hot meal. Her work was to make a song that gives comfort to those who (like many of us today) sometimes feel like their in-laws and extended family are trying to kill them.

The erotics of celibacy

Abstaining from sexual activity does not always mean the end of erotic life, as the example of Mirabai makes clear. Celibate persons who refrain from sexual activity may nevertheless have robust erotic imaginations and ecstatic experiences of sexual bliss. Mira certainly did. Sometimes sequestered from the world, frequently given ample time to study and contemplate higher order realities, religious people who opt for permanent celibacy are often in a position to cultivate practices that link them to divine beings in amorous ways. Medieval Christian nuns like Hadewijch saw themselves physically coupled with the body of Jesus. Ecstatic union with a heavenly bridegroom could be earned by the very disciplines of chastity and sexual abstinence that made a girl or women sexually unavailable to human partners. Virginia Burrus (2004) details the erotics of celibacy for Christians in *The Sex Lives of Saints: An Erotics of Ancient Hagiography*. Chapter 7 explores visions that Christian and Hindu mystics report, visions that give them access to ecstatic states of mind that could be described as orgasmic, within the mystical realm of religious life.

Benefits of celibacy

Sexuality is clearly a key aspect of what it means to be human. The two case studies presented here beg us to take up several questions. First, there is the question of why so many religiously and philosophically inclined people have argued that sexuality distracts us from what really matters in human life. Across the centuries and across the globe, there have been persuasive voices suggesting that sexual activity should be renounced so that other virtues and pleasures can be cultivated. Buddhist examples in Case Study 1 show how voluntary celibacy can bring a person freedom to author their own existence. Case Study 2 illustrates how celibacy might have given some Hindu women in North India scope for self-expression in the sixteenth century. Although both case studies focus on religious traditions that developed in India, they indicate the kinds of rewards that religious and philosophically minded people around the world have associated with sexual renunciation. Roman writers such as the Stoic philosophers of late antiquity saw celibacy and the regulation of sexual life as a prized weapon in the arsenal of self-control that gave a person authorship over their health and their state of mind. Christian writers developed the idea of sexual regulation as a sphere of personal development and self-authorship. Control of outward circumstances can be enhanced by control over one's sexual life. For Christians who had little control over decisions their family would make about whom they were to marry and at what age, temporary or permanent celibacy could offer enhanced agency. Elizabeth Clark (1981, 2008) has documented how many premodern Christian girls and women used voluntary celibacy to reject or modify prescribed gender roles of their times.

Celibacy and the social reproduction of religion

We saw in the Buddhist metaphor of the celibate renunciant monastic as a powerful rhinoceros that a celibate way of life can help a person define their own existence. Celibacy can be a way of defining oneself in relation to those aspects of society that are organized around family and vocational ties. By eschewing sexual activity, a religious person can stand apart from the world of reproduction and the responsibilities that are entailed by having children. By refraining from sex, such a person can also stand apart from the world of material productivity and opt for a life of scholarship, activism, artistic expression, or contemplation instead. Other people will bear children and ensure intergenerational continuity. Other people will make useful objects and sell them in the marketplace. The celibate person is called to something different – a different vocation. The work of the celibate religious person often involves memorizing, interpreting, and composing sacred texts or sacred songs and poems. Celibate religious persons also take as their vocations sacred practices such as chanting incantations or scripture, meditation, contemplative artistic endeavors such as painting, and contemplative athletic activities such as archery. By removing herself from the demands of the world of production and reproduction, the celibate person frees up time and energy that she can devote to reproducing religious practices and sustaining religious communities across space and time. Hence celibacy is often a key component in the social reproduction of religion. Across Asia and now across the world, celibate Buddhist monastics teach meditation and do scholarly work that suggests how to interpret the words of the Buddha in today's world. In historical Christian communities, monastics committed to permanent celibacy have played major roles as educators offering both religious and secular education. This is not to say that *all* religion is transmitted and passed down by celibate people. Many people, celibate and sexually active alike, are involved in the social reproduction of religious traditions. But celibate people do more than their share of spreading religion.

Types of celibacy

Celibacy is as complicated as sexuality. Sex occurs between the ears every bit as much as it does between bodies and sets of genitals. A person's sexual desire is conditioned by her age, education, social location, class identity, gender identity, sexual identity, and various other intersecting factors. Many forms of sexual pleasure are acquired tastes that are cultivated through exposure to certain social scenes and certain people. Like sexual activity, celibacy is immensely complicated. With so many intersecting aspects of human identity, what it means to be celibate is much more than simply refraining from sexual expression.

   Some of the types of celibacy to consider are: (1) temporary and permanent celibacy (including temporary abstinence from sex based on religious regulations), (2) voluntary and involuntary celibacy, (3) celibacy as a way of getting around social and religious regulations, and (4) celibacy that is desired but not attainable.

Temporary and permanent celibacy

Some of those who choose to be celibate opt for permanent celibacy. Religions whose most advanced practitioners live celibate lives offer institutional support for this choice in the form of places where a person committed to permanent celibacy can live and a community that she or he can join. But celibacy offers opportunities to transition through difficult passages in life, such as birth, illness, and death. Many religions that do not value the permanent renunciation of sexual activity nevertheless prescribe celibacy at key moments in life. Some Jews and Muslims observe scriptural commandments to avoid sexual contact on certain days in the religious calendar as well as on occasions of mourning and ritual impurity. As we will see in Chapter 2, religious people connect to the sacred in observing regulations about when, where, and with whom to engage sexually. Temporary celibacy is often part of the fabric of religious life, even in religions that have no place for people who undertake celibacy as a permanent lifestyle. Times of mourning and times of transition to a new social status are occasions when celibacy is often required of a person. The death of a loved one is an especially powerful moment when the community of the living must mark the change and help close the circle disrupted by death. Religious people often mark the mourning period by refraining from sexual activity for a time, as well as by fasting, wearing special clothing, and avoiding certain people, places, and activities.

Rituals that require temporary celibacy give some Buddhists a taste of institutional support for religious life and the benefits of celibacy without any expectation that a permanent vow of celibacy is required. In some South Asian cultures where Theravada Buddhism offers a framework for rituals of passage to adulthood, boys undertake temporary celibacy during a limited time spent as a novice monk. Time as a celibate monk helps to mark the transition between childhood and adulthood, but it is not expected that all boys who wear the robes of novice monks will remain in the monastic order. Some do, but many others leave the monastery to get married.

Seasonal renunciation makes sense as a response to changing conditions in work and income. Likewise, in some Buddhist and Hindu communities in Asia, celibacy can be practiced on a seasonal basis. Some Hindu and Buddhist renouncers observe celibacy for a time and then, when circumstances change, resume membership in the sexually active social world in which one must work to support a family. For example, on occasion Hindu and Buddhist renouncers work on a seasonal basis; these renunciant women and men typically renounce the social world of production and reproduction when the weather is inclement (monsoon time) or when work is scarce.

Voluntary and involuntary celibacy

We began this chapter with examples of voluntary celibacy, Buddhist and Hindu. Voluntary celibacy is often a path freely chosen by individuals that is often associated with a transformative experience that redefines the world of that individual. These are often exemplary individuals who are gifted self-narrators, establishing celibate communities where others can follow in the footsteps of the founder.

In some cases, celibacy that is based on religious regulations is involuntary, based on adherence to rules rather than personal choice. Such regulation-based celibacy is often temporary, such as that required when one is in mourning or undergoing a rite of passage to adulthood. Involuntary celibacy can stretch out for longer periods of time, however. Many of us are celibate before marriage. For some, that is a personal choice.

For others, social constraints limit opportunities for romance and sexual activity. Celibacy is imposed by parents or community leaders who keep young people under observation and punish those who engage in sexual activity. There are often grey areas that fall in between these two extremes. When you think of how peer pressure operates in your own life and in the choices that people in your peer group make, you have a good sense of the grey area that exists between free choice and coercion. We might speak of constrained choice, in recognition of those situations (and they are many) when one can exercise choice but the options one can choose are limited.

Celibacy and sexual identity

People who experience only same-sex sexual attraction may opt to be celibate in order to join or remain in a religious community that holds heterosexual marriage to be the bedrock of religious virtue. Many factors might convince a person to abstain from acting on same sex attractions. Such a person might refrain from same-sex erotic activity to accede to family wishes, such as the family's desire for grandchildren and continuation of the line through heterosexual marriage and childbearing. Such a person might enjoy deep ties of friendship with other adherents to that religion. For that person, the solidarity experienced in religious circles of their peers might be central to their sense of identity. While such horizontal ties with peers may be central for some, others may be more sensitive to vertical dimensions of relationships. Such people might value the institutional support that comes with adherence to a set program of sexual behavior as defined by institutional mandates. Some opt for celibacy in order to continue to be mentored by religious leaders and spiritual guides.

Eve Tushnet, author of a book titled *Gay and Catholic: Accepting My Sexuality, Finding Community, Living My Faith*, focuses on the horizontal ties of friendship that she has found in the Catholic community. Tushnet describes herself as an out queer Catholic who lives as a celibate person. Her story begins as a teenager coming out of the closet as a lesbian. Raised as an atheist, the author formally converted to Roman Catholicism in college. In an article (Tushnet 2014b, 20) on how religious communities with historically established stances against same-sex eroticism are being transformed by people like herself, Tushnet describes a Christian blog site (https://spiritualfriendship.org/) that she contributes to. This blog site features the work of a range of writers with different sexual preferences and different denominational affiliations who advocate "Christ-centered chaste friendships." For Tushnet, coming out as a celibate lesbian is part of a larger movement within her community – people who are out of the closet and who bring their identity as same-sex attracted people to the religious communities in which they participate. Some writers who contribute to the blog site regard their same sex attractions as out of line with the historic teaching of their denominations of Christianity. Some support civil rights for same-sex attracted persons while believing that acting on their own erotic desires would be impermissible. Some are single and intend to remain so. Some are married to heterosexuals and intend to remain loyal to their marriage vows.

Like Eve Tushnet, some Muslim women in communities that frown on same-sex eroticism remain celibate in order to maintain ties with loved ones and the larger religious community. While Islamic law has been explicit in the condemning male same-sex behavior as illicit, it has been much less clear on the issue of female same-sex behavior. For the same sex attracted Muslim woman in Scotland with whom anthropologist Afisa

Siraj conducted a series of interviews, it was more important to stay connected to her community than act on same sex desires. Like Eve Tushnet, this Muslim Scotswoman chose to forego sexual pleasure with other women in order to continue to enjoy intimate ties with family and friends.

Voluntary celibacy for people with same sex attractions can take many forms. People like Eve Tushnet abstain sexually by refraining from all sexual activity. Some maintain celibacy with regard to marital sex while pursuing sexual pleasure with same-sex partners. Others make arrangements with their heterosexual spouses to engage in some limited heterosexual activity perhaps in order to generate children or to conform to religious mandates about permitting a spouse sexual fulfillment. Religious institutions and authorities sometimes offer a great deal of latitude in what is permissible in the way of sexual imagination, sexual expression, and sexual activity. Marital arrangements can be established that allow scope for both spouses to satisfy primary needs. It's important to see that the authority that religion holds is rarely monolithic. Regulations that govern sexual life are composed of both formal and informal mechanisms of control, and these mechanisms operate differently. Moreover, not all individuals are equally subject to control and enforcement. It depends how visible one's personal identity is – in some cultures there is a great deal of surveillance and regulation of male behavior, but little is known or expected of female behavior. This is often true of cultures that practice gender segregation: the activities of women and those marked as female fall outside the purview of the realm of men and those marked as male. Some people's sexual activities are legible and some are not. Hence when we speak of celibacy based on religious regulations, we should be aware of horizons of possibility that go beyond the simplistic picture of religions as monolithic ideologies that compel all adherents to give up all sexual pleasures.

Celibacy as a way of getting around social and religious regulations

The third variety of celibacy that we dealt with in this chapter is potentially a subversive one. Celibacy can be a way around social regulations. The Hindu poet saint Mirabai exemplified for us the potentially rebellious power of celibacy. Mirabai loved a man whom she could not physically be with because the man she loved was the god Kṛṣṇa. We saw in Case Study 2 how Mirabai's ardent devotion to Kṛṣṇa enabled her to endure an unsatisfactory marriage to a human man. Mirabai shows how refusing sex and claiming celibacy as the correct path can be a deft subversive move for some, enabling them to avoid the limitations of a lifestyle that may be disempowering.

Likewise, Buddhist women and men have found a subversive power comes with opting for a life of Buddhist monastic celibacy which gives them options that their sexually active peers cannot exercise. Many nuns who joined the women's monastic Buddhist community in India, especially those who came from working-class backgrounds, left behind dangerous and exhausting lives as low-wage workers and domestic servants. Many records left by these women suggest that the celibate life of a Buddhist nun was a refreshing alternative to the endless labor and subservient social status that they would have suffered as married women in their modest socio-economic class of brides. Likewise, men who might have lost limbs in dangerous agricultural labor found alternative work in the monastery.

Celibacy wished–for but not attained

Celibacy can be desirable but unattainable for some classes of persons or some people at certain times in their lives. In some communities (for example, Muslim and Jewish), the very concept of celibacy is anathema and anyone who attempts to practice it would likely be shunned. In other communities, it is acceptable to practice celibacy in old age but never in youth. Differences in age and social power often affect one's ability to make decisions about what kinds of romantic and sexual relationships one will explore. As we saw with the case of the Scottish Muslim woman discussed above, there are some communities where a young person can only exercise very constrained choices when deciding how to conduct their sexual and romantic lives. Sometimes, poverty limits the choices available to a person. The celibate life often comes with a price tag that very poor people cannot afford. One might guess that impoverished and working–class people suffer the most constraints in choosing how to conduct their romantic and sexual lives, but this is not always the case. In the pre-modern world, aristocratic young people were often married off while still young, before they had any glimmering of sexual desire. For many elite families, the stakes would have been too high to allow their children to choose for themselves. Now if the spouse wedded to a young person through an arranged marriage should die and the young person were to marry a second time, there was often more latitude in the choice of a marriage partner. There might also have been the option of a celibate life, if desired by the person whose spouse had died. But for a first marriage for a young person of an elite social class, choices were often very limited. Hence a young North Indian woman of an elite family like Mirabai's would have been married off to a man of another elite family before developing an attraction to a chosen partner or developing a desire to live the celibate life.

Some gender fluid people must make a living as sex workers when they would prefer to remain abstinent. For example, in India today intersex and transgender persons known as *hijras* live in major cities. Hijras are often assigned male identities at birth but live lives marked by feminine modes of dress and presentation of self. Some are born with intersex genitalia. Some hijras are males who do not experience erections. Some undergo a castration ritual, known as *nirvan*, that is said to make the person a vessel of female divine energy. As we will see in later chapters, gender-variant and intersex people have played important roles as ritual specialists. Some cultures regard people who are "in between" genders and "in between" sexes as endowed with special abilities to cross over into other realms; such persons are sometimes seen as freely moving between human and divine realms. Hijras have traditionally been ritual specialists who use explicitly sexual innuendo in bawdy dance and song performances to confer fertility on newly married couples and on newly born children; in addition to this ritual role, some hijras engage in sex work (Nanda 1986; Reddy 2005). Hijras serve as conduits conferring fertility by drawing on the power of Hindu deities: goddesses representing fertile feminine energy coupled with disciplined male energy (represented by the god **Shiva**). Endowed with the power to bless couples with fertility, hijras also have the power to curse families with infertility. Their presence at weddings and the birth of babies is the occasion for gifts in exchange for giving their blessing to the family and the baby. If gifts are not given to the hijras who perform on these occasions, insults and curses will result.

Prior to the advent of British rule in India, hijras played an institutionalized, state-recognized religious role as ritual specialists. Today, it is more difficult to make a living in this way. While sex work has always been an option for hijras, economic pressures today make it difficult to remain celibate. Serena Nanda (1986, 157–158) shows that colonial era laws that removed state protections, disallowed land grants in support of hijra communities, and criminalized the castration ceremony had the effect of delegitimizing and impoverishing the hijra community. In the cities where many hijras live, Westernized education and a general decline in interest in traditional life cycle ceremonies have also made ritual work less reliable as a means of livelihood.

These changes explain why sex work might be desirable as a means of gaining income for hijras today. The hierarchically organized communal life of today's hijras can also make celibacy difficult. Many hijras live in domiciles known as houses (from the Hindu word *gharana*) that are organized along clan lines. In their structure, these houses draw on the traditional Hindu religious authority of the guru, or religious teacher, who is responsible for the religious education of disciples. The leadership of a gharana operates on the basis of seniority and can be quite authoritarian (Thomas 2013, 12ff.). Gurus maintain control over the hijras under their care and cover expenses through income garnered by sex work performed by junior hijras. If a junior hijra wishes to remain celibate and avoid sex work, it is generally impossible to do so until such time as the junior hijra reaches a certain number of years in the organization. Rising to the rank of guru, a hijra who wishes to be celibate is free to do so. Constraints on forming intimate bonds with sexual partners also limit the choices that hijras can make. In the communities where Tissa Mariam Thomas did her fieldwork in Bangalore, she observed that gurus often discourage their disciples from cultivating exclusive bonds with sexual partners (Thomas 2013, 107–108). Such bonds can make a hijra less available for sex work and have an impact on the revenue that the enables the house to run successfully.

Conclusion

Celibacy has appealed to many persons across time and space. As a means of empowerment, temporary celibacy has given sexually active people ways to mark sacred times and sacred places. It has been a means of concentrating power and consecrating oneself for ritual activity. Celibacy that is temporary helps people transition during critical passages of life; it appears often in rites of passage to adulthood or rituals of mourning that mark the death of a family member or spouse. Permanent celibacy has given many religious people ways to take authorship over the arc of their lives, offering self-definition and roles as religious teachers who reproduce the religion for the next generation. Celibacy offers a strategy that gives some people with same sex desires a way to remain deeply connected to their extended families, their religious institutions, and their chosen communities of friends. Monastic environments such as that established by the Buddha in ancient India or those of medieval Europe provide one context in which to pursue a celibate life. But celibacy can also be pursued within marriage, as we saw with the Hindu saint Mirabai. Called to a passionate love affair with the god Kṛṣṇa, Mirabai found in marital celibacy a way to deal with an unsatisfactory marriage. She pursued her own path and was eventually given the freedom to wander the countryside and compose poems that are still sung by Indians of all walks of life today.

Review: chapter highlights

- Case study 1: the Buddha and celibate Buddhist nuns and monks of early India;
- Case study 2: Mirabai, the celibate Hindu married saint;

- The erotics of celibacy;
- The benefits of celibacy;
- Celibacy and the social reproduction of religion;
- Types of celibacy;
- Temporary and permanent celibacy;
- Voluntary and involuntary celibacy;
- Celibacy and sexual preference;
- Celibacy as a way of getting around social and religious regulations;
- Celibacy wished-for but not attained.

Applications and reflections

1 Do you consider voluntary celibacy appealing? Why or why not? Was there a time in the past when you were drawn to celibacy as a temporary choice? Would you consider celibacy as a permanent practice? Why or why not?

2 For those drawn to it, how does celibacy that is chosen offer opportunities for self-expression and self-development? How does celibacy, even though it is chosen voluntarily, sometimes operate as an instrument of social control? Reflect on different kinds of celibacy that might be placed in a grey area in between voluntary celibacy and imposed celibacy. For example, how might same sex attracted people find possibilities for religious vocation in organizations that require them to be sexually abstinent? How does celibacy – temporary or permanent – offer possibilities for same-sex attracted people who wish to resist compulsory heterosexuality?

3 If you practice a religion, does celibacy play a role in the lives of people in your religious community? Do celibate persons that you know understand their abstinence in ways that offer a challenge to the conceptions of celibacy discussed in this chapter?

4 Reflecting on the example of Mirabai discussed in Case Study 2, can you think of contemporary examples of celibacy as a way to subvert or get around social regulations? Reflect on different kinds of celibacy that might be placed in a grey area in between voluntary celibacy and imposed celibacy.

5 Are you aware of secular groups of celibates? How do communities that identify as secular celibates differ from the kinds of religious communities practicing celibacy discussed in this chapter? Are there affinities between these groups?

6 If you are or can imagine yourself to be a same sex attracted person, what factors might make you desire to join or remain in a religious community that holds heterosexual marriage to be the bedrock of religious virtue? Can you see yourself practicing celibacy with regard to marital sex while pursuing sexual pleasure with same-sex partners?

Resources for further study

Bly, Robert, Mirabai, and Jane Hirshfield. *Mirabai: Ecstatic Poems*. Boston, MA: Beacon Press, 2004.

Clark, Elizabeth A. "Ascetic Renunciation and Feminine Advancement: A Paradox of Late Ancient Christianity." *Anglican Theological Review* 63, no. 6 (1981): 240–257.

Kinsley, David. "Devotion as an Alternative to Marriage in the Lives of Some Hindu Women Devotees." *Journal of Asian and African Studies* 15, no. 1 (January1980): 83–93.

Siraj, Asifa. "Isolated, Invisible, and in the Closet: The Life Story of a Scottish Muslim Lesbian." *Journal of Lesbian Studies* 15, no. 1 (2011): 99–121.

Thomas, Tissy Mariam. *The Clan Culture of Hijras: An Exploration into the Gender Identity and Status of Hijras Inside and Outside of Gharanas.* Bangalore: Centre for Research Projects, Christ University, 2013.

Tushnet, Eve. *Gay and Catholic: Accepting My Sexuality, Finding Community, Living My Faith.* Notre Dame, IN: Ave Maria Press, 2014.

Wilson, Liz. "Buddhism and Gender." In David McMahon (ed.) *Buddhism in the Modern World.* New York and London: Routledge, 2012: 257–272.

Wilson, Liz. "Buddhism and Family," *Religion Compass* 8, no. 6 (July2014): 188–198. http://reli gion-compass.com/sections/buddhism/.

2   Regulation

Case study 1

In Nepal's Kathmandu valley, surrounded by majestic Himalayan mountains, there is a religious institution in which girls and young women are assigned the job of running the world, or at least keeping forces of evil at bay and destroying any army that might wish to take over the country. Girls and young women known as **Kumārīs** have powerful roles to play in the religious and political spheres of Nepalese life. They incarnate a powerful warrior goddess and in order to make that power available to protect the people of Nepal, live cloistered lives following a strict regimen of rules that regulate how they eat, sleep, bath, and comport themselves in daily life, as well as where they go and with whom they interact.

In Hinduism, *shakti*, divine female power, is said to be the force that runs the world, animating and maintaining the manifest aspect of a supreme reality that also has an immaterial, unmanifest aspect. It is shakti that gives life to all creatures and animates all things. All the female deities of Hinduism are said to be forms that this female energy takes to accomplish specific tasks such as creation and destruction. Even the male deities venerated by Hindus are said to be animated by a shakti. Shakti works through them too; it is the energy that keeps the world going. Kumārīs are identified as individual manifestations of the shakti that is behind all embodied existence. They are specifically thought to incarnate the warrior goddess Durgā in her wrathful form as Taleju. Through the spiritual power of these girls, the goddess defends the Nepalese people and keeps invaders from taking over this crossroads Himalayan country. Nepal is a place where commerce has gone on between different ethnic and cultural groups for millennia: it is a common marketplace for Indian merchants who bring spices and other goods up from the hot plains of the south and for Tibetans who come down from high altitudes of the north with mountain products.

There are various legends about how the practice of venerating girls as living goddesses began in Nepal. One version says that the goddess **Durgā–Taleju** used to come down to earth and play dice with a particular Hindu king who ruled in the Kathmandu valley. She came night after night until one evening, the king could not control his lust and attempted to have sex with her. Durgā left the palace in anger (manifesting herself as the wrathful Taleju) never to return again. But she later revealed to the king that he could still enjoy the benefit of her patronage. Henceforth, the goddess declared, she would take the form of human girls who belong to a Nepalese Buddhist ethnic group, the Newars, and in that form she would henceforth provide protection for the Nepalese people. The Newars have a long history in the Kathmandu valley, where they constitute over half of the population. Newar Buddhists practice a Tantric form of Buddhism that meshes with the Hinduism brought to Nepal by Hindu kings from India. Thanks in part to the common veneration of a goddess who incarnates in the form of human girls, Buddhists and Hindus have built a society together and cemented their alliances by reference to a common stock of deities and sacred powers.

There are many Kumārīs who incarnate divine female power in Nepal. At one time, the Kathmandu valley was divided into three kingdoms with three capital cities. Each city was protected by its own Kumārī. In time, the kingdom was consolidated by one dynasty of Hindu rulers who built their royal complex in the city of Kathmandu. The Kumārī of the city of Kathmandu came to outshine the others, but there are still important living goddesses venerated in places outside the city of Kathmandu. The monarchy of Nepal was abolished in the early twenty-first century, but the institution of the Kumārīs continues.

To be selected as a Kumārī, a girl must exhibit bodily perfection. If a girl has shed blood, lost any teeth, or been afflicted with disease, she is ineligible to serve as a vehicle of the goddess. In addition to these aspects of physical wholeness, she is expected to have auspicious physical endowments such as a chest like a lion's. The Kumārī of Kathmandu is selected when very young and proves herself a worthy vessel of the warrior goddess by showing great courage during her installation ceremony. Performed on the eighth night of a fall festival in celebration of the goddess, a "black night" in which hundreds of buffaloes, goats, sheep, chickens and ducks are sacrificed at goddess temples throughout the country, she is ritually made into the terrible goddess Durgā-Taleju in a display of courage. The ritual is held on the evening that celebrates the famous military exploit in which Durgā killed a demon in the form of a buffalo, a demon that none of the gods were able to slay. A few hours after midnight, the Kumārī-elect is brought to the entrance for her final test after a month-long period of observation in which the girl is closely watched for any behavior incommensurate with those expected of a living goddess. As long as she showed the requisite focused, calm, and courageous personality expected of the goddess during the prior month, the Kumārī-elect is installed in a final test of her bravery: while being observed by the selection committee from an upstairs verandah, the girl must walk by herself around a courtyard that had been strewed with the decapitated heads of buffaloes. The buffalo heads represent the demon vanquished by the goddess Durgā-Taleju. Each head has been made visible by a lighted wick placed between the horns. The Kumārī-elect shows the committee her moxy by walking fearlessly along a raised edge on the border of this bloody courtyard. If she passes their final test, she is taken into the temple for a ritual of installation that removes all previous life-experience from the little girl's body so as to offer the goddess a pure vessel in which to enter into human life and Nepalese politics.

The life of a Kumārī is bound by discipline. The little girls who embody the goddess are expected to be virgins. They also lead cloistered lives and avoid not only sex, but also going out in public places and meeting people who are not close relatives. They are to sit without fidgeting on a throne or a cushion for hours at a time. They always wear red clothing and gold jewelry, and their hair must be worn in a knot on the top of the head. Their foreheads are marked with vermillion and other substances to give form to the eye of wisdom, known as the third eye in Hindu and Buddhist mappings of the subtle body. They eat a restricted diet of unspiced foods.

In Kathmandu, the royal Kumārī lives an especially sequestered life, enshrined in the heart of the city. She lives in a building that is called her home, a three-story building by the old royal palace in Kathmandu. The Kumārī's own family lives elsewhere. They may visit her, but they are not to hug her or speak to her. Her family must treat the royal Kumārī with the utmost respect, just like the other people who visit her in her capacity as a living goddess. Like ordinary devotees who worship the goddess seeing recovery from illnesses, success in business and school, and other forms of good fortune, her parents must visit the Kumārī in her home. They show her honor with the ritual gesture of putting their forehead on her feet, a gesture often seen in South Asian religious life as a way of showing respect for superiors: even the lowly feet of a superior are more pure than the highest and purest part of one's own body, the head. The Kumārī receives her parents and other visitors in a shrine room; on upper floors of her house, there is a throne room for the king and meeting rooms where men of her clan and caste group gather to settle disputes. Most of the time, the Kumārī stays "at home" receiving worship at set times of the day. She does not leave her home to go to school but instead received visits from tutors. She remains sequestered there unless needed to perform at state rituals that occur about a dozen times a year. Other non-royal Kumārīs live with their parents, but lead cloistered lives, maintaining purity through isolation from situations that could threaten their state of purity. Their dress, makeup, and comportment are similar to that of the royal Kumārī.

When the royal Kumārī leaves her home for state rituals, she is carried by male relatives so that her feet do not touch the profane ground and bring her ritual impurity. She is to exhibit extreme self-control on these ritual occasions. For example, once a year the royal Kumārī goes out on a chariot procession around the city of Kathmandu. She is not allowed to eat or drink or leave her chariot to go to the bathroom. She is expected to radiate a supernatural calm while, during the chariot procession, the city of Kathmandu erupts in festive merriment. Her placid demeanor is made even more evident by ritual combat going on all around her. The city is filled to capacity with exuberant festival goers, many of them fueled by drinking ceremonial alcohol, who engage in raucous games of tug of war involving her sacred chariot and the chariots of other deities.

When there are signs that a reigning Kumārī is human rather than divine, signs such as the loss of blood, the child is replaced by another girl. Any serious illness could be an indication that a girl is no longer a goddess. But the most watched-for sign is the loss of blood. Most girls are installed at a very young age. By the age of five or six years, some show signs of mortal status by the loss of blood associated with "baby teeth" falling out. Others are disqualified by first menstruation or a wound that brings blood loss. When such signs occur, they indicate that Durgā-Taleju is about to make herself present in another child.

On leaving office, a royal Kumārī receives a small stipend from the state in recognition of the services she rendered as a child goddess and she is henceforth required to be present at certain festivals where rituals that maintain the welfare of the Nepalese people are performed. Other Kumārīs also continue to play ritual and political roles. In an interview with Julie McCarthy (McCarthy 2015), a former Kumārī of Patan named Chanira Bajracharya described the transition to ordinary mortal as "tough" (McCarthy 2015). According to Nepalese anecdotal tradition, former Kumārīs often remain single. Many men are afraid to take former goddesses as wives. They are said to emit shakti energy long after the goddess has departed. That energy can take the form of an electrical charge that could be dangerous to potential husbands.

Case study 2

We will see in subsequent chapters how some cultures give important roles as religious leaders to gender-variant and intersex people. Sometimes being in-between sex and gender categories is linked to the ability to cross various cosmic barriers and help other people to cross them too. In those cases, people who cannot easily be classified as female or male are considered sacred beings or people who can enter sacred realms without difficulty. In other places and times, the structure of the religious world requires that a person be classifiable as one sex and not another or one gender and not another. Binaries of woman and man, female and male are, in these places and times, thought to be divinely created or inherent in the sacred order of nature. In such places and times, one wonders how gender-variant and intersex people navigate religious worlds that are divided into two separate spaces. Are gender-variant and intersex people able to move in religious settings where sex and gender binaries are held dear and thought to protect people against immorality? Are they welcomed, and if so, what regulations govern their actions? This case study may surprise you if you assume that gender-variant or intersex people have no place within religious communities that hold a strictly binary view of sex and gender differences.

In contemporary Iran, a theocratic state that enshrines Shia Islam as the basis for rule, sex change surgery is not only possible but receives moral and financial support from governmental agencies and religious leaders. Today's Iran offers an instance of a how a religion that proclaims the binary of male and female to be divinely created makes a place for intersex and gender-variant adults. Since the 1930s, intersex conditions and sex change surgeries have been part of journalistic, scientific, and religious discourses in Iran. With the establishment of the Islamic Republic in the 1980s, the regulation of sexual life in Iran has made gender-variant and transsexual persons legible and provided state support for sex change surgeries for people who feel that the sex assigned at the time of birth does not express their identity. Ayatollah Khomeini, the influential leader of the revolution in Iran that led to its establishment as an Islamic republic, set the tone for Iran's current state support for sex change surgery. Khomeini noted in a legal proclamation that in the foundational scriptures of Islam, there are no grounds on which to categorically prohibit sex change surgery (Bucar and Shirazi 2012, 420). Since this type of surgery is not mentioned in the Qur'an or the hadith, it can be considered within the realm of permissible interventions for those assigned a label at birth that does not suit their felt identity.

From the time that revolutionary forces ousted a CIA-backed regime in Iran that kept a puppet of the American government on the throne and was finally toppled with the establishing of an Islamic Republic, Iranians have organized their sexual lives in a much more public way than under the secular government of the Shah of Iran (the American-backed ruler whose fall from power occurred in the 1979 revolution). The Iranian state has an interest in social ethics and has many rules that are meant to guide appropriate romantic and sexual behavior of all people living in Iran. Sex within heterosexual marriage is highly valued as a sacred act and an expression of the gendered world that God created. State support for gender reassignment surgery is thus consistent with what the Iranian government wants to accomplish with regulations and incentives that influence how people arrange their lives (as persons with bodies that respond to stimuli from other people and impulses to have sex with other people). The government of Iran regards gender identity disorder as a treatable medical condition. For eligible persons who cannot afford the cost of surgery, the government pays expenses partially or in full (Bucar and Shirazi 2012, 420). With the support of Shia Muslim religious authorities, several hundred Iranian women and men have gone through sex change surgery since the 1980s.

Children with intersex conditions have always existed. Obviously, such children have been born to parents who belong to religious communities that divide the world by strict binaries of sex and gender. As these religious communities grapple with how to classify a child with atypical anatomy or an adult whose felt gender does not match their assigned gender, they generate regulations that make a place for people that do not fall on one side or another of strict binaries. In the case of Iran, medical discourses are put in the service of making gender-variant and intersex people legible and including them in the life of the religious community.

It would be naïve to celebrate Iranian support for sex change surgery as an example of a permissive country that puts no limits on the expression of sexual desire. Far from it. In contemporary Iran, same sex eroticism is illegal and same sex marriage is not permitted. Some people find it odd when they hear that Iran treats gender-variant people differently from same-sex attracted people. Scholars who look globally at the way that cultures get stereotyped warn against rushing to judgment when hearing about such places (Bucar and Enke 2011; Bucar and Shirazi 2012). These scholars suggest that the legacy of Western sexology as a science and liberal Western philosophical discourses on rights has given many Westerners the mistaken impression that freedom from social stigmas surrounding sex and gender is a Western achievement. People are surprised by what they hear about Iran because they expect all cultures and societies to follow a trajectory of freedoms progressively gained in the West. In the case of the West, it was the category of the gay or the lesbian person as a member of an identity class that opened the door to many other political gains for people marginalized by gender variance or sexual preference. The concept of rights that are based on a person belonging to a certain identity class (in this case, "homosexuals") is one that has a Western history. Some scholars insist that it should not be used as a yardstick to measure progress in other countries. A gay/straight alliance that gives a lesbian teen a voice in her Wisconsin middle school is an important place of support for her. But this does not mean that what some people in America regard as a separate identity based on same sex attraction must be expected to exist and be legible in those parts of the world that have not been informed by Western histories. The scholars cited above suggest that while identity-based groups are the basis for political power in liberal political philosophies of the modern West, we should not expect that this is universally the case all around the globe.

There has been much sensationalism that reveals broad stereotypes of Muslim majority cultures in media coverage of Iran's religious support for sex change surgery. Muslims are represented in frothy media coverage as backwards and oppressive towards women and minority groups. Some journalists, filmmakers, and scholars have suggested that the only reason the state of Iran promotes sex change surgery is to force same-sex attracted people to conform to compulsory heterosexuality. By going under the knife and taking on an "opposite" sex identity, the gay or lesbian person emerges as a heterosexual. Some commentators even insist that sex change surgery is inflicted punitively on unwilling participants. Afsaneh Najmabadi, a scholar who has voiced concerns about social pressures on same-sex attracted people in Iran, has looked into these allegations and found no evidence that sex change surgery has been forced on same-sex attracted people and no evidence of the use of the surgery being utilized as a form of punishment (Najmabadi 2008, 39).

This case study suggests that when looking at religious regulations pertaining to sexual expression in Iran, one can separate out how gender-variant people are treated from how same-sex attracted people are treated. This is one of the things that makes Iran an informative case study illustrating the diversity of religious life across the world. Iran is a complicated case to consider; it is important not to deny the tremendous difficulties that a same-sex attracted person can face in today's Iran. For such people, to live in a country where homosexuality is a crime punishable by death surely requires extraordinary courage and the capacity to suffer trauma. The ability to flourish as a human being cannot be easy in such a place. One-size-fits-all thinking, however, will not help, as Bucar and Shirazi suggest in their analysis of how sensationalistic Western media coverage focusing on sexuality in Iran has affected lesbians living there. Religious authorities in Iran now "work harder to appear tough on all non-normative sexuality" (Bucar and Shirazi 2012, 430). Gray areas of Muslim religious law that used to allow latitude for women to engage in same-sex eroticism are disappearing as new codifications that regulate sexuality are emerging.

Purity, pollution, wholeness, and holiness

The human body is fertile ground for religious practice. Anthropologists speak of a special kind of bodily impurity that is different from being physically dirty and in need of a cleaning; this kind of impurity cannot be removed simply by taking a shower. This is a type of religious impurity that comes when biology intrudes into community life. Life-changing events such as birth and death often require a response that acknowledges the fact that a new social moment has dawned and needs human effort to bring it to fruition. Birth is often said to bring ritual pollution on the birthing mother, her family, and those with whom she associates. A new human being emerges in a tremendously powerful biological event which can feel to the mother and people in attendance like a tidal wave. In childbirth, nature breaks into the human realm in powerful, unpredictable, and often uncontrollable ways; the ensuing state of ritual pollution marks the intrusion. It is much the same with death. With death, it is often the case that everyone in the family or clan of the deceased is considered to be temporarily polluted. A biological event has irrupted into human life; people mark the occasion by changes in their behavior. Necessary as death is, it is still something that breaks down human solidarity and interrupts cultural transmission of knowledge and wealth from one generation to the next.

Ritual impurity results from natural processes such as childbirth, disease, and death. As people move through the life cycle, they are sure to encounter other moments that bring contact with primal life forces and their disrupting power. Transitioning between the status of a child and that of an adult is often seen as a fraught passage. In those societies, girls and boys who transition into adults are subject to many regulations that mark the difficulties of the passage. Sometimes the child in transition to woman or man is to be treated as a corpse and avoided by community members for the time of transition to adulthood.

In many religions, rituals for restoring a person's purity lost through natural processes are thought to restore wholeness in the body in a way that matches the holiness of the divine or the sacred. Rituals restore wholeness by regulations of many different types. Some control the body's movement, leading to solemn, stylized, or markedly constrained movements of the body. Some control the times of waking and sleeping, of eating and drinking, and the types of foods and drinks consumed. Some dictate circumscribed interactions with other humans, such as separation and isolation from others and the avoidance of sex and other forms of intimacy. Some limit interaction with animals and plants; some place limits on the kinds of work that a person can do.

Regulation of the sexual body

Adult bodies with the capacity to connect sexually with another body have orifices that require attention. Sexual emissions need to be cleaned; the hygiene of the body is enhanced by regular attention to fluids that emerge from organs of the body associated with reproduction. But clearly the attention to the body that religious regulations impose is about more than hygiene. Many religions view the body's powers of generativity as sacred. Reproductive organs are the source of intergenerational continuity, generating children who pass the financial, social, and cultural legacies of one generation on to the next. The sexual body that can bring new life into the world must be cared for and restored to wholeness and holiness with ritualized behaviors that range from private cleansings to public rituals of purificatory bathing. For cleaning, a variety of agents of purification are used. Water is commonly used in many purification rituals, but other substances such as smoke are also used. In Orthodox Judaism and conservative forms of Islam, regulations speak to questions of when and where seminal emissions are appropriate as well as methods for cleaning the body after ejaculation. These religions speak of permissible times and places for sexual activity. While many folks consider talking about bodily emissions undesirable, religions are often garrulous about people's sex lives. Codes of purity in religions such as Orthodox Judaism and Islam devote much attention to sexual fluids such as vaginal emissions, breast milk, and semen.

In some societies, physiological substances like menstrual blood and semen are categorized as polluted. In others, blood and other bodily emissions are simply regarded as powerful but not necessarily as polluting. The menstruating woman or the man who has had a nocturnal emission is not considered unclean. Rather, this person is in a state marked by the irruption of sacred forces into human life. In the case of menstruation, the appearance of blood at the time when the uterus has been prepared for conception marks this blood as fertile. Such blood offers the potential of childbirth, and in childbirth there are often questions of paternity and responsibility. Whose child does she bear? Was the woman or girl raped? What family or clan will the child belong to? Menstrual blood is thus an eloquent symbol of all that can complicate or challenge present social arrangements. Menstrual blood symbolizes the potential of childbirth to bring chaos; childbirth can challenge human hierarchies and other social arrangements. In response to a substance that carries powerful symbolism, the menstruating woman or the man who has had a nocturnal emission needs to act in a ritualized way to mark the occurrence of such indications of fertility. Whether considered impure or merely powerful, emissions associated with the sexually active body are the focus of regulations that mark their appearance with ritualized, self-conscious forms of private cleaning or public rites of purification.

In many societies, the reproductive and sexual lives of girls and women are more closely regulated than sexuality in men. Menstruation, sexual intercourse, and childbirth are often occasions for girls and women to conform to set patterns. Purity rules speak to how a girl or woman should conduct herself when she is menstruating, having sex, pregnant, or in a state of post-partum impurity, having recently given birth. Where a girl or woman dwells during her menstrual period, what she does with shed menstrual blood, what she wears, who she associates with, whether she cooks for others or not, and whether she allows sexual and other forms of access to her body or not – these are often matters about which religion has much to say.

Regulation of the body in menstruation and childbirth

Menstrual blood and fluids emitted during childbirth are the focus of purity laws in Orthodox Judaism, traditional forms of Islam, and in various Asian religions. While more liberal forms of these religions are less concerned with matters of purity and pollution, more traditional forms focus on such matters as a way of recognizing the sacred in everyday life. For example, the Hebrew Bible specifies an extended period in which a woman who gives birth to a child is to sequester herself due to ritual impurity. The holiness code in the Biblical book of Leviticus tells men not to have sex with women during their periods. According to this code, women are to live apart from their husbands during their menstrual periods and cleanse themselves in running water, in a **mikveh** or religious bathing place, at the end of their periods. Jewish men who follow the Hebrew Bible's holiness code also immerse themselves in a men's mikveh when in a state of ritual impurity due to ejaculation. Some Jewish people today immerse themselves in the men's or women's mikveh when they wish to observe what their sect or group believes to be mandated by the Biblical holiness code. As we will see in Chapter 6 on Instrumentalization, for some contemporary Jewish people who are undergoing Jewish gender transition rituals in the U.S., the mikveh plays a central role in the process.

Hindu texts also speak of menstrual blood as a source of impurity that can be transmitted to others, mandating that women stay out of the kitchen and eat apart from their families. A Hindu guide to religious law, the *Laws of Manu*, declares that a man who has sex with a menstruating woman will lose his wisdom, strength, and shortens his life-span (Doniger and Smith 1991, 78). Like Orthodox Jewish and traditional Muslim women, traditional Hindu women attend to their bodily emissions and observe regulations about contact with others during their menstrual periods. Some live in a separate dwelling on the porch of their home or in a courtyard, being considered too impure to dwell with their husbands in the bedrooms. Menstrual seclusion is a double edged sword. It cuts against the freedom of females to move about and conduct themselves as they wish. But it also means that during their periods, many Hindu and Orthodox Jewish girls and women do not have to tend to men's needs, perform cleaning tasks in their homes, and cook meals. They are not even to enter the kitchen when in a state of menstrual impurity. Many Hindu girls and women consider the time of menstrual flow plus four-days to be the time required for impurity to pass. This could mean for a potential of eight, ten, or more days in which to be relieved from the ordinary responsibilities of a Hindu female householder. They are not required to entertain and bathe children. Others in her family bring her food and take care of her duties while she bleeds. So one might imagine a Hindu woman who happens to be burdened with too many domestic responsibilities, especially dull or unpleasant ones, looking forward to getting her period.

As a substance that is life-giving but dangerous in its capacity to transmit states of ritual impurity to others, menstrual blood has been a topic of immense concern for Hindus and Buddhists. In places such as China and Japan, mythic depictions of Buddhist realms of post-mortem punishment illustrate the workings of karma and warn that deviant female behavior leads to miserable places of rebirth. East Asian Buddhist legends tell of women suffering post-mortem pollution as a result of thoughtless shedding of polluted fluids from their bodies (Momoko 1983; Faure 2003; Glassman 2008). Texts such as the *Blood Bowl Sutra*, a Mahayana text attributed to the Buddha that was probably composed in China in the twelfth century, present graphic scenarios of unpleasant afterlives where women are forced to drink their own menstrual blood for an entire afterlife. Women in these realms must ingest disgusting fluids and be immersed in bodies of filthy liquids because they were not careful in the handling of blood and fluids coming from the uterus in past lives. This text and others like it also suggested that women should worry about the ecological circulation of blood and its miasmic effects. Menstrual blood, shed monthly, and post-partum fluids associated with childbirth can sully the earth and its guardian deities as well as deities associated with ponds, streams, and rivers. As Amy Paris Langenberg (Langenberg 2017) shows in her analysis of Buddhist menstrual blood taboos in comparison to ritual impurity systems in other religions, there is a tendency in some Mahayana texts circulating in China and Japan to blame the female womb for all kinds of impurities. Such texts use the rhetoric of female impurity to air worries about the vulnerability of men, especially monks who attempt to lead celibate lives detached from the realm of sexual reproduction. Women end up going to hell (or more accurately, one of a number of special hells that have the punitive, didactic purpose of teaching women who spread the miasma of menstrual blood what it feels like to receive impurity). Glassman notes a particular concern that female fluids could blend into the tea that the holy men drank (Glassman 2008, 137ff.).

The regulation of sexuality in marriage

The regulation of sexuality forms a bedrock of social control in most societies. Marriage is an obvious example that illustrates the power of sexual regulation to organize human life and encourage things that a society deems good and virtuous. With marriage vows and marital regulations, lust is harnessed for social ends and channeled productively. To appreciate the immense social labor that is performed by the regulation of sexuality in marriage, consider the procreative emphasis found in some religions. The demand that sex be dedicated to procreative ends tells us that marriage is often geared toward redirecting the couple's energies to larger social goods. This makes the marriage bed a place of sexual self-control as much as a place of sexual indulgence. During the late imperial age of Rome, when many lives were lost to early infant mortality and warfare, the emperor Augustus saw that the need for more citizens was becoming dire. He proclaimed new legislation geared toward controlling the practices of those aristocratic couples whose marriages did not yield children. Only those who coupled productively with their spouses could inherit wealth from their parents.

For early Christian thinkers who looked forward to the imminent return of their crucified savior Jesus and his establishment of an ideal millennial reign of perfection, marriage and family were looked at with suspicion as a source of conflict for the believer who should be ready to drop everything and follow Jesus. As Peter Brown shows so lucidly in *Body and Society* (Brown 1988), many early Christian thinkers were openly opposed to marriage as a perpetuator of a dominant social order that they believed to be on the verge of disappearance, to be replaced by a heaven on earth. As time went on and Christianity went from a countercultural religion to a state-supported religion, Christian thinkers needed to justify marriage as a social good. The identification of the marriage bed as the arena of moral action was a crucial rhetorical step. Christian thinkers developed regulations to govern sexual life, drawing on pre-Christian ascetic and medical practices for the proper channeling of amorous impulses. The idea that sperm should not be squandered by having a lot of sex, for example, was one that many found compelling in the Greco-Roman world of antiquity. Sperm were thought to concentrate a man's vital essence or life-force. Christians drew on such pre-Christian ideas about the need for sexual self-discipline in order to give marriage legitimacy.

For those religions that encourage but do not require people to practice celibacy on a permanent basis as renunciants or members of monastic orders, the regulation of the minutia of sexual coupling is often the moral equivalent to the disciplined life of the full-time celibate person. It makes possible those religions (Roman Catholic Christianity, for example) that esteem members of monastic orders but also regard sexually active married couples as exemplars of the morally proper life. Monogamy in such traditions is itself a moral exercise, a disciplining of the amorous impulses that makes it the lay counterpart to the monastic call to total self-discipline.

In Jewish ethical life, marriage is an arena for the expression of religious piety. Gratitude for a God who created the world along with bodies marked by sex and gender makes sexual activity on Shabbot a **mitzvah**, a commandment that Jews take as an obligation to do good. Sex on Shabbat is a mitzvah, provided that the sexual act meets the regulations that govern what is appropriate. Sexual desire, a natural desire like thirst and hunger, is a good deed when expressed appropriately in marriage. In the marital bond, desire is channeled by religious regulations. Attention to women's sexual needs is required of an observant man. Sex should be geared toward what biologists would call "strengthening the pair bond." It is not just for procreation but also for sustaining mutual attraction and commitment in a couple. Regulation is key to ensuring that sexuality is harnessed to appropriate ends. Regulations govern not only the activities of people engaging in sexual activity but the intentions that shape the patterns of arousal.

Likewise, for Muslims sexuality is celebrated as a natural part of human life. Marriage is ordained by God and sex within marriage is a desirable aspect of human life. There are mandates that ensure that men pay attention to women's sexual pleasure in the marital bed. As we will see in later chapters, the Prophet Muhammad founded a new religion that gave girls and women in the Arabian Peninsula considerably more rights than they enjoyed at the time of the Prophet's birth, including rights within marriage.

Social status and marriage regulations

In many cultures, the more important you are in the social hierarchy, the more you must abide by regulations that limit your freedom. Such was the case when it came to marriage for elite girls and young women in medieval and early modern Europe. While their less affluent age-mates could tumble into the arms of lovers in the barn or forest and engage freely in sexual intercourse prior to marriage (as long as betrothal took place if pregnancy occurred), aristocratic young women were not permitted such sexual liberties. In addition, they were often denied the physical freedom that their peers enjoyed – the freedom to wander and play far from home. As historian Marilyn Yalom (2002) has demonstrated, elite women in the West have historically done some of the heaviest lifting in terms of the social labor that their marriages have been expected to perform. The higher the social class or position of authority within the society, the more likely it is that her sexual activities have consequence not just for her but also for others. The purity of descent lines which elite women's legitimate offspring support only matter if there is an inherited authority or wealth that depends on there being no illegitimate children to sully those pure lines of descent. While non-elite girls and women of premodern Christianized European cultures often selected their own mates, females whose families owned land in early medieval Europe might have endured pre-adolescent betrothals and marriages, locked chastity belts, and constant surveillance by nannies and servants. Girls whose families did not own land could often follow their amorous feelings and, having made their selection, be betrothed to a mate in a simple ceremony such as hand-fasting. For peasants in medieval Europe, sexual activity was permitted after the betrothal as long as the couple presented themselves at the altar for marriage before any offspring were born (Yalom 2002, 49). Illegitimate offspring posed more serious problems for the landed gentry, where girls and women were arranged in marriages that were intended to foster solidarity among elites and produce legitimate children to transmit elite patrimony to the next generation.

As we will see in later chapters, the intertwined social and economic status system known as caste has operated in South Asia as a regulator of social life that is also open to improvisation and experimentation. In the traditional caste system, caste is inherited. Like some societies' understandings of class as a hereditary trait, caste limits a person's options for occupation as well as the person's place in society. Unlike some hereditary class systems, though, caste specifies precisely what a person's occupation will be. Marriage within the caste of one's family is thus a means of keeping a high rank: perpetuating a family's occupation, income, and social status. Their role as guardians of caste rank makes marriage a serious pursuit for high caste females within traditional South Asian Hinduism and also within those forms of traditional Buddhism that have been heavily influenced by the caste system, as in Nepal. Married women typically go to live with their husband's extended family; children that they bear will be counted in their husband's line of descent.

Where caste is a consideration at the top of the social hierarchy, a girl's potential to bear children that will grow up to carry their father's names and continue their occupations is a precious asset. An unmarried girl who is a virgin has in her the potential to bear legitimate children. Since this unrealized potency means a great deal in a highly stratified social system, a high caste Hindu or Buddhist girl's potential to maintain caste purity compels expressions of respect and veneration. As we will see, the veneration that she is given and the regulations that she must follow to be worthy of such respect make this high caste unmarried girl a counterpart to the living goddesses, the Kumāris of Nepal's Kathmandu valley.

In Hindu and Himalayan Buddhist wedding ceremonies, the father of the bride strives to give his daughter to another man of equal or higher caste, a man who appreciates what the girl's potential fertility can do for his family and recognizes what a precious gift a virginal bride is for the sake of caste purity. The father who gives away his daughter at the Hindu wedding rite is giving the gift of a virgin. Hindu legal treatises use terms in Sanskrit that can be translated in English as "virgin-gift" or "maiden-gift." A father who so gives knows that his daughter's true value is her *potential* fertility. Her hymen should be intact; there should be no risk that she is already pregnant with the child of man of a lower caste (or subcaste, to be more precise, since each caste is divided into hundreds of subdivisions). Should her capacity to be fertile be known to have been tested or be in evidence at the time of the wedding, this could lead the bridegroom's family to stop the ceremony and call the marriage arrangement off.

Traditional Hindu and Buddhist bridegrooms who worry about maintaining the religious values of their parents seek women who will allow their paternal lines to flourish
without any concerns about adultery.

There is some flexibility in marriage within the traditional caste system. For example,
hypergamy (marriage in which the woman marries a man of higher status) is an ideal
form of marriage according to some Hindu texts. In cases of hypergamous marriage,
regulations surrounding the bride are particularly strong. The bride is being given to a
family who, by association, can lift the status of the bride's family. If a girl is being
prepared for hypergamous marriage to a higher caste family, she may be subject to
extensive surveillance. A potential source of upward social mobility, she must avoid
anything that would compromise her family's reputation and bid for identification with
a higher caste people.

Gender segregation

Among high caste women in Nepal and other parts of South Asia where caste stratification plays a significant role in society, many regulations dictate women's comportment, dress, speech, and other aspects of self-expression. Women not only care for the
bodies of children but pass along caste identity and caste values; they are key figures in
guaranteeing that the next generation knows their rank in society and knows how to
live accordingly. The job of reproducing religion and culture in succeeding generations
falls heavily on the shoulders of elite Hindu and Buddhist women in Nepal. Because of
this, such women must be circumspect in their actions and speech. Such tasks as
childcare and domestic instruction are often thought to be better done by a woman
who is trained, who is selective in the company she keeps, and who is self-aware and
careful in the words that she speaks to outsiders, than by a woman who has not been
trained in these facets of life. The well trained woman who observes caste codes governing conduct for her gender always pays attention to kinship relations. She knows
who is kin to her and who is not and seeks to avoid interactions with men who are
outside her family or clan. Unless it is a matter of urgency or strategy, she will avoid
initiating conversation with strangers.

High caste women in some parts of South Asia observe rules of gender segregation. If
a family can afford to do so, it's considered prestigious for girls and women to stay at
home rather than working outside the home. Rather than going out of the home for
schooling, tutors are brought in to the home. When medical care is needed, doctors
come to the home to treat the girls and women there. Men in the family or servants do
the shopping. Even within the home, women and girls maintain a boundary between
themselves and adult men in the house or domestic complex. For example, the inner
courtyard is often designated as female space and adult men are normally not expected to
appear there. If an adult male wishes to enter that space, he needs to send a child to tell
the women that he plans to visit. Men who are not kin to the women may only enter
parts of the domestic complex designated for men.

Not all high caste Hindus and Buddhists practice gender segregation. But the custom
of sequestering young women and restricting their movements is common. It is often
the case that for a high caste family that does not practice gender segregation, there is a
feeling that girls and young women need to transition to a more restricted sphere of
movement as they approach puberty. In traditional Hinduism, high caste girls were
given in marriage before their first menstruation. At this moment when her potential

fertility is at its peak, a daughter is in need of the kind of training that makes her able to preserve caste purity. The young woman who is not yet married has the potential to do a great deal of social labor for her family and her caste. The recognition of this potential is ritualized in a Hindu custom of setting up a temporary platform for the display and worship of girls who have not yet reached puberty. This custom is observed in many parts of India, but particularly in Punjab and Bengal. Pre-pubescent girls are the focus of rituals of veneration that draw attention to the good fortune that they can bring families. In Bengal in the northeast of India and Punjab in the northwest, as well as in parts of the south, pre-pubertal adolescent girls are ritually displayed for their families and clans to venerate in a ritual called *kumāri pujā* (Fruzzetti 1982, 96–98; Allen 1996, 3). In this *pujā* or worship ceremony, the girl is temporarily elevated to the status of a goddess such as the warrior goddess Durgā or Kālī, who manifests Durgā's fierce aspect. Sometimes the girl is identified simply as shakti, the divine female energy behind all manifest existence. However the girls are identified, they are to behave as sacred beings. Like the Kumārīs of Nepal, these pre-pubescent girls are expected to sit placidly for prolonged periods of time while relatives bow before them and offer foods, flowers, lights, and other gestures of veneration normally offered to goddess icons in the home or temple.

The festival calendar of Hinduism offers a symbolically rich occasion for kumāri pujā rites. In many parts of north India, Hindus celebrate the good fortune brought by the goddess Durgā when she slayed the Buffalo Demon Mahīṣa Asura. During this time, the goddess is thought to visit her natal family on earth. Artists create handcrafted icons of Durgā that can range from a small icon suitable for table-top display to gigantic icons the size of small houses. In places like Kolkata (Calcutta), people band together with others in their neighborhood to build temporary outdoor shrines large enough to display these icons of the goddess. During the height of the fall goddess festival, people of Kolkata and visitors who come for the festivities wander from place to place admiring the artistry of the displays. At the end of her visit to earth, the goddess is said to go back to her legendary heaven to take care of business required of her until festival time next year. Her icons are then ritually immersed in bodies of water as a way to dismiss the goddess. Likewise, the girls who are venerated as a goddesses during Durgā Pujā return to the status of human girls.

Conclusion

Religious regulations are crucial markers of the sacred in many religions. Regulations govern all aspects of life, marking powerful biological events such as birth and death and underscoring the necessity for humans to acknowledge these events as primal forces that demand attention. By paying deliberate attention to the body as a field of powerful forces, religions use the life of the body to effect a state of wholeness or holiness. The life of the sexual body often demands special attention. Cleansing after sex or the emission of sexual fluids during erotic dreams marks sexual expression as an arena in which deeply held values are expressed and a person registers the desire for wholeness or holiness. Nothing is too ordinary to be overlooked. Rules about contact with blood, semen, post-partum fluids, breast milk, and other physical excretions are the stuff of religious law codes. In addition, the sexual body is often closely regulated during moments of major transition in life, such as the transition from childhood to adulthood.

In some societies, physiological substances like menstrual blood and semen are categorized as polluted. In others, blood and other bodily emissions are simply regarded as powerful, but not necessarily as polluting. These fluids are understood to mark the irruption of a potentially chaotic power into the structures and order patterns of human society. To restore wholeness and holiness, the menstruating woman or the man who has had a nocturnal emission needs to act in a ritualized way to mark the occurrence of blood or semen.

We often think of religion as a sphere of privation in which pleasures are prohibited. But when sex is enacted in a regulated, permissible manner, it is often given high value in religions as a way of doing good or keeping the cosmos in balance. The channeling of sexual desire in marriage is a good example. Societies have used regulations to harness lust to enable the cultivation of virtues like loyalty, reciprocity and compassion for others and as a way to promote such social goods as the bearing and training of children. In societies that are highly stratified by class, marriage is an important means for highly ranked people to maintaining their social status. Among those at the top, regulations governing the lives of adolescents of marriageable age can be quite demanding. Likewise, for married elites at the top, the regulations that govern behavior, dress, comportment, and other aspects of lifestyle can be elaborate. Gender segregation is common in some places as a marker of status. Those who can afford to keep women sequestered from public view thereby make their status conspicuous.

Review: chapter highlights

- Case study 1: Kumārīs in Nepal;
- Case study 2: gender-variant people in Iran;
- Purity, pollution, wholeness, and holiness;

  a   Primal forces and human responses;
  b   Ritual purity and pollution;
  c   Wholeness and holiness;

- Regulation of the sexual body;

  a   Sexuality and chaos;

- Regulation of the body in menstruation and childbirth;

  a   Social control;

- Regulation of sexuality in marriage

  a   Regulating desire toward social goods;
  b   Ascetic and medical self-discipline;

- Social status and marriage regulations;

  a   Hierarchy and restriction;
  b   Elite women versus non elite;

- Gender segregation;

  a   Divisions of social space;
  b   Sequestration of females as a signal of high rank.

Applications and reflections

1   Reflect on a religion that you know something about – perhaps one that you practice, or perhaps that is practiced by a friend or family member. What kinds of regulation do you see operating in that religion? Are people likely to follow regulations in the way they conduct themselves based on their gender? What about social class or rank: are people at the top or the bottom more likely to be subject to such regulations? What is the role of age and stage of a life?
2   Are there religions that do not posit the need to regulate the life of the body? In those religions, what marks major transitions such as birth and death?
3   How might religious forms of regulation lead to social solidarity? How might they enforce differences between group members?
4   Reflect on the difference between bathing for hygiene and bathing to mark the end of menstruation. What is it that makes one a religious act? For those who have engaged in religious rituals that relieve the body of a condition of impurity, what marks ritual cleanliness? Is it something more than the passage of a set number of days? Are there types of impurity that do not go away with the passage of time or the application of ritual effort?

Resources for further study

Bucar, Elizabeth, and Anne Enke. "Unlikely Sex Change Capitals of the World: Trinidad, United States, and Tehran, Iran, as Twin Yardsticks of Homonormative Liberalism." *Feminist Studies* 37, no. 2 (2011): 301–328.

McCarthy, Julie. "The Very Strange Life of Nepal's Child Goddess." National Public Radio. May 28, 2015. Accessed Aug. 15, 2018. https://www.npr.org/sections/parallels/2015/05/28/410074105/the-very-strange-life-of-nepals-child-goddess.

Tree, Isabella. *The Living Goddess: A Journey into the Heart of Kathmandu*. New York, NY: Eland Publishing, 2015.

Wilson, Liz. "Embodiments of Shakti: Cosmic Power Displayed by Kumārīs, Incarnate Goddesses of Nepal." In Jeanine E. Viau and Otto von Busch (eds.) *Silhouettes of the Soul: Meditations on Fashion, Religion, and Subjectivity*. London: Bloomsbury Press, Dress Cultures series, edited by Reina Lewis and Elizabeth Wilson. Release date 2020.

3 Controversy

Case study 1

Polygyny (a practice that allows a man to marry and to be married to more than one woman) is a controversial practice in many societal contexts. Even in places where polygyny is an accepted marital practice on religious or cultural grounds, it is often debated internally and among religious communities, by national legal authorities, the society in general, as well as by international organizations working in the areas of women's rights and sexual and reproductive health rights.

The practice of polygyny is commonly perceived to be a religious practice and in our contemporary world it is often associated with Islam. It is important to note that although polygyny is associated with Islam, it does not mean that all Muslims subscribe to the practice. In fact, in some countries where Islam is the dominant religion, as for example in Tunisia, polygyny has been declared illegal. This type of negation of a religious practice in contemporary times illustrates that religious practices are contested and subject to change over time. Polygyny also constitutes part of the accepted marital regimes in many African societies, some of which have accorded polygyny legal recognition through the implementation of customary law.

In South Africa, Muslim communities, which make up approximately 1.5% of the total population, have sought legal recognition for Muslim marriages. Muslim marriages are potentially polygynous as a Muslim man is allowed to take up to four wives. Although there exists many contestations pertaining to interpretations of Qur'anic verses that allow for polygyny – some of which uses other verses in the Qur'an to delegitimize the practice – the traditional view is that a Muslim man is allowed to marry up to four wives. During **apartheid**, a system of institutionalized racial segregation and hierarchy (white supremacy) that existed in South Africa from 1948 until the early 1990s, polygynous unions were considered to be entirely immoral. Since 1994, democratic South Africa has redressed some of the discriminatory apartheid politics by, among other things, drafting and implementing laws that recognize African cultures and practices. The Recognition of Customary Marriages Act of 1998 is one such legal framework. Under the Customary Marriages Act, polygynous marriages, observed by many indigenous peoples of South Africa, are recognized and regulated. Despite foreshadowing legislation that recognizes marriages under *any* tradition or religious system in the South African Constitution of 1996, Muslim marriages are still not legally recognized. Internal disagreements and ideological contestations over who gets to decide what and how inform the battle over recognition of Muslim marriages.

Muslim communities in South Africa are not one homogenous group, rather, South African Muslims are a diverse group that reflects complex histories and distinct practices. When the Muslim Marriages Bill was released in 2010 – a bill that seeks legal recognition and regulation of Muslim marriages (including polygynous unions) – it was given the nickname "the *kufr* bill" by those who are committed to the primacy of **Shari'ah law** (that is, moral and ethical principles set out in the Qur'an) over South African Constitutional Law. *Kufr* is an Arabic term used to refer to a person who has rejected God and is often translated to mean "disbeliever" or "infidel". In the colloquial use of the term, *kufr* commonly refers to a person who acts immorally or who holds anti-Muslim sentiments. In the context of the Muslim Marriages Bill, then, the term *kufr* indicates that the Bill did not represent "true" or "authentic" Islam. Rather, the Bill was like an infidel! Not only because of what the Bill contained but also because it was to be included in a legal framework that did not prioritize God as the ultimate lawmaker.

The Muslim Marriages Bill was also contested by many **ulama** (religious clergy) who would much rather formalize a parallel legal system where Shari'ah courts function alongside the South African legal system. This solution reflects current practices where a number of *ulama* bodies – without any state regulation or control – cater to the needs of the South African Muslim population with regard to contracting marriages (including polygynous unions), matters of divorce, custody, and inheritance.

There were also those who opposed the Bill as its provision to allow polygyny, in particular, was seen as contrary to the constitutional value of gender equality. Women's rights activists and advocacy groups argued that religious laws (in general) are so steeped in patriarchal discourse that including such provisions (such as that of allowing polygyny on religious grounds) into constitutional law is like giving religious patriarchy license to continue to treat women like second-class citizens. The Bill was also opposed on the grounds that religion is a private matter. These, predominantly dedicated secularists, advocated for the strict separation of state and religion. They cared less about the content of the proposed Bill than the need to keep secular law secular!

What are the experiences of South African Muslim women? And, would the recognition of Muslim marriages have a positive impact on Muslim women's lives? A keen attention to the real bodies and experiences of Muslim women is missing from the above contestations over the Bill. One of the most persuasive arguments for recognition, as articulated by Muslim NGOs and networks lobbying for support for the Bill as well as researchers involved in mapping the experiences of Muslim women in South Africa, is that non-recognition has proved to negatively impact the lives of Muslim women. In particular, this has to do with the need to ensure rights for Muslim women who are in polygynous unions, the need to regulate the contractions of these unions, as well as to alleviate the difficulty of attaining divorce for women. Two excerpts from Hoel (2010) serve as examples to illustrate some of the contextual texture of current marital practices in Muslim communities:

> I was about 3 months pregnant, [and] he had a [sexual] fling the whole year before that, [because] I was pregnant I wasn't working, [and] I couldn't support him. Every time I don't support him he performs [has sexual relations and doing drugs]. So he got married to her because the drugs was free ... he took another wife, and I didn't know about it ... [You] don't just take another woman because that is when all these diseases come in, AIDS and all this. I did it [HIV-test] afterwards at work,

because now sometimes … he stays away … if he can cheat on you once, he can cheat on you again, you know what I mean, and what do you do? Now I must go for a test, I did twice a test, because I had to protect myself.

When we got married none of his family was there … because do you know what, they blamed me. I was the dirty rag, I was stealing him away from his wife, and in the meantime I didn't even know [that he was already married]. I was very scared of her [first wife]. After he admitted to me he was married, she came one day to point a finger in my face and said to me that I was really the bad one because I stole him away and I messed up his life.

The excerpts signal that polygynous unions are contracted in secrecy, that is, without the knowledge of the first wife (as in the first excerpts) or without the knowledge of the second wife (as in the second excerpt). Obviously, the contraction of polygynous unions also happens with the knowledge and consent of wives – and Hoel's study also documents examples of this. However, the point is that the current practice of polygyny does not require the knowledge or consent of wives. To complicate matters further, *ulama* bodies hold marital reconciliation as an Islamic ideal and women therefore often go through protracted procedures in order to attain a religious divorce. In Islam, men have a unilateral right to divorce, whereas women have to seek recourse through religious bodies such as the *ulama*. To make matters even more complex, women in polygynous unions whose marriages are not registered elsewhere – as they are not legally recognized – can (officially) not seek protection under South African constitutional law.

South African Muslim women's experiences in dealing with marriage and divorce practices – particularly in relation to polygynous unions – is incisive when it comes to debates over Muslim marital recognition. In 2018 the High Court in South Africa ruled in favour of producing legislation that extends constitutional protection under the law to individuals in Muslim marriages. In particular, concerns related to women and children were highlighted. Although the judgment signals willingness on behalf of the Court to provide protection, the extent of regulation particularly as it pertains to the male privilege of divorce and polygyny remains to be seen.

The controversy over recognizing Muslim marriages involves many actors and spheres of society both internal and external to Islam and Muslims. The Muslim practice of polygyny, in particular, also opens up interesting debates that relate to legal dimensions (both religious and secular law) and push back against international laws such as the legal systems evolved through the United Nations (for example, Human Rights), which operates through a notion of collective rights. Women's rights and advocacy groups are concerned about religious patriarchy, particularly as it pertains to provisions on gender equality and women's sexual and reproductive health rights, and the extent of its power if/when religious law is implemented as part of constitutional practice. Moreover, the controversy over Muslim marriages and Muslim polygyny in particular, can also be interpreted through the lenses of colonial, racist and Christocentric discourses, which beg a contemporary privileging and acknowledgement of diverse indigenous cultures and religions. The controversy over Muslim marriages signals the many and complex ways in which religion gets intertwined in multiple connecting discourses and the wider public and moral implications that the debate fosters in society at large.

Case study 2

In 1988, a "Statement on AIDS" was released by the National Association of Evangelicals (NAE). The statement foregrounded the intimate connection between the transmission of AIDS and morality. More precisely, the statement reflected that the transmission of AIDS occurred because people were having immoral (sexual) relations in the context of the United States. According to most evangelicals, what was needed in order to deal adequately with the epidemic was a Biblical approach. That is, to remain chaste before marriage and to remain faithful within marriage. For most evangelicals, the AIDS epidemic signaled the need for and importance of Christian morality, which was believed to hold civilizing capacities where sexual behavior (read: promiscuity) was concerned.

Importantly, the 1980s was also the decade where AIDS was primarily associated with homosexual sexual behavior, a view held among many evangelicals in the United States. Ron Sider, a leader in the Christian justice movement, wrote "AIDS: An Evangelical Perspective" (1989, where he made this link clear. While arguing that homosexuals who are infected with AIDS should be cared for and given support, he also notes that he believes that the Bible teaches that homosexual practice is wrong and, as such, it is not presumptuous to assume that such sexual transgressions will have negative consequences. Although not arguing that AIDS is God's punishment for homosexuals, Sider does amalgamate homosexual sexual behavior with immoral and un-Christian sexual behavior (Petro 2015).

Within evangelical circles, AIDS continued to be a disease that had to do with homosexual sexual (im)morality until the turn of the twenty-first century when many evangelical missionaries heard about or came across the epidemic during their trips to sub-Saharan Africa. The "face" of AIDS changed from that of a gay (often white) man in the United States to that of heterosexual Black Africans. However, the Christian moralizing rhetoric – the Biblical approach – remained similar. The battle to prevent AIDS transmission had to do with cultivating a Christian morality (read: abstinence and fidelity), not promoting condom-use or administering drug cocktails. Many evangelicals saw themselves as particularly well suited to engage in the moral education of Africans (Petro 2015). The Saddleback Initiative, founded by Rick and Kay Warren, is one such evangelical initiative. Prompted primarily by Kay Warren's motivation to help the "innocent victims of Africa," that is, women and children, the Saddleback initiative employs the S.T.O.P. strategy to end the AIDS pandemic. S.T.O.P. consist of four strategies: "Save sex for marriage," "Teach men and boys to respect women and children," "Open the door for the Church," and "Pledge fidelity to one partner for life" (Petro 2015).

The S.T.O.P. strategy and the Saddleback Initiative, overall, are troubling for a number of reasons. Reflective of colonial approaches to civilize Africa and Africans, including the belief that Christianity is superior and/or more evolved than any indigenous religious system, the Saddleback Initiative posits the church as the ultimate moral authority in sexual matters. Hence, people's sexual behavior needs to be modified in order to reflect "correct" Christian morality. The focus on African male promiscuous behavior – through the portrayal of innocent women and children infected with AIDS – can be read as a result of the lack of Christian morality in African men. Colonial imaginaries of African men are ripe with portrayals that render African men excessively sexual (and predatory), portrayals that find resonance in contemporary evangelical discourses. The solution according to evangelicals is moral education. In practice, this means abstinence and fidelity. It becomes clear when taking into consideration the S.T. O.P. strategy that monogamy is the only acceptable Christian sexual relation. In contrast to the previous case study, which, among other things, presented a rationale for polygyny in South Africa, the S.T.O.P. strategy implicitly links all relations but monogamy to the sphere of sexual immorality.

Looking at the ways in which evangelicals have dealt with the AIDS crisis since the 1980s up until today, it is interesting to note the similarities between how evangelicals dealt with AIDS as a "gay problem" and, then, AIDS as killing innocent women and children in Africa. In both cases, the Christian evangelical rhetoric has to do with changing sexual behavior in men. Moreover, moral training provided by evangelicals – into the proper Christian norms of abstinence and fidelity – will help address the promiscuity of homosexual and African men, and, eventually, stop the pandemic. The AIDS pandemic, then, from the perspective of these evangelicals, is ultimately about the lack of Christian morals, which necessitates a paternalistic governing of when and with whom sex can happen.

Religion and controversy

Religions as a whole, its myths, symbols and main figures, for example, have caused tremendous controversies throughout human history. Just think about a few of the founding figures of some of the largest religions of the world: Jesus, the Prophet Muhammad, and Siddhartha Gautama (the Buddha) – each of them symbolized and represented major shifts in the religious landscapes of the world. Their respective visions and religious missions did not sit easily with many folks at the time, rendering them deeply controversial figures – even rebels. Their lives, embodiments and epistemologies, challenged accepted politics of being and belonging. They symbolize both continuity and change, disrupting the "old" and reimagining "new" ways of believing, of being, and communities of belonging.

Controversial religious figures continue to inform and reconfigure the religious landscapes of the world, not least through their very embodiment. In addition to being controversial due to holding or promoting particular ideas or practices (such as the queerness of God or same sex marriages), many religious figures are perceived to be controversial, or cause controversy, because they – as opposed to the religion-founders referred to above – are women or queer. Of course, it might be that many of the founding Fathers were also queer, however, dominant understandings traditionally cast them as heterosexual. The point here is that bodies and sexualities are particular sites wherein controversy emerge and create broader contestations, inside of religious traditions and relating to broader community and national contexts, about who gets to say what, when, and where.

Religion, or religious communities and individuals might also engage in particular practices that cause great controversy. As seen in the introductory case study on South Africa, the practice of polygyny – an accepted religious and cultural practice in some contexts – becomes a deeply contested issue that affects and involves many spheres of society. The case study illustrates that polygyny is not only a matter of being for or against, but that it is a practice that is deeply embodied and its resolution (in its religious, juridical, and societal dimensions) has real-life consequences for women in particular.

The case study on evangelical engagements with AIDS, illustrates the various ways in which a Christian preoccupation with morality casts certain practices (sexual relations before marriage or having multiple partners) and folks (homosexuals and African men, in particular) as immoral. The controversial practice of moral education, enacted by some evangelicals, shows how moralizing discourses on sexual relations and "correct" sexuality are steeped in heteronormative and problematic colonial narratives.

Controversial practices might also involve scandals and many of you are probably familiar with the many cases of child sexual abuse that have been exposed within the context of various Catholic religious orders, for example. Another controversial practice is that of female genital cutting or female genital mutilation (FGM), a theme discussed in more depth in the chapter on instrumentalization. Controversies can manifest in very violent ways and controversies can also be dangerous or have dangerous effects and results. Controversial practices are informed by complex and intricate relationships between religion and culture (like that of South Africa) and the ways in which power and the dynamics of power shift depending on what is considered normative, or even, "truth" (as in the case of the evangelicals). Controversies in their more scandalous forms are primarily caused by religious leaders or members who violate (often sexually) individuals in less powerful positions (children and women).

Controversy also has to do with conflicting opinions, disagreements and contestations that bring to light the possibility of multiple perspectives and understandings. Controversy can be about challenging orthodoxy or **orthopraxis** (correct conduct). Controversy can create disruptions or rupture normativity and "the ways things have always been." As with most controversies, at least in the modern period where the circulation of news is more and more a cyberspatial activity, media plays a major part in making controversies visible and accessible. Also on a global scale – by giving voice to, covering, or speaking about a particular phenomenon. Media can thus also help to sustain certain controversies, as in the case of the numerous hijab-debates that have been going on for decades. Have we not been over this before? Additionally, and in the contemporary period to an even greater extent, media are also complicit and/or the driving force in the creation of controversies.

We have divided the chapter on religion and controversy into three primary themes: (1) controversies internal to religion, (2) controversies external to religion, and (3) religion as a cipher for broader controversy.

Controversies internal to religion take as starting points something that happens within a particular religion. This "something" is of such quality that it draws the attention of other religious actors within the religion. Commonly, the attention is negative in character, but it can also include having a heated discussion or argument over certain religious perspectives or doctrines. This "something" often challenges status quo or religious normativity and is, at times, perceived to be a form of transgression or "irreligious" doing/saying. Hence, issues of belonging, religious authenticity and who is allowed to say what, how, and where become important questions informing controversial matters. Controversies can be internal to particular religious communities in specific locations but can also transcend regional or national boundaries and become a broader international religious controversy. Controversies internal to religion can also be taken up and engaged with by the broader society. As such, controversy need not *remain* internal to the religion but in various ways interweave into the broader society. The role of the media plays an important part for the ways in which controversies travel, from internal to religion to societal, from local contexts to national contexts, and from one geographical region to another.

Our second theme, controversies external to religion, involves controversies that emerge from outside of religious discourses but that engage and provide a critical commentary on religion and religious themes. Of course, it is difficult to delineate in a clear manner where religion "ends" and the "external to religion" begins. As we know, societies are much more complex than that. However, for the purpose of differentiating between different types of controversy, we have chosen "external" as a useful analytical category. Primarily, we focus on controversies external to religion that offer critical perspectives on the ways in which bodies and sexualities are understood and approached in religion. This includes, but is not limited to, the various ways political and legal discourses may debate and contest religious norms or doctrines. Examples of this abound, from issues around the use of contraception and the right to abortion to interfaith and same sex marriage practices. Similarly, in the NGO sector, a variety of human rights and gender/queer activist organizations, in particular, challenge and make visible the many ways in which religions discriminate and dehumanize women and LGBTIQ+ people. Of course, many NGOs are also situated within religious discourses; we understand this kind of organizational/activist work to be internal to religion. The external societal dimension that this chapter focuses on the most is the many controversies relating to religion that are produced by popular culture. Popular culture, such as music and the arts, is a rich resource when examining the (often, controversial) relationship between religions, bodies, and sexualities. Expressing timely and poignant critique through song or photography, for example, popular culture creatively reimagines religion in new and sometimes intentionally provoking ways. Moreover, the mediatization of such creative and critical expressions allows for a more extensive audience and possibilities for engagement.

Our final theme in this chapter is that of religion as a cipher for broader controversy. By this we mean that the controversy has wider implications or ramifications for society at large. Religion acts as the cipher – alternatively, lens – that the controversy emerges through but then spirals into the broader society and is taken up by a number of actors/discourses. To a larger extent than controversies that are internal to religion and controversies that are external to religion, religion as cipher engages a number of societal discourses. The case study about Muslim polygyny in South Africa, introducing this chapter, exemplifies religion as a cipher for broader controversy. In this case, Muslim polygyny is entangled in complicated questions about the legal recognition of Muslim marriages in a democratic South Africa, the status of African Customary Law, gender equality and rights-discourses, religious and secular feminist discourses, Muslim diversity, questions of authority and the need to prioritize the empirical realities and contextual needs of contemporary women. Likewise, the case on evangelical engagements with AIDS through morality education can be seen as a cipher for broader controversy. Although the case is reflective of the manner in which many evangelicals approached the issue of AIDS, it transcends internal disputes and national borders as it engages with sexual behavior (or, sexual immorality) in the United States more broadly and also in Africa.

Employing historical, sociological and ethnographic approaches to examine the relationship between religion and controversy pertaining to the three themes outlined here, the chapter primarily focuses on controversies that inform or foreground understandings and/or experiences of particular bodies and sexualities. It also considers cases of controversy where bodies and sexualities have become the focus of religious intolerance or religious contestation.

Theme 1: controversy internal to religion

Within the study of Islam, Professor Amina Wadud is a pioneer. Her writings (particularly *Qur'an and Woman*, published in 1992, and *Inside the Gender Jihad*, published in 2006) framed and paved the way for a flourishing body of work on Islam and gender. Although Professor Wadud might be perceived by some scholarly traditionalists to be a controversial figure within the field of Islamic Studies, as she unapologetically positions the female subject as central in her analysis of Islam, it is her embodied performance of ritual leadership – in particular, that of giving the **khutbah** (the Friday sermon) in the mosque that sparked great controversy.

We are in South Africa. It is 1994 and the year of South Africa's first democratic election. Professor Amina Wadud is invited to the Claremont Main Road Mosque in Cape Town to deliver the Friday *khutbah*. The event coincided with the commemoration of the thousands of women who on August 9, 1956, marched on the Union Buildings in Pretoria to protest against the apartheid **pass laws** (an internal passport used as a means to control the population). A hopeful era is on the horizon in a new democratic South Africa.

The Claremont Main Road Mosque is known for its progressive and inclusive approach to Islam. Amongst other things, they focus on women's participation in the mosque and welcome talks that are attentive to societal concerns such as gender violence, drugs, and the prevalence of HIV/AIDS. In particular, from the 1980s, under the tenure of Imam Rashied Omar, the Claremont Main Road Mosque increasingly engaged sociopolitical issues through sermons, political activism, and community outreach programs. As an extension of their already inclusive engagement, the invitation of Prof. Wadud was not seen as controversial by the Claremont Main Road Mosque board. However, for reasons we will discuss briefly, segments of the South African Muslim population found the decision to be unlawful according to Islam. The decision was met with tremendous criticism, there were reports of violent attacks, both physical and verbal, against the main protagonists hosting the event. Imam Rashied Omar received several death threats and the Forum of Muslim Theologians (an organization that was formed as a result of Wadud being invited to give the *khutbah*) lobbied to remove him from his position. The controversial nature of the event, that is, a woman giving the *khutbah*, also reached across the Atlantic, to the United States, where members of Wadud's local mosque demanded her dismissal from her academic position at the Islamic Studies Department at Virginia Commonwealth University (Wadud 2006).

Why did the event cause such fierce opposition? What was the controversy about? First and foremost, the controversy has to do with gender, more specifically, with normative assumptions concerning gender norms and roles. That a Muslim woman was to perform the *khutbah* did not sit well with traditional understandings of what a Muslim woman should or shouldn't do. Secondly, in preparation for Wadud's *khutbah*, the Claremont Main Road Mosque board decided to implement new gender-inclusive spatial arrangements in the mosque. The normative male mosque space was divided into two parallel sections separated by a single rope. Women were invited to occupy one side of this space, rendering the main prayer area shared and gender-inclusive. Prof. Wadud inhabited the prestigious space traditionally reserved for men, in the main section of the mosque facing the congregants.

The debates that ensued, commenting on the controversial nature of the event, revolved around certain bodies – women's – occupying a particular space – the mosque – in ways that were deemed inappropriate. Not only was there a sense of women's bodies being in the wrong place (in the main section of the mosque and in front facing the congregation), but these bodies (through their gender-mixing, although separated by a rope) meddled with and would likely have implications for the "purity" of Islam, as it was stated by the Forum of Muslim Theologians (Gamieldien 2004). Hence, there is more at stake than bodies being in the wrong place. Wadud and the female congregants occupying the main prayer space somehow upset and destabilized an exclusively male space, and in so doing – by virtue of their female bodies – jeopardized the "purity" of Islam. What is it about women's bodies, and the visible presence of them in the mosque space, that introduces *impurity* or de-sacralize a space? Are women's bodies more sexual than men's and as such constitute an obstacle for (male) worship? The existence of particular gendered discourses on sexuality became visible in responses from the Muslim Judicial Council (the largest body of religious authority in the Western Cape), who opined, amongst other things, that a woman's voice is *'awrah* (lit. nakedness) and as such, a Muslim woman cannot address men in the mosque as her voice (and moreover, her embodiment as a woman) can stir desire in men. Linked to notions of modesty, *'awrah* emerges as a particular gendered comportment as a similar rationale for men addressing mixed gatherings does not form part of what constitutes *'awrah*. Similarly, a number of religious institutional, clerical and ecclesiastical structures have prohibited or restricted women's participation and leadership in sacred spaces and places due to particular assumptions about women's difference to men. Although much has changed in terms of bringing women in – from the margins to the center – patriarchal understandings concerning purity and pollution specifically targets women's bodies, often due to their ability to do things that men's bodies don't (like bleeding and giving birth).

In the context of the discussion of women's religious leadership in Islam, *'awrah* becomes a property of the female body, which thus precludes her from speaking in public. In short, following this line of argument, the issue of women's religious leadership in Islam is controversial because women – and the visible presence of their bodies – sexualize the mosque space and prevent men from religious devotion. Women disrupt male worship!

The controversy pertaining to Wadud's *khutbah*, as commented on by actors within the South African Muslim community, brings to the fore a keen attention to sexuality or sexualization of people and places, as a key "concern" in the broader debate on women's religious leadership in Islam. But what did Prof. Wadud really say?

> I will talk about this [engaged surrender] from a woman's perspective, starting with an important part of many women's lives: giving birth. ... This is a marvelous example of engaged surrender. The mother cannot take a day's rest. She cannot lay the child down beside her on the bed and say, 'Just for today, I think I will not be pregnant.' ... This image of a mother carrying her child under her heart, then bringing that child forward consciously as she participates in labor, is not only a reflection of engaged surrender, it is also not unlike Allah Him/Her/It Self who describes Himself ... as *al-Rahman* [the Merciful], *al-Rahim* [the Mercy-giver]. ... Both His names of mercy, *rahman* and *rahim*, comes from the same root word as *rahm*: the womb. (Wadud 2006)

Wadud's *khutbah* was perceived by many to be cathartic. Not only did she speak to notions of being human and the importance of establishing a good relationship to God, her notion of engaging in surrender – which for her is the meaning and purpose of being Muslim – is explicitly linked to the metaphor of a woman giving birth to a child. Through this evocative metaphor, Wadud powerfully decenters the normative male religious subject by situating women at the heart of religious performance and surrender to God.

Controversies, such as the one described here, often fail to be attentive to the deep motivations that inspire such initiatives and thoroughly engage the substance of words spoken. Instead, the language of controversy concerns who is allowed to do what and where. In 2005, Amina Wadud was again the focus of great controversy when she led a congregational prayer, this time in New York. To a more extensive degree than the *khutbah* she led in Cape Town, the New York event was sensationalized in the media and was debated on a global scale. Heavy police presence and security checks surrounded the entrance of the Synod House of the Cathedral of St. John the Divine, where Prof. Wadud delivered the *khutbah* in front of journalists and camera lights (Hammer 2012).

In Chapter 5 on Innovation, we note how such disruptions impact religions as a whole, not only in that the ensuing debates often reflect the patriarchal landscapes wherein "official" religion is pronounced, but also, that disruptions can act as opportunities for increased inclusion and visibility. Since Wadud, several gender-inclusive and queer-friendly mosques have emerged. These represent a significant challenge and break with tradition, while also foregrounding the ways in which certain bodies and sexualities constitute controversial sites for religious contestation and broader social engagement.

Connecting to issues of disruption, increased inclusion and visibility of multiple voices, the autobiographies of three nineteenth-century African American women preachers – Jarena Lee, Zilpha Elaw, and Julia Foote – give powerful testament to women's religious leadership. Collected by William L. Andrews in *Sisters of the Spirit* (1986), the autobiographies in different ways argue for women's spiritual authority in ways that challenged the traditional female roles at the time. Moreover, the autobiographies illustrate that in the midst of the struggle for Black independent churches, women's spiritual authority as preachers in official capacities was not particularly welcome. Similar parallels can be found in a number of religious liberationist discourses wherein the struggle for more inclusive communities and theologies often retain patriarchal privilege and power when it comes to positions of religious leadership.

In the context of these three nineteenth-century African American women, their calling to ministry legitimated their preaching careers. In other words, God authorized their preaching! In addition to challenging the men in their lives, they were also at odds with their local religious institutions, which were controlled by men. Although it was not uncommon for women to hold prayer meetings or even address the congregation once licensed male ministers had completed their sermons, women preachers were not perceived to be a Christian practice. It was believed that women preachers were "unscriptural" (contrary to Biblical teachings) and taking into consideration traditional female roles, such a practice was also coded as "unseemly" for women (Andrews 1986). Nevertheless, they all pursued their calling to ministry – some at great risk to their individual freedom as they travelled to slave states to conduct their preaching mission. Jarena Lee, Zilpha Elaw, and Julia Foote's autobiographies collectively celebrate women's resistances to and maneuvering of racism and male religious authority. Establishing their ministries on the primacy of the experiential, namely, their individual experiences of

God's calling and understandings of God's will, Jarena Lee, Zilpha Elaw, and Julia Foote challenged orthopraxis by locating God at the center of their lives. The privileging of a good relationship to God is eloquently illustrated by Julia Foote when she notes: "you will not let what man may say or do, keep you from doing the will of the Lord or using the gifts you have for the good of others. How much easier to bear the reproach of men, than to live at a distance from God." (Andrews 1986)

Theme 2: controversy external to religion

Police sirens intensify in the background as we witness a woman being killed by a gang of white supremacist men. Ku Klux Klan crosses are burning on the plains. A Black man is mistakenly arrested for the murder. Madonna who witnesses the murder of the woman seeks refuge in a nearby church where she encounters a statue of a Black saint. Madonna gently touches the face of the statue and the saint becomes alive – unmistakably becoming one and the same as the Black man who was arrested. The saint whispers something in Madonna's ear before he leaves the church. Madonna, who seems to be longing for the saint, picks up a knife and accidentally cuts both the insides of her hands, resembling **stigmata** (manifestation of wounds on the body that resemble the wounds inflicted on the body of Jesus Christ when he was crucified). In a dream, Madonna and the saint embrace and kiss, passionately. The saint returns to its form as a statue. Madonna awakens. She runs to the police station to inform the police officers about the innocence of the arrested Black man. He is subsequently released.

Such is the storyline of the music video, roughly recapped. Released in 1989, Madonna's *Like a Prayer* is perhaps unfamiliar to many of you and the controversy it caused might be surprising to some as its storyline, seen through twenty-first century lenses, appears rather ordinary. For those of you who are somewhat familiar with Madonna's music, her later work might be more provocative. Nevertheless, at the time, the music video's religious themes and symbols and their intimate coupling with the erotic, stirred controversy particularly in the Catholic Church. The Vatican condemned the music video and many religious groups took to the streets in protest. Pepsi-Cola cancelled a five-million-dollar contract with Madonna due to groups of Christians threatening to boycott the brand, which had made a number of ads starring Madonna. In particular, the Vatican found Madonna's romance with the saint blasphemous. As we have noted earlier, the relationship between religion and sexuality is, amongst other things, tenuous and the case of Catholicism is no exception. Madonna's play on sexual passion as one way of relating to religion and to God – through her intimate encounter with the saint – can be read as a critique of Catholic suppression of sexuality and sexual passion as significant for expressing religiosity and connection with the divine.

The fact that the saint is a Black man is by no means a coincidence and deserves special mention. Inspired by Martín de Porres, one of the few Catholic saints of color and by some hailed as the great patron saint of interracial relations (as he himself was of mixed-race background), the saint features in the music video as a critical commentary on white normativity. Being accustomed to images of white (asexual) Jesus, in the music video God's love is revealed though a Black saint whose embodiment is both pious and erotic. Marcella Althaus-Reid's notion of "indecent theology", a theology which among other things problematizes accepted scripts of gender and sexuality, appears as a suitable descriptive in illustrating the "theological work" enacted in the music video (Althaus-Reid 2000).

Madonna's intimate encounter with the saint, particularly seen in the context of the scene that depicts burning crosses – a practice primarily associated with Ku Klux Klan – can be read as a commentary on the discourses that perceive interracial relations to be an insult to the white race. Indeed, reflecting the pervasive racism of our time, with nationalist discourses vividly present, the opening scene where the Black man (who is later revealed as the saint) is wrongfully arrested in place of the white supremacists responsible for the murder, remains central. From a critical race perspective, the narrative could also be read in a slightly different way: it is a story about how a white woman saves a Black man, or perhaps more poignantly, it takes a white woman to save a Black man! Although we would not possibly assume Madonna to take on another role than that of the protagonist in her own music video, the empowerment potential that the video represents is suggestively limited to that of the protagonist (read: the white woman) who is the only one capable of navigating through the hegemonic racism that we encounter in the video.

In its totality, Madonna's *Like a Prayer* stirred great controversy particularly as it challenged Catholic sacramentality and norms related to (sexual) decency. Some of her later provocations, like her masturbation simulation that accompanied her performance of *Like a Prayer* on her Blond Ambition tour (1990), her suspension from an enormous mirrored cross while singing *Live to Tell* on her Confessions tour (2006), and the pole-dancing nuns in hot-pants on her Rebel Heart tour (2017), have caused numerous cardinals and bishops to call for her excommunication. To this day, Madonna continues her mission to provide a critical commentary on the relationship between religion and sexuality. Having incorporated sexual diversity and queer sexual relations as poignant themes quite early in her career, she has also been hailed as a "gay pop culture icon."

Many artists have followed the controversial path Madonna has trodden in terms of her coupling of graphic sexual relations with religious themes. One such artist is Tooji Keshtkar, who released his music video *Father* in 2015. In this music video as well, a church features as the primary locus of embodied (sexual) experience. However, where Madonna and the saint kiss in the pews, a naked Tooji straddles the equally naked priest of the congregation at the altar. Some of the congregants in the pews lift their eyes and hands towards the heavens in prayer, whereas others, seemingly lustfully, enjoy the spectacle. The erotic encounter reaches its climax when Tooji penetrates the priest, only covered by his **stole** (liturgical vestment). The storyline early on establishes that Tooji and the priest are together, as partners and as lovers, but that an argument has caused the couple to drift apart. Re-united through the sexual performance at the altar in front of an audience, the music video ends with Tooji and the priest embracing in front of the altar while a set of massive angel-wings unfolds behind them.

Addressing a Norwegian audience, although the video was released online and thus opens up for much broader social engagement and commentary, the music video calls attention to the exclusionary practices of the church. The video challenges several assumptions: *who* commonly are allowed in as well as *how* people relate to each other within the church space. Tooji, who used the release of the music video as a timely opportunity to "come out" as a gay man, wanted to highlight the church as a significant discriminatory space. In the music video he reconfigures this space to be inclusive of queer folks and sex. The legitimation of queer relationalities and sex as a human activity (perhaps also as an expression of worship?) that can find expression within a church, is arguably symbolized by the unfolding and enfolding angel-wings at the end.

The music video caused controversy within Christian denominations and parts of the queer community in Norway. Most reacted to the explicit display of erotic intimacy taking place at the altar. The altar, which commonly is where religious sacrifices are made (and in many Christian denominations where the ritual of Holy Communion take place), was believed to be de-sacralized by some commentators. Others noted that sexual intimacy had nothing to do in the church space (no matter where or who was engaging in it). Predominantly, it seemed that most folks commenting on the video in the news and on social media felt as though the sex scene was a religious transgression of sorts. The video was indecent. Inappropriate. Sacrilegious. As with Madonna's *Like a Prayer*, Tooji's *Father* illustrates a flirting and blurring of the imagined juxtaposition between religion and sexuality. Historically, however, religious imagery of sex abounds and so does sexual imagery of religion.

Notably, voices from the queer community also critiqued Tooji's music video. It was argued that the video perpetuated the idea of homosexual relations as primarily sexual and as such did not do much to help reconfigure the image of homosexual people as preoccupied with sex. Granted that the music video might fuel the continuing stereo-typing of homosexuals as preoccupied with sex, particularly among homophobes, still, by bringing sex (back?) into the church, Tooji's music video can also be read as an attempt at naturalizing queer sexuality, not fetishizing it. Acknowledging human bodies as deeply sexual and erotic while also religious, Tooji's *Father* speaks back to traditions of religious orthodoxy that has de-eroticized theology and kept queer bodies on the fringes of religious communities.

Another notable group that loudly has spoken back to orthodoxy is the Russian feminist protest punk rock group, Pussy Riot. Founded in 2011, Pussy Riot rose to international fame after staging a number of **guerilla performances** (the staging of an unannounced concert, commonly performed in a non-traditional setting) in public spaces. Making good use of social media by posting their performances online, and as such reaching an international audience, their songs are primarily concerned with challenging Putin's politics and the Orthodox Church's misogyny. Pussy Riot is perhaps most known for their performance inside the Cathedral of Christ the Savior in Moscow in 2012. The music video entitled, *Punk Prayer: Mother of God Drive Putin Away*, which features footage of the group's occupation of the Cathedral, urges the Virgin Mary to become a feminist and dethrone Putin from his position of political leadership. Pussy Riot were condemned by the Russian Orthodox Church, who deemed the band sacrilegious. Later that year, three members of Pussy Riot were arrested and charged with "hooliganism motivated by religious hatred." They were later convicted to serve a sentence of two-years in prison.

The strict punishment spurred a global interest in Pussy Riot and for many, the convicted members represent (s)heroes who became the victims of authoritarian political and religious dogma. Much more can be said about Pussy Riot, who in 2016, two weeks prior to the U.S. election, released a music video entitled *Make America Great Again* in anticipation of Trump's victory. The video vividly portrays a dystopic United States where President Trump enforces religiously conservative and right-wing politics by physically branding the bodies of women who are perceived to be illegal immigrants ("outsiders"), women who fail to comply with the bodily ideal of what a woman should look like ("fat pigs"), women who are lesbian ("pervert"), and women who have had an abortion ("she made an abortion"). The video ends with a still picture that prophesizes: "this is the end."

Although music constitutes a potent contemporary resource in addressing the many problematic ways in which religions engage (or fail to engage) issues of gender and sexuality, it is not the only resource. Visual art is another valuable resource that frequently provides a critical social commentary on religion. One such example is the visual art exhibition *Ecce Homo*. Produced by the Swedish photographer Elisabeth Ohlson Wallin, the exhibition was first launched in Stockholm, Sweden in 1998 and later, the same year, the photographs were exhibited in the central cathedral of Uppsala, Sweden, before hitting the international scene. The exhibition of 12 photographs caused great controversy and international debate. What was it about these photographs that stirred such emotive responses?

The photographs depict a variety of well-known biblical themes and narratives, like the Pietà motif, the crucifixion of Jesus, and the Last Supper, in contemporary contexts. However, as opposed to romanticized re-appropriations of these motifs, the photographs depict people from LGBTIQ+ communities in their everyday struggles. One of the photographs, the recreation of the Pietà motif, displays an emergency room in a hospital with Mary, dressed in a greenish-blue surgical robe, holding Jesus, who is dying from AIDS, on her lap. In the photograph recreating the Last Supper, Jesus is depicted with a group of transgender people. The photographs were exhibited in conjunction with passages from the Bible and together they evocatively address the various ways in which queer folks have been marginalized and stigmatized by religious communities. The photographs importantly parallel Biblical "outsiders" with contemporary outsiders, that is, the queer community, and Jesus' compassion and love for people who were on the margins of society. The photographs speak powerfully to the need to take seriously the various ways in which queer embodiment relate and can relate to a loving God. However, as in the case of Tooji, the photographs were understood to be sacrilegious, by some, and reinforcing stereotypes of the queer community as preoccupied with sexuality and eroticism, by others. Others again, perceived the photographs as radical expressions of Christian love.

The examples given in relation to the theme, controversy external to religion, illustrate that popular culture in the form of music and visual art provides important critical commentary on religion and religious themes. In privileging particular bodies and sexualities, public culture stirs controversy primarily among those who hold on to traditional or conservative norms, on the one hand, while providing empowering resources for those seeking greater inclusion in various religious communities, on the other.

The circulation of popular culture in the form of social media, sharing-mechanisms and other forms of mediatization, enables an expansive dissemination that was unimaginable not so long ago. For many artists and performers, such as that of Pussy Riot, their work and message is known *because* it "goes viral," allowing for rich international conversations and engagements that have the potential to disrupt patriarchal and heteronormative religious regimes.

Theme 3: religion as a cipher

In contemporary times, particularly in the West, few religious symbols have received more widespread attention than the ubiquitous Muslim veil. Although many scholars, us included, are tired of the continuous obsession with the Muslim veil, it serves as a compelling example to illustrate the various ways in which religion works as a cipher for broader controversy. Hence, the focus of this section is not on whether or not Muslim women should or should not wear the veil, or whether or not it is a requirement in Islam – or even what Muslim women themselves believe or chose to do in terms of dress. Rather, we are interested in the various ways in which the veil has been employed (at times, hijacked) by broader sociopolitical discourses to support and buoy particular political agendas and ideological goals. By situating the veil as a central symbolic marker for the ways in which religion works as a cipher for broader controversy, we wish to particularly highlight a critique of European and American political discourses.

"Under western eyes," to borrow a famous phrase from postcolonial scholar Chandra Talpade Mohanty (1991), the veil has come to represent women's subordinate position in Islam. Muslim women who wear the veil are frequently depicted as women who are victimized, without agency and incapable of self-definition. Conversely, a Muslim woman who has discarded her veil (in the Western context) is hailed as someone who has been liberated from a patriarchal, misogynist religious tradition. These dichotomized stereotypes are not only (if even) about the nature of Muslim women, that is, whether Muslim women are imprisoned or free. Rather, such representations act as visible boundary markers to delineate the West from "the rest", or, in this case, the West from Islam. The veil has become the central symbol of a new **"clash of civilizations"** (Huntington 1996) and thus serves as a politicized symbol that signifies Islam's difference ("backward," "oppressive," "masculinist") to the West ("developed," "liberatory," "egalitarian").

The politicization of the veil in the contemporary era is not a new "invention" as the veil frequently has been employed, in contexts like Iran, Turkey and Egypt, to name a few, to symbolize support or opposition to political regimes. In the context of Western nation-states, the politicization of the veil gained momentum after the 9/11 attacks on the World Trade Center and the Pentagon. In particular, right-wing neoconservative political discourses linked the Muslim veil to Islamic terror and to the impending Islamization of the United States and Europe. At the same time, the veil also continued to symbolize Muslim women's oppression in Islam, which further perpetuated the idea that Islam was opposed to "Western values."

In the context of the United States, Islam gradually emerged as the new, post-Cold War enemy. The U.S. War on Terror, legitimized by the 9/11 attacks, also generated grave concerns over women's rights in Muslim majority contexts. The War on Terror, beginning with the U.S. invasion of Afghanistan in 2001, was buttressed by the need to save and liberate Muslim women. In other words, Muslim women's bodies were mobilized and used in the service of military intervention. In many ways, feminist ideas of gender equality were hijacked and problematically aligned with right-wing neo-imperial projects. These projects have, of late, also (mis)appropriated the struggle for LGBTIQ+ rights to further position Islam, with their "conservative" views on sexuality, as the enemy of the West. These right-wing ideological polemics is underlined by an increasing Islamophobia, which can be clearly traced in political strategies such as President Trump's executive order on "Protecting the Nation from Foreign Terrorist Entry into the United States" in 2017. Commonly referred to as the "Muslim ban," as the executive order targeted Muslim majority countries, it signals an intent of social control and regulation of particular minority and immigrant populations that are associated with the "threat" of Islam.

In Europe, increased concerns about migration have emerged among right-wing political parties, in particular. What has come to be termed the "Muslim migration crisis" is underpinned by a heightened fear of Islamic terror (as a result of the attacks carried out in Paris, Brussels, and Berlin) and an intensified fear of sexual assault (after reports of sexual assaults committed by Muslim men). The Muslim male migrant, then, is often portrayed as a sexual predator who will blow shit up! The right-wing vilification of Muslim migrants occurred in tandem with controversies around the Muslim veil, in particular, the **niqab** (veil covering the face). In a number of European countries, such as the Netherlands, Austria, Switzerland, Germany, the United Kingdom, Denmark, and Spain, political debates revolved around possibilities for implementing a ban. National security and the liberation of women were employed as central arguments. In France, in 2009, the (then) president Nicolas Sarkozy stated that "face-veils" (niqab) are not welcome in the secular Republic. In 2010, the ban was passed in France.

In 2010, prior to the passing of the ban, Naima Bouteldja and Fatima Ali produced a protest video to oppose the passing of the ban. The video, entitled "Thriller in Paris," uses the tune of Michael Jackson's *Thriller* to provide a critical commentary on French culture where niqabi-clad women are portrayed as monsters and where Islam, as a whole, is perceived to be diametrically opposed to "secular values" such as gender equality. The video shows two niqabi-clad people dancing in front of the Eiffel Tower in Paris to the beat of *Thriller*. The video can be read as a response to secular neo-conservative attempts (and indeed, accomplishment) at regulating and controlling Muslim women's bodies in the contemporary era. Artistic expressions, such as this, render visible the various ways in which social media have become avenues for protest and contestation as multiple religious and secular communities lay their claims to investing public spaces with different meanings.

Within the context of modernity, neoconservative regulation and control, commodification and appropriation of the veil (and indeed, of Muslim women's bodies) have aided and abetted political and politicized discourses that have a clear vested interest in making Islam the "other" – the enemy. Limiting migration and engaging in large-scale warfare is done in order to "protect" the West from Islamic terror and defend secular values, of which gender equality occupies a central space. It is perhaps timely to note that the envisioned rational subject of modernity was distinctly gendered, largely limiting women's roles to that of wife and mother in the sphere of the private. That is to say, the separation of church and state in Western societies, which launched the era of Western modernity, did not – as many might think – change the politics of gender. Rather, it was only in the wake of increased focus on questions about Islam that gender equality became a central (perhaps even foundational) aspect of secular discourse (Scott 2018). The "politics of the veil" includes, in the contemporary period, an intensified attention to the visibility of bodies. It is the presence of Muslim women's veiled bodies, in particular, that constitute the "objects" that inspire and "legitimise" ideological contestations.

Conclusion

The relationship between religion and controversy has to do with continuity and change. It has to do with contestations over theologies and epistemologies and the politics of being and belonging. Controversy also brings to light the possibility of multiple perspectives and understandings. Controversies might emerge as a result of disruption – over meaning and over "truth." Often, bodies and sexualities become centrally entangled in controversies as they represent or are portrayed as problematic, dangerous, or other. Or, they are abused, paraded, or killed. Violence can be one manifestation of controversy, which also illustrates that controversy can be dangerous. This chapter has shown that controversies can take many forms and in all of the three central themes outlined herein, power and relations of power play critical roles. Power – acted out within patriarchal, hegemonic, nationalist, or clerical frameworks – sets the stage for and enables possibilities for controversy. At times, controversies reflect deeply problematic situations and developments, such as the deployment of embodied religious symbols to legitimize neocolonial ideologies and projects. At other times, controversies might result in radical change in ways that take seriously the experiences of real and diverse bodies.

Review: chapter highlights

- Case study 1: contestations over Muslim marriages in South Africa;
- Case study 2: evangelical approaches to AIDS in the United States and in sub-Saharan Africa;
- Religion and controversy;

  a Religion and controversial figures;
  b Religion and controversial practices;
  c Religion, controversy, and the media;
  d Outline of three main themes: (1) controversies internal to religion, (2) controversies external to religion, and (3) religion as a cipher for broader controversy;

- Theme 1: controversy internal to religion;

  a Islam and women's ritual leadership: the case of Amina Wadud;

    - 1994: The Claremont Main Road Mosque;
    - Gender, sexuality, and worship;
    - 2005: New York;

  b Nineteenth-century African American women preachers: Jarena Lee, Zilpha Elaw, and Julia Foote;

- Theme 2: controversy external to religion;

  a Madonna's *Like a Prayer*;
  b Tooji's *Father*;
  c Pussy Riot;
  d *Ecce Homo* by Elisabeth Ohlson Wallin;

- Theme 3: religion as cipher;

  a The ubiquitous Muslim veil;
  b The politicization of the veil: the United States;
  c The politicization of the veil: France.

Applications and reflections

1 Identify a controversy or a controversial feature internal to a religion you know. What was controversial about it and why? In what ways did the controversy relate to particular bodies and sexualities? Did the media play a role? If so, in what way?

2 Many of the controversies discussed in the section on controversy external to religion focused on critically addressing the ways in which religious communities engage with

issues of gender and sexuality. Looking to popular culture (to your own favorite musical archive, for example), provide an example and explore how your own example addresses similar issues. Reflect on the role of the media in the example that you provide. Do media (print, online, etc.) play an important role in the circulation or dissemination? What might the implications be of the role of media?

3   Reflecting on your context, what are the religious symbols or practices that you know of that are intertwined or appropriated in broader societal contestations? In what ways can these religious symbols or practices be seen as ciphers for broader controversy? And, what roles do gender, bodies, and sexualities play in these broader contestations?

4   Are there other categories of controversy you can think of (more than what we presented in this chapter)? If so, what are the different ways in which they relate to religion, bodies, and sexualities?

Resources for further study

Abu-Lughod, Lila. *Do Muslim Women Need Saving?*Cambridge, MA: Harvard University Press, 2013.

Hammer, Juliane. *American Muslim Women, Religious Authority, and Activism: More than a Prayer.* Austin, TX: University of Texas Press, 2012.

Petro, Anthony. *After the Wrath of God: AIDS, Sexuality, and American Religion.* New York, NY: Oxford University Press, 2015.

Scott, Joan Wallach. *Sex and Secularism.* Princeton and Oxford: Princeton University Press, 2018.

van Klinken, Adriaan S. *Transforming Masculinities in African Christianity: Gender Controversies in Times of AIDS.* Surrey: Ashgate, 2013.

Wadud, Amina. *Inside the Gender Jihad: Women's Reform in Islam.* Oxford: Oneworld, 2006.

4 Violence

Case study 1

We are in the **favelas** (underprivileged area/slum) in Rio de Janeiro, Brazil, where the spirits of the street are actively cultivated to protect devotees against violence and sexual assault and to empower them to work toward a better life, a more successful life. The favela is home to the marginalized and the disenfranchised. The poor and the under-privileged. Drug gangs and prostitutes. Extreme violence, much due to drug trafficking, occurs on a daily basis. Not only are the favelas known to house and produce rampant criminality, but also, at least in Brazilian imaginary, the favelas foster types of indecency and immorality that threaten the social fabric that is carefully constructed around gen-dered notions of respectability and decency. What better place for the **Pomba Gira** (female spirit being) to do her work.

The Pomba Gira is a complex female spirit being whose embodiment is reflective of the realities of the poor and marginalized. Relatedly, her devotees primarily belong to poor and working-class neighborhoods. Often identified as a sex worker, the Pomba Gira embodies feminine qualities associated with the notorious femme fatale. Oozing of eroticism and desirability, the Pomba Gira symbolizes uncontrolled and independent female sexuality or female sexuality "gone wild." She poses a dis-tinct threat to the established norms around gender power relations and of women's propriety in particular. In a context wherein women's primary responsibilities involve taking care of the household, children and husband, and where a woman's sexuality is expected to be under the control of a father, then husband, the symbolisms of the Pomba Gira pose an imminent moral threat. Together with Maria Molambo, one of Pomba Gira's most popular and fierce incarnations, she challenges patriarchal and hegemonic (read: Christian) discourses concerning gender and gender relations. In the favelas, women's realities are complicated and messy and, although many may hold romanticized ideas pertaining to the ideal of a gendered division of labor, it is seldom reflected in their reality. Women in the favelas do not necessarily live in households where the husband is the main breadwinner. Women work and, often, they are the primary breadwinner. Gendered expectations, in which men are envi-sioned as heads of households, result, in some cases, in domestic strife and, in worst cases, in partner violence. The Pomba Gira posits an alternative moral imaginary that is inclusive of, and makes space for, different and transgressive ways of being in the world and one that is responsive to many of the contextual challenges people in the favelas experience (Hayes 2011).

Kelly E. Hayes, in her vibrant ethnographic account of the Pomba Giras in Brazil, writes about Nazaré – a **zelador** (a caretaker/custodian) – whose body and life have become channels for the powerful spirit Maria Molambo. Sharing some of the same experiences – both Nazaré and Maria Molambo rejected the arranged marriage organized by their fathers and instead opted for choosing their own lover – their relationship is characterized by reciprocity and ritual exchange. In addition to making offerings consisting of food, drinks and praises, Nazaré provides the corporeality needed for Maria Molambo to act in-the-world. In exchange, Maria Molambo offers protection for Nazaré and her family. Nazaré's experiences with spirit possession started when she was about four years old. At that time, Maria Molambo intervened so as to stop her father from hitting her. Later on, Maria Molambo saved Nazaré from a marriage organized by her father by taking possession of her body and "running away" with her. In Nazaré's current marriage, Maria Molambo has acted as a protector and avenger. She has made Nazaré aware of her husband's infidelities and intervened in ways that have reconstituted the relations of power in their marriage. Having Maria Molambo as a protector and, indeed, an ally, Nazaré has spent much time learning how to best be a *zelador* to the extent where she now performs consulting work, working with the spirits of the streets to resolve people's problems. The reciprocal relationship between a *zelador* and a Pomba Gira that results in guidance and protection demands keen attentiveness to the needs of the spirit being. Failing to serve the spirits, neglecting their needs for food and praise, for example, will result in misfortune and difficulties of various kinds – often befalling persons to whom one's relationship is particularly close (Hayes 2011).

In the context of helping others, the figure of the Pomba Gira is central in challenging normative claims to women's propriety and docile role in the domestic sphere. For most female clients, domestic conflict is what prompts them to seek help and, in addition to providing spiritual support, the Pomba Gira – through her very existence and particular embodiment – offers valuable resources for maneuvering gender relations and sexual norms that are rooted in patriarchal and Christocentric paradigms. This is not to say that the Pomba Gira necessarily is able to resolve the conflict – particularly, when it comes to situations of gender power asymmetry, such as intimate partner violence. Nonetheless, her transgressive and forceful embodiment speaks to the potential for transformation and empowerment for people living on the margins of society and for whom envisioning a better life is paramount for their survival (Hayes 2011).

Case study 2

"Kill the Indian, save the man," declared Colonel Richard Henry Pratt, the founder and superintendent of the first federal off-reservation boarding school for Indian children in the United States. Carlisle Indian School, established in 1878, was a boarding school intended to "civilize" and "Christianize" Native American children for the purpose of assimilation into the greater society.

Similar to that of other colonizers for whom conquering vast territories inhabited by indigenous people was essential to the imperial project, indigenous peoples and their ways of living were commonly perceived to be "primitive," "savage," and "uncivilized." Colonials described indigenous peoples as people without religion, or peoples whose practices were characterized by superstition and the use of magic. Similarly, Native Americans were viewed by the colonizers as culturally and religiously inferior. A variety of Christian organizations, such as the Jesuits, Russian Orthodox, Anglican, Presbyterian,

Catholics, Protestants, and Quakers, among others, established and ran boarding schools in various parts of the United States and Canada. Although differing slightly in terms of practice, the education of Native American children primarily focused on civilizing efforts and "saving souls"; that is, indoctrinating and converting Native American children into the Christian faith and European cultural norms (Trafzer et al. 2006).

Colonel Richard Henry Pratt's establishment of Carlisle Indian School, which coincided with the end of the Indian Wars, marked a new era wherein military action was abandoned in favor of educational projects. Pratt's well-known statement, "Kill the Indian, save the man," reflects a shift in the thinking of the time. That is, that Native Americans with their "savage" and "uncivilized" ways could be saved, and, thus, wouldn't need to be exterminated through violent genocide. Nonetheless, the so-called saving of Native American children, a mission that included a process of "humanization" – of making human that which was perceived to be less-than-human – was a project that replaced the explicit violence of genocide with cultural genocide, that is, the violence of forced assimilation through education.

Pratt, together with other boarding schools' officials and superintendents, instituted a range of different "civilizing" strategies. First, it was believed that Native American children needed to be separated from their parents and communities. By physically removing children from their environments of "savage practices" and "superstition," colonials believed that Native American children stood a chance of becoming civilized. Pratt and others also believed that what they thought to be "primitive languages," "superstition," and "savagery" needed to be destroyed. As a consequence, Native American children were often separated by tribal affiliation to ensure that those speaking the same indigenous languages were unable to talk to one another. All students were required to speak English. Failing to comply resulted in disciplinary action, which could include corporeal punishment and/or solitary confinement (Trafzer et al. 2006).

The indoctrination of Native American children into the Christian faith was one of the strategies employed to destroy indigenous cultures and "superstition" and formed a central part of the overarching civilizing mission. Forced conversion as well as mandatory name change were common practices. Pratt firmly believed that the taking of Christian names (such as Mary and Ruth for girls, David and James for boys) helped the process of civilizing the Native American children – who were to function in the broader society at one point (read: in the white man's society). Other civilizing strategies adopted so as to combat "savagery" were that of stripping the children of their "primitive" clothes (including ornaments and jewelry) and dressing them in Western style clothes that were more akin to military uniforms. Native American children's hair was cut off or cut short as it was believed that their usually long hair was dirty, swamped with bugs, and "wild." Visual archives attesting to this cultural genocide have been kept much due to boarding school staff both needing and wanting to document the *successful* transformation of Native American children. In the archives are notable images of Native American children on their knees praying – demonstrating successful conversion to the Christian faith – and before-and-after photographs, some of which were commercially reproduced as post cards, displaying the transformation of Native American children from "savage" to "civilized," making the children into spectacles for public consumption.

In the gloomy history of the boarding schools in the United States and Canada, Christianity played a central role. For the many Christian organizations that ran the boarding schools, the Christian faith represented a resource that would enable Native

American children to become "civilized." Christianity was the solution to bring to an end "primitive beliefs" and practices ("superstition" and "magic") and "savagery," more generally. By converting to Christianity, Native American children would be "redeemed," it was believed, and although the strategies employed were coercive and sometimes explicitly violent, the objective of "saving souls" seemingly legitimated the use of force. It has been widely documented that Native American children sustained tremendous amounts of physical abuse at the boarding schools, sometimes ending in death. Native American boarding schools survivors recount episodes of having their heads smashed against walls, being thrown down stairs, and deprived of food. Additionally, many children were exposed to brutal sexual violence, including rape. These dehumanizing and atrocious acts, carried out by adult priests and nuns in the business of "saving souls," have inflicted extensive intergenerational trauma.

From a critical contemporary perspective, the boarding schools and their vile abuses of Native American children, were central in the project of cultural genocide. In many ways, Christianity, and the process of Christianization – a task carried about by the boarding schools – acted as an important ally in the production of "acceptable" citizens more broadly. After all, it was in the interest of the white majority to continue the process of cultural erasure. Assimilation, by force, into the world "outside" of the boarding school was the long-term objective. Relatedly, the boarding school system was intricately connected to the project of ensuring colonial control over indigenous land. Dispossessing Native American peoples of land was central to the colonial project. The colonial mission of Christianizing and civilizing indigenous populations at the many boarding schools in the United States and Canada can be seen as instrumental to sustain the continuation of the violent conquest of land in that it dispossessed generations of Native American children not only of their culture but also of their relationship to indigenous land.

Religion and violence: bodily intersections and interjections

For many religious people, religion carries within it a message of peace. Followers greet each other "with peace" – *as-salamu alaykum* ("peace be upon you") – are encouraged to "turn the other cheek," practice **ahimsa** (non-violence) and live in the spirit of **ubuntu** (a state of being that contribute to the well-being of others and of community). Yet, we don't need to look far to realize that religion and violence are interrelated in many different and complicated ways. Interactions between religion and violence daily unfold in the news, on social media, and in and through our social surroundings and everyday lives. The relationship between religion and violence has a long history and continues to remain a frail but powerful intersection in our contemporary world.

The two case studies introducing this chapter on religion and violence are meant to draw your attention to the range of registers wherein the intersections of religion and violence function. As the title of our book project, we are particularly interested in foregrounding the various ways in which religion and violence deeply intersect with human bodies and sexualities. What kinds of violence towards bodies and sexualities are enacted by religions, its leaders, and followers? What kinds of bodies and sexualities are being violently acted upon? What are the various ways in which bodies are instrumentalized for violent purposes? What resources do religions have to offer to respond to violence in ways that empower marginalized and stigmatized bodies and sexualities?

In order to address the questions above, the chapter focuses on four main themes, which represent ideal types and are not fixed categories. Our first theme is that of religion being a source of violence. Religious imaginaries, such as that provided by literary, mythic, and symbolic materials have been used to create and justify violent practices by religious institutions, religious leaders, and individual followers of religious traditions. Violence has been, and still is, motivated and legitimized by religious beliefs and normative practices. Carrying out violent acts in the name of religion is a familiar phenomenon. However, not all violence is physical. **Epistemic violence**, a term coined by Gayatri Spivak (1988), constitutes another form of violence, namely, violence that is caused through discourse. The erasure of Native American cultures and belief systems by colonial powers, with the assistance of a range of Christian organizations — although utterly violent in its expression — was also an act of epistemic violence. A systemic destruction of indigenous regimes of knowledge, languages, beliefs, and practices took place at the boarding schools where Native American children were forced to convert to Christianity and drilled in its norms. Christianity, then perceived to be a higher form of religious expression and civility, marginalized indigenous traditions by demonizing them and rendering them savage. Our first theme, then, religion as a source of violence, addresses these two different registers of violence — physical and epistemic — and provides examples that interweave these registers of violence with real bodies.

Our second theme engages religion as a resource in violent situations. In the first case study you get acquainted with the Pomba Giras who protects devotees against the threats of daily violence. Embodying enfleshed human beings, these female spirit beings act as religious resources that empower marginalized and underprivileged people. At the same time, the female spirit beings do not ask permission to take their corporeal form. Women's bodies, in particular, are instrumentalized by the Pomba Giras so as to perform their work in-the-world. In return, however, she offers protection. For many believers or followers of religious traditions, religion constitutes a source of empowerment and can provide healing when having to deal with violent situations, such as domestic abuse and homophobia/queerphobia/transphobia. Religious resources, such as songs, myths, symbols, imagery, rituals, and spirit beings, for example, can act as powerful mechanisms that provide individuals and collectives with a sense of purpose, affirmation, and community belonging. Using religion as a resource in violent situations signifies the centrality of religion in peoples' lives and constitutes an important contrast to the previous theme on religion being a source of violence.

Our third theme explores religion as accessory to violence. Under this theme we focus on how religion can act as an ally or collaborator together with other segments of society (e.g. political parties or ruling elites) to achieve particular goals. During colonial times, for example, Christianity acted as a powerful accessory to violence. It followed imperial expansion and territorial annexation, exported its ideology aimed at mass conversion through establishing missions. Religion, its beliefs and practices, can also offer much-needed legitimation for the sculpting of militant nationalisms or the implementation of repressive state ideologies that marginalize or criminalize particular bodies and sexualities. As seen in the case study on the Indian boarding schools in the United States and Canada, Christianity acted as a legitimizing framework for forced and violent assimilation of Native American children.

The Anti-Homosexuality Act in Uganda, passed by parliament in 2014, is a contemporary example wherein particular Christian understandings of homosexuality — in essence, homosexuality being incompatible with Christian values and beliefs — are employed to legitimize its criminalization. Notably, the Anti-Homosexuality Act also functions as a contestation of a colonial past. Arguing that homosexuality is a Western import, Ugandan politicians in support of the Anti-Homosexuality Act attempt to forge a new, "more authentic," Ugandan national identity. Religion as accessory to violence thus also entails using religion for purposes that are not necessarily religious.

Our fourth and final theme explores religion as a target of violence. It includes the ways in which religions as a whole are targeted by the broader community or other religious communities for holding beliefs or practices that are perceived to be primitive, false, outdated, or ethically unjust, for example. The targeting of Native American people was not only legitimized due to colonial interest in possessing indigenous land, but also because they were perceived to be "savage" and "primitive"; thus, at least from the Christian organizations' perspectives, they needed to be saved from their "superstitious ways." Targeting in this way can have serious consequences for religions as a whole and for followers whose identities are seen as representative or illustrative of a certain way of life/ideology. Think about Islamophobia as another example and the ways in which some Muslim women who wear the niqab have been spat at and had people attempt to remove their face-covering. Or, the recent mass shootings in New Zealand (2019) where two mosques were attacked by a white supremacist, killing 51 people. Religions as a whole can be targeted due to changes in the political climate (for example, the increase of far-right extremism), pervasive racist and xenophobic discourses, or rivalry between or among various co-existing religious groups. Religion as a target of violence can have detrimental effects on religious individuals, communities, the religion as a whole, and the broader community.

This chapter also engages two particular forms of violence and is attentive to different levels of violence. As mentioned already, the chapter engages both physical and epistemic forms of violence and you will find examples of both under the different themes outlined. Additionally, violence – both physical and epistemic – can affect individuals (both real and imagined/mythical/metaphysical); violence can affect groups or collectives of people (often those who identify in contradistinction to the norm, such as women, queers, and racial minorities); and violence can affect whole religious communities through, for example, large scale warfare. The different themes in the chapter address violence through these three different levels: individual, groups/collective, and whole religious community. Not all themes engage all three levels as sometimes examples at the level of the individual can also pertain to groups/collectives or the religious community as a whole. Now, let's move on to explore each of the four themes in more detail.

Religion as a source of violence

Religious frameworks, through their literary, mythic and symbolic registers, hold potent resources for violence, both physical and epistemic. Drawing up the contours of physical forms of violence, we know that religious individuals and collectives intentionally and calculatingly have taken the lives of others so as to "stand up for justice" or "fight a righteous cause." At times, killing the enemy, and, perhaps more importantly, what the enemy represents, involves taking one's own life. By some perceived to be an act of martyrdom; by others, an act of terrorism.

In contemporary times, it is undoubtedly the figure of the Muslim suicide bomber vociferously uttering "Allahu Akbar" (Allah is the greatest) who has received widespread attention, particularly in the West. For many, the Muslim suicide bomber epitomizes an "ultimate" type (a climax) when considering religion as a source of violence. Not attempting to diminish or reduce the pains and losses for those who have lost their loved ones in terror attacks, we find it important to draw your attention to the ways in which the body of the suicide bomber not only functions physically through bodily performance but also discursively. Being the one who causes terrible deaths, the body of the suicide bomber is commonly perceived to be naturally or essentially violent. However, the body of the suicide bomber is also a religious body – a Muslim body – and, as such, the body of the suicide bomber may intertwine with and project particular understandings of Islam. For Islamophobes, the Muslim body of the suicide bomber commonly becomes conflated with what Islam *is* (essentially). Moreover, the body of the suicide bomber is also a gendered body and thus holds particular assumptions pertaining to masculinity in Islam. Dominant stereotypes about men in Islam – i.e. they are prone to violence and aggression – are inextricably linked to perceptions about Muslim women, or how Muslim men treat Muslim women, and by extension, the position of women in Islam. Universalizing generalizations pertaining to Muslim women being oppressed and marginalized by Muslim men and Islam as a whole, are familiar and form part of antagonistic geopolitical discourses. The discursive functioning of the suicide bomber is in this context religion-specific and gendered. Race also comes into play as the racialized bodies of Muslim men are particularly policed and regulated through increased security measures implemented at airports, for example. The War on Terror, which justified the United States' invasion of Afghanistan in late 2001 (after the 9/11 terrorist attacks), was also intertwined in politics of race and gender. Gayatri Spivak's famous phrase "white men saving brown women from brown men" (1988) has been employed by anthropologist Lila Abu-Lughod in her book *Do Muslim Women Need Saving?* (2013) to problematize the United States' invasion of Afghanistan. Although the declared aim of the invasion was to destroy al-Qaida and remove the Taliban, examining some of the discursive tensions at the time, the invasion was also buttressed by the need to "save" burqa-clad Afghan women from misogynist Islam. As articulated by then First Lady, Laura Bush, "The fight against terrorism is also a fight for the rights and dignity of women" (Abu-Lughod 2013, 32). In other words, a liberatory, even feminist agenda, legitimized the U.S. War on Terror. Following this trajectory, it becomes clear that individual acts of violence such as that of suicide bombers, at least when considering religion being a source of this particular form of violence, is discursively rich and incredibly complex.

Interestingly, studies done on female suicide bombers found that, as opposed to disrupting some of the gendered scripts referred to above, typically female suicide bombers were cast as victims whose bodies were instrumentalized by masochistic religious groups to perform acts of terror. Women who were unable to have children, women who had broken honor codes related to being sexually pure until marriage or women whose bodies for some reason or other were seen as "damaged" or "broken" were targeted to maximize tactical advantage (Narozhna and Knight 2016). In this way, the gendered scripts illustrious of the victim/aggressor dichotomy are retained, despite the equally horrific ramifications caused by the acts of suicide bombers.

Gendered and racialized bodies being violently sacrificed in the pursuit of religious goals not only involve practices of death and dying, but also permanent bodily modifications such as forced castration or female genital cutting – practices commonly linked to ethnic cleansing and sexual purity, respectively. The use of sexual violence as a weapon of war is a particularly brutal dimension of warfare. Often, religion and religious difference constitute the central node through which the sexual brutalization of bodies (particularly female bodies) happen. In the context of war, bodies are instrumentalized and may serve a particular religious purpose. The chapter on instrumentalization discusses this at greater length.

The violent civilizing strategies employed in Native American boarding schools (e.g. cutting of children's hair) are examples of forms of violence that, although perhaps causing permanent scars, are temporarily deployed so as to effect change and transformation in particular bodies. Likewise, punishments resulting from transgressing religious morality codes or punishment created to assess whether religious morality codes have been transgressed – commonly linked to sex and sexuality – are, among other things, religious mechanisms that seeks to discipline the body. A well-known example of the latter – punishment to assess – is that of Sita, the Hindu goddess, married to Rama, who had to undergo trial by fire so as to prove her fidelity to Rama after having been abducted by the demon-king Ravana. The familiar tale of the relationship between female sexuality and male honor, which constitute the pulse of many patriarchal societies, reaches a climax when Sita begs Mother Earth to take her back. Disappearing into a fissure in the earth, becoming one with the earth mother, Sita represents female perseverance and resistance. For many contemporary Hindu women, Sita is a survivor of violence and provides women with the strength to fight violence in their own marital relationships.

Religion being a source of physical violence is further compounded by particular politics of religious inclusion/exclusion. Scripting rules for who's in and who's out, where and when, religions are notable sources of epistemic violence. For many religious women and queer folks, epistemic violence means belonging to belief systems where they are commonly positioned as wholly other, or not positioned at all. Their existence is either peripheral or non-existent within the normative tradition. Dominant beliefs and practices silence and marginalize religiosities that are embodied by the wrong body, or names you heretic, sodomite, or less-than-human. Some folks who are at the receiving end of such violence have turned to self-inflicted violence, sometimes ending in suicide. We may ask, who constitutes the religious human being – the Eliadean *homo religiosus*? We don't need to look far to see the ways in which patriarchy and heteronormativity have informed religious anthropology. *Homo religiosus* is usually a heterosexual white alpha male. Paying attention to gender and sexuality when it comes to who or what counts as normative or taken for granted in religion, reveal systemic practices of othering and form part of the ways in which violence is caused through discourse (epistemological violence).

Epistemological violence is, amongst other things, redressed through queer folks' engagement in the re-reading and re-interpretations of religious texts, for example. Refusing to be sidelined, banned or inhabiting the margins of their own religious communities (much like the Pomba Giras!), queer folks for whom religion matters have developed empowering and liberatory alternatives to challenge religious normativity. In the chapter on innovation we learn about how the emergence of queer religious authorities and spaces, for example, disrupt religious normativity (although not only with positive consequences).

Acknowledging religion as a source of various forms of violence is important in order to reimagine "truths" and reconfigure the structures that render particular bodies vulnerable to acts of violence, be they physical or epistemic. However, it is also important to acknowledge that religion can act as a resource in violent situations, and it is to this topic we now turn.

Religion as resource in violent situations

We find ourselves in a violent, potentially deadly, situation. Our environment, our earth community, is in crisis. And, the crisis is definitive; it will not "go away." Humanity might not make it. Discourses of colonialism, capitalism and consumerism, characteristic of the era now known as the **Anthropocene** (the current geological age where human activity has constituted the dominant influence on climate and the environment) have informed human practices and our relationship to the earth. The logic of domination so present in this era has been challenged by ecofeminists, among others, who also have pointed out the similar parallel oppression of women and earth – described as rape. Mary Daly in *Beyond God the Father* (1973) uses the term "rapism" to describe patriarchal domination. In her later work, *Wickedary* (co-written with Jane Caputi 1987) she defines rapism as "The fundamental ideology and practice of patriarchy, characterized by invasion, violation, degradation, objectification, and destruction of women and nature; the fundamental paradigm of racism, classism, and all other oppressive-isms" (Daly and Caputi 1987, 91). The dystopic novel *The Handmaid's Tale* (1985), by Margaret Atwood – a novel now popularized by the Netflix series with the same name – raises similar parallels. In *The Handmaid's Tale*, the rape of the land – which has rendered the land toxic and infertile – is intimately connected to the Gileadean practice of institutionalized rape of women (the handmaids).

Recognizing the violation of the earth and the violation of women through the lens of rape (both real and metaphoric) does much to highlight relationships of domination and exploitation. More so, for ecofeminists, recognizing the earth as *a body*, the earth-body, establishes a strong connection to women's bodies. In ecofeminism, the earth-body and women's bodies are similarly violated, abused, and battered. For practitioners of earth-based spiritualities, spiritual ecofeminism and ecofeminist theologians, religious resources such as ritual and goddess symbolism inspire new ways of relating to the planet. Often, the earth-body is perceived in terms of maternal symbolisms such as "mother" and "goddess." Ecofeminist theologian, Rosemary Radford Ruether, who problematizes the link between women and the earth (so as not to continue to perpetuate the nature/culture dichotomy where women are like nature and men are like culture) also advocates for the critical need of healing – of women and earth. The title of her edited volume, *Women Healing Earth* (1996), is reflective of this commitment. In this book, women from Global South contexts outline and discuss their struggles to overcome the violence committed against women and nature, and deliberate on the liberatory and empowering aspects offered by religion in affirming life, broadly understood.

Practices of healing to restore the broken bodies of the earth (which includes human bodies) commonly find expression in ritual. Many people have looked to religion to find empowering ritual and symbolic resources that can address and challenge anthropocentric norms, while also providing opportunities for healing and re-connection with the earth and, at times, one's own body. Rituals developed to heal the earth, or earth-healing rituals are intended, amongst other things, to foster a sense of community of belonging – a community that is reflective of the intimate connections with non-human species. The Council of All Beings, a ritual developed by Joanna Macey and others, is aimed at cultivating an ecological or biocentric consciousness and serves as a spiritual preparation for social action. In the Council of All Beings people take on the identities of other natural beings and speak to that being's position within the earth community, often highlighting the kinds of human violations and abuses experienced. "Thinking like a mountain," a phrase used by the renowned environmentalist philosopher Aldo Leopold (1887–1948), captures the profound inter-species relationality that the Council of All Beings aims to achieve. Macey and others believe that rituals, such as the Council of All Beings, have the ability to empower human beings to foster radically different ways of relating to each other and to the environment, relationalities with the earth and the earth community that are marked by a profound sense of interconnectedness.

Wicca is a religion that incorporates diverse ideas and practices that commonly relate, in some way or another, to developing a sacred relationship with the Earth. Nature is perceived as a source of revitalization, and for many Wiccans, the divine exists in all of nature. Caring for nature in the midst of human exploitation and destruction, is for many Wiccans a central concern. Many Wiccans are dedicated to environmentalist struggles as one particular way of putting their beliefs into practice. Starhawk, an American activist, is one of the most well-known feminist Wiccans. Involved in protests such as anti-nuclear demonstrations and redwood forest activism, she is also widely known as being the main initiator of the reclaiming movement. Reclaiming is a movement that is underpinned by ecofeminist frameworks and feminist spirituality and highlights the idea of nature as sacred as well as Goddess symbolisms in their ritual practices. Many members of reclaiming are environmental activists. Importantly, reclaiming is also about empowerment and the need to establish a good relationship with the Earth and with its creatures. Annually, the Spiral Dance ritual is enacted. Developed by Starhawk, and echoing the title of her landmark book published in 1979, the Spiral Dance, amongst other things, commemorates the deaths of those who dedicated their lives for peace and justice (Salomonsen, 2005).

Considering the earth-healing rituals of a contemporary reclaiming community in Canada, Rosemary Roberts (2011) found that rituals such as Waters of the World, a meditative ritual wherein collected water from different parts of the world is displayed on an altar, instil in many practitioners feelings of compassion and connection. On display is both water that is life-giving (healthy and pristine) as well as water that is polluted and toxic. For some practitioners, the ritual allows for a deep sense of interconnectedness to be cultivated – as one comes to recognize that water is central to one's being (central to the materiality of the body) and, as such, relatedly, acknowledging the precarity of one's water-dependent existence. The human body, as a body of water, intersects with other bodies of water, such as rivers, oceans, fjords, groundwater, and rainfalls, and are similarly threatened by the degradation of aquatic ecosystems, which ultimately can result in disease and death.

Earth-healing rituals can be closely interlinked with the need for personal healing as well. In the community examined by Roberts (2011), participants also engaged in rituals where sharing of experiences pertaining to sexuality were important to the broader establishment of a community of belonging. Rituals of sharing with regard to sexual identity, experiences of sexual abuse and/or gender-power relations, contributed to create a supportive environment invested in collective healing. Likewise, Roberts found that participants in need of personal healing due to experiences of sexual assault, dealing with how to live with HIV/AIDS or other traumas, were drawn to earth-healing rituals as it provided a shared sense of purpose, mending the disconnects and brokenness of human bodies and the earth-body and their powerful entwinement. As such, earth-healing rituals, through their capacity to foster a sense of community and *being in* community, hold the capacity for healing and empowerment and constitute a fecund resource for individuals and collectives for whom a sense of belonging/interconnectedness to the earth community is central to being and staying alive.

For many religious queer people, that is queer folks for whom religious belief and practice remains a central commitment, experiences of violence (such as **corrective rape**; a hate crime in which one or more people are raped due to their sexual orientation or gender identity with the aim that the person will become heterosexual or conform to society's gender norms) or threats of violence form part of their everyday lives. For many who have experienced violence or threats of violence, religion constitutes a profound source of empowerment. Religion and religious belief functions as a resource and inspires religious queers to develop and join activist projects so as to fight for social justice. Additionally, such commitments also inform new theological epistemologies or liberatory readings of religious texts.

The work of Scott Siraj al-Haqq Kugle (2010 and 2014) is exemplary in showing how queer Muslim activists use religion actively as a discourse that gives hope and moral guidance and provides a sense of community of belonging. In fact, Kugle argues, being in community is an essential part of Muslim personhood. Kugle foregrounds that being Muslim involves being active in the struggle against injustice and oppression. Being Muslim, then, provides a sense of purpose, a common struggle – a queer **jihad** (struggle) – to challenge and destabilize the structures (religious and otherwise) that continue to perpetuate heteronormativity and that are complicit in the violence done to queer bodies. Employing religion as a resource in violent situations, in situations of injustice and dehumanization, provides for many religious queers an empowering and supporting framework. Refusing to "let go" of their religious identity, even when being marginalized, sometimes violently, by members of their own faith tradition, profoundly speaks to the notion of religion as resource. Religion acts as a resource not only in terms of its empowering dimensions, but also for its capacity to be used to challenge authoritative and heteronormative versions of itself.

Examining the centrality of religion in peoples' lives form an important aspect of the relationship between religion and violence. In the context of religion as a resource, particularly for people whose embodiments are perceived to be non-conforming and whose lives have been permeated with violence and threats of violence, or whose bodies are experienced as broken and in need of healing and a deeper sense of interconnectedness, religion provides life-affirming and empowering resources.

Religion as accessory to violence

> Normality in our part of the world is a bit like a boiled egg: its humdrum surface conceals at its heart a yolk of egregious violence. It is our constant anxiety about that violence, our memory of its past labours and our dread of its future manifestations, that lays down the rules for how a people as complex and as diverse as we are continue to coexist – continue to live together, tolerate each other and, from time to time, murder one another. As long as the centre holds, as long as the yolk doesn't run, we'll be fine. In moments of crisis it helps to take the long view.
>
> Arundhati Roy, *The Ministry of Utmost Happiness*

Arundhati Roy's *The Ministry of Utmost Happiness* (2017), offers an incisive and critical commentary on the right wing Hindu nationalist Bharatiya Janata Party (BJP) through the lens of the fictional Indian characters Anjum and Tilo. Anjum is a Muslim **hijra** woman who turns a cemetery in Delhi into a guesthouse that serves as a protective sanctuary from the turbulent violence outside. Tilo, the (illegitimate) child of a Dalit man and a Syrian Christian mother, is an architect who travels to Kashmir to join a group of Kashmiri independence fighters. The lifeworlds of Anjum and Tilo, and their intersections, tell the powerful story of the ways in which the emergence of Hindu nationalism situates particular bodies at the margins of society (by way of their embodiment) and the atrocious violence, dispossession and dehumanization, committed as part of **Hindutva** (Hindu nationalism). Is the yolk runny?

The BJP, the ruling party in India (in 2018), taps into religious discourses so as to legitimize the need for Hindu nationalism (also in its militant forms). In particular, women's bodies (real and mythical) are employed to advocate specific understandings of Hindu-ness and the need for Hindu patriarchy. Discourses that expound on the violation of women by Muslim men and thus the need for women's protection by Hindu patriarchy, form a core of the group's ideology. Depicting Hindu women's bodies as naturally pure and innocent, and as Bharatmata (India as a mother goddess), stands in stark contrast to the demonization of Muslim men as rapists. While some BJP members considered the raping of Muslim women to be a just response (to Hindu women being raped by Muslim men), others highlighted the pollution this would cause to the bodies of Hindu men. Either end of the spectrum projects Muslims as the ultimate other – they are defilers or deserve to be defiled; Muslims are the enemy that necessitates Hindutva and nuclearization. The BJP's symbolic ammunition consists of figures like Sita, Savitri, and Draupadi, Hindu goddesses representing ideal forms of womanhood in dire need of protection. Perhaps you recall the story of Sita in the section dealing with religion being a source of violence? In the context of the BJP's project of establishing Hindu nationalism as *the* central pan-Indian identity, the story of Sita's capture by the demon-king Ravana morphs into the abduction and rape of Hindu women by Pakistani Muslims.

Interestingly, it is not only pure, docile, and subservient Hindu goddesses that function as potent symbolic justification for the protection of Hindu women and nation. The independent, powerful, demon-slaying goddesses Kali and Durgā are also invoked as part of the BJP's symbolic arsenal so as legitimize nuclearization. Kali and Durgā function in the Hindu nationalist imagination as aggressive and militant avengers who go to battle to slay demons (Pakistani Muslims). As such, they also symbolize goddesses who protect. The Hindu goddesses of destruction – in their manifold representations as enraged slayers – are instrumentalized by the BJP so as to perpetuate the idea of an outside enemy that threatens the nation (and its women) and that needs to be destroyed (Das 2006).

The symbolic religious resources employed by the BJP function to frame the need for protection (and a potential armed struggle, or worse, nuclear war) in religious terms. The justification for nuclearization is provided by invoking discourses of gender that play on the dichotomous construction of goddesses who need protection and goddesses who protect. In the same way, Hindu women need to be protected from the Muslim men who rape them, while simultaneously, Hindu female members of the BJP express certain levels of militancy – particularly accentuated through their anti-Muslim sentiments. Nonetheless, Hindu patriarchy is the dominant discourse through which Hindu "womanhood," or women's ideal roles and responsibilities, are articulated. In the context of the BJP project of nuclearization, religion – its symbols and narratives – is re-appropriated to further political nationalist and militant agendas.

Likewise, the emergence of Buddhist nationalism in Myanmar (Burma) gains legitimacy through particular religious discourses; however, interestingly, the discourses on religion primarily involve anti-Muslim sentiments. That is, particular negative understandings and projections about Muslims (as a group) justify the need for a Buddhist political and militant nationalism and, as a consequence, an "active" dehumanization of Muslims. In 2012, in the Rakhine State, home to the Rohingya Muslim minority, anti-Muslim riots erupted after rumors spread that a Buddhist girl might have been raped by a Muslim man. Similarly, in 2013, a group of demonstrators, among them Buddhist monks, targeted and destroyed local mosques and ended up killing several Muslims after having heard rumors about the rape of a young Buddhist girl. Through these events, and many more, a particular form of militant nationalism emerged as a perceived adequate response to the "Muslim-threat." As in the example of the BJP, it is often women's (and girl's) bodies, and the potential violation of these bodies, that constitute an important lens through which militant nationalism is legitimized. And, again, the threat of the religious other (here: the Muslim man) shape the kinds of preventative measures and protective mechanisms that are instituted at the political level.

In contemporary Myanmar, the Rohingya are not recognized as citizens, rather their official status as a population is that of "illegal immigrants." Although a number of sources document Rohingya presence in Myanmar since the fifteenth century, the current government contests this fact. Since 2012, hundreds of thousands of Rohingya have fled over the border to Bangladesh, thousands have been internally displaced, and hundreds have been killed. In some areas of Myanmar, Buddhist nationalists have been calling for the establishment of Buddhist-only areas. This have resulted in, amongst other things, many Buddhists explicitly and literally "flagging" their national identity as Buddhist. Some households hoisted their **dhamma flag** (a Buddhist flag commonly symbolizing faith and peace). Others stuck **969** stickers on their businesses and homes (969 is a Burmese nationalist movement; the number 969 signifies the nine attributes of the Buddha, the six attributes of his teachings, and the nine attributes of the Sangha, or monastic order). Whereas others again proudly advocated living in "Muslim-free" villages. In this way, a Buddhist identity was overtly proclaimed, with the effect of alienating and publically marking or "ousting" non-Buddhists in certain areas, while also rendering other areas religiously homogenous and "free-of" Muslims (Fink, 2018).

Furthermore, the Organization for the Protection of Race and Religion, an organization whose mandate it is to monitor the religions in the country, drafted a set of laws intended to regulate the rights of religious people. Reviewing the set of laws proposed it is clear that, although delineating the rights of all religious people, it is the regulation of Islam, and Muslims, who are the primary target. Another important aspect worth highlighting here is that the laws mainly engage issues of family law. For example, the laws regulate (or, more precisely, criminalize) the practice of polygyny as it suggests jail sentences for those (men) who are married to more than one spouse. Interfaith marriages are regulated particularly with respect to conversion. The laws regulating interfaith marriage reflect a need to protect Buddhist women from conversion to Islam in particular, as the law requires Buddhist women and men of other faiths to register their intent to marry with local authorities. Additionally, it was proposed that the state can intervene in matters concerning population-control where they see fit and how they see fit (including taking such extreme measures such as coerced contraception, forced sterilization, and abortion). The population control bill was enacted in 2015 and mandated birth spacing of 36 months in "overcrowded" areas. In the wake of the increased Islamophobia that seems to inform severe de-humanizing discourses in Myanmar, many argue that the legislation is aimed at policing and reducing the high birth rates among the Muslim communities in the region (Crouch 2016). The laws (both drafted and endorsed) are in clear conflict with Myanmar's obligation to honor human rights conventions, in particular, the Convention on the Rights of the Child and the Convention on the Elimination of all Forms of Discrimination against Women (CEDAW).

The discourses informing particular negative understandings of Islam and Muslims in the context of Myanmar are international in scope and part of a broader Islamophobic current. They range from Buddhist nationalists conflating Islam with terrorist groups like al-Qaida and ISIS, to familiar Islamic "take-over" narratives, seen throughout Europe, and thus an increased need to protect the nation. The current situation, wherein Buddhist militant nationalism constitute the dominant political system, has led to a certain tolerance or, perhaps even normalization, of violence against Muslims.

It is clear that religion holds great symbolic and mythical resources. At times, these resources are utilized to justify the functioning and purpose of militant regimes. In the BJP example, Hinduism gives legitimacy to the project of nuclearization through its mythical narratives and goddess imagery. In the latter example, on Buddhist nationalism in Myanmar, discourses on the religious other and Islamophobia to a greater extent functions so as to legitimize the need for Buddhist militancy. In both examples religion acts as an accessory to violence, not unlike what we saw in the introductory case dealing with the colonial use of (but also collaboration with) Christian organizations through the boarding school system. Here indigenous peoples' "savagery" was pitted against Christian "civility" so as to enable colonial access and ownership over indigenous land.

Religion as target of violence

Between 1600 and 1692, 91 people were sentenced and killed (burned at the stake) under the witchcraft legislation in Finnmark, in north Norway. The witchcraft trials in Finnmark reflect a widespread European phenomenon, namely, the witch-hunt, or witch-craze, that took place from about 1450 to 1700. Also spreading to some parts of colonial America, the horrific witch-craze resulted in the deaths of approximately 100,000 people, most of them women.

The persecution of witches emerged, in part, as European theologians developed **demonological** treatises (the study of demons or beliefs about demons) so as to obtain complete juridical control over the "heresy" of witchcraft. Perhaps the most well-known, the *Malleus Maleficarum* ("Hammer of the Witches"), written by the Catholic clergyman Heinrich Kramer in 1487, emphasized the natural link between female sexuality (which was believed to be insatiable) and heresy. Hence, in the demonological treatises, it is primarily women who become equated with witchery and black magic, much due to their insatiable carnal lust. Inspired by Tertullian's notion of women being the "devil's gateway," the figure of the witch became demonized as an incarnation of evil, a "servant of Satan" and an "enemy of God." The witch, it was assumed, was conspiring with the Devil so as to destroy the Church and the Christian civilization more broadly (Salomonsen and Pike 2017). Taking part in nocturnal gatherings (orgies) and performing sacrifices and black magic resulting in child-murder and the spoiling of crops, amongst other things, the witch presented a primary moral and spiritual threat to Christian dominance. The need to obliterate paganism – as a response to the Devilish warfare waged against the Church – granted the Church, and later the State, license to torture and perform public executions.

In Finnmark, the number of witch-trials carried out is amongst the highest in Europe, relative to population ratio, which was approximately 3,000 at the time. Some scholars have argued that the North represented, at least in the European symbolic geography, a profoundly magical place (in the negative sense) – described by some as the Devil's abode. It is possible that the high number of witch trials performed in Finnmark was underpinned by this belief of the North being associated with evil. Interestingly, and arguably related to this belief, is the fact that in Finnmark, also **Sami** men (indigenous people inhabiting Norway, Sweden, Finland and parts of Russia) were persecuted. Of the 91 people who were burned to death at the stake, 16 were Sami men assumed to be engaged in shamanic practices. Comparatively, this is a high percentage of males. The remaining 75, were all women, most of whom had migrated from the southern part of Norway to different villages in Finnmark to perform domestic work or to marry (Salomonsen and Pike 2017).

The 91 people who were killed in Finnmark, Norway, were targeted and persecuted because they were assumed to perform magic and rituals perceived not only to be un-Christian, but also Satanic or devilish and a threat to the Church's authority. The assumed witches of Finnmark were charged with the poisoning of food, causing the deaths of people and domesticated animals through the performance of magic, and casting spells causing storms, shipwrecks and disease, amongst other things. Whereas folk beliefs at the time commonly held that certain people had unique natural powers, the development of Christian demonology, in particular, enforced the belief in the strong association between the witch and the devil.

The targeting and killing of assumed witches in Finnmark, and across Europe, more broadly, speaks to contemporary notions of difference and processes of othering. In our varied religio-political contexts, individuals are targeted – and persecuted – for holding beliefs and performing practices deemed to be different to or in contrast with the accepted context-specific norm. Not only are people targeted because of what they believe or do, but also for what/who they are, that is, their particular embodiment. Often, discourses of othering are underwritten by a particular demonology that is relative to place, being, and belonging.

Steilneset Witchcraft Memorial, located in Vardø, a municipality in Finnmark county, Norway, is one of the few memorials in Europe that commemorate the victims of the witch-craze. Inaugurated by the Queen of Norway in 2011, the memorial both acts as a site that commemorates the 91 people who were killed as part of the witch-craze in Finnmark, and constitutes a visible reminder of victims of contemporary prosecutions.

The memorial is built on the grounds where many of the actual executions are assumed to have taken place. As such, the memorial site renders visible a particular textured geography and situated history that previously was erased (Salomonsen and Pike 2017). The memorial consists of two separate architectural structures, by Peter Zumthor, one of which houses an installation by Louise Bourgeois. The memory hall, a structure that stretches for 125 meters along the rocky beach of Steilneset, resembles a **hjell** (a wooden rack used to dry stockfish, especially cod). Inside the dark tunnel structure one finds 91 memorial plaques – all complemented by lights in small windows – containing short inscriptions about each individual who was killed as part of the witch-craze. The second structure, a square house, contains Louise Bourgeois' installation "The Damned, the Possessed and the Beloved," which consists of a chair and an eternal flame.

The chair and flame may allude to the so-called "witch's chairs," one of the techniques of torture during witch-trials where the accused was placed on a metal, fire-heated chair so as to confess her or his crimes. Above the chair, attached to the roof, are seven round mirrors that reflect the burning flames, perhaps indicating something about bearing witness and self-in-relation, but the mirrors also tap into notions of hierarchy, judgement, and the authoritarian position of looking at something from above. The reflection of the flames, the emptiness of the chair, as well as the title of the installation may signal the many ways in which the historical prosecution of those perceived to be *other* constitute a bridge into contemporary prosecutions of people who experience processes of othering. It speaks to those being targeted and positioned at the margins of contemporary societies through their particular embodiment as queers, people of color, religious minorities, or migrants (the damned); it speaks to those who believe or practice differently to the norm (the possessed); and it also speaks to those whose embodiment is that of a beloved for whom being-in-the-world is informed by their relationship to the lover (the beloved). In this way, the memorial at Steilneset not only makes visible that which was hidden, but also acts as a contemporary reminder of the horrific enactments ensuing from the polemical "us" versus "them."

It is important to consider also the ways in which processes of othering happens within religious traditions. In other words, the enemy is not only "out there," where different religions or ideologies are pitted against one another, but processes of othering, or the targeting of difference, also finds expression within particular religious traditions. As alluded to in the chapter on experimentation, religious queers are attempting to increase inclusion within their respective religious communities by establishing places of worship that are inclusive of LGBTIQ+ people. For the folks who pursue these goals, their endeavors often come at a cost and are not risk-free.

The Ibn Rushd-Goethe mosque in Berlin, established in 2017, is a mosque which allows men and women to pray together and the founder, Seyran Ates, a human rights lawyer of Kurdish-Turkish decent, has been quite vocal about the mosque's inclusion of LGBTIQ+ people. When the mosque opened, the Egyptian Fatwa Council at the prestigious al-Azhar University issued a **fatwa** (an authoritative legal opinion or ruling made by a qualified jurist or mufti) that condemned the mosque and called it "an attack on Islam." The mosque, its founder and fellow worshippers have, after the opening of the mosque, received multiple threats of violence. In particular, the founder, Seyran Ates, received more than a hundred death threats and is currently under police protection. The establishment of the Ibn Rushd-Goethe mosque is an example of religion – or a particular understanding and practice of religion – being targeted by people who considers themselves religious authorities and whose version of religion is the true or most correct form of religious understanding and practice. Responding to these threats of violence, the community of the Ibn Rushd-Goethe mosque expressed that they fight "Islamic terror" by engaging in readings of the Qur'an that foreground tolerance and respect and that are inclusive of those who commonly are excluded from Muslim places of worship (read: women and queers). Moreover, the community of the Ibn Rushd-Goethe mosque also responds to violence through their very existence, as a place of worship that is inclusive of religious queers. As such, resources for responding to the violence and threats of violence experienced are found within the same Islamic tradition as that which is used to target and persecute non-conforming Muslims.

Conclusion

For many people religion is inextricably tied to different registers of violence. This chapter has shown some of the ways in which religion can act as a source of violence and as an accessory to violence, but also how religions constitute empowering resources and inform responses to violence. In particular, the chapter has highlighted the kinds of violence enacted by religion (physical and epistemic) and foregrounded the kinds of bodies and sexualities that religions commonly enact violence upon (women, queer folks, and other *others*). Simultaneously, the chapter provides important examples of the ways in which bodies and sexualities that have been marginalized, stigmatized and violated, physically and epistemically, respond to violence by using religion as a resource for empowering personhood, developing community and reconfiguring religious traditions in ways that are inclusive of diversity.

Review: chapter highlights

- Case study 1: Pomba Gira in Brazil;
- Case study 2: boarding schools and First Nation children;
- Religion and violence: bodily intersections and interjections;

  a   Outline of four themes: religion being a source of violence, religion as a resource in violent situations, religion as accessory to violence, religion as a target of violence;
  b   Forms of violence (physical and epistemic) and extent of violence (individual, groups/collective, and whole religious community);

- Religion as a source of violence;

  a   Suicide bombers;
  b   Body modifications and disciplining of the body for religious purposes;
  c   Sita's trial by fire;
  d   Epistemological violence and otherness;

- Religion as a resource in violent situations;

  a   Our environmental crisis;
  b   Ecofeminism; rape of nature and rape of women;
  c   Rituals of healing; earth-healing rituals and personal healing;
  d   Religious queers and faith commitments; religion as empowering;
  e   Queer Muslims;

- Religion as accessory to violence;

  a   Arundhati Roy; *Ministry of Utmost Happiness*;
  b   Hindutva, BJP, and Hindu patriarchy;
  c   Hindu goddesses and the need for protection of Hindu women and India;
  d   Buddhist nationalism in Myanmar;
  e   Rohingya, a Muslim minority in the context of Myanmar;
  f   Islamophobia and regulation of religion;

- Religion as a target of violence;

  a   The European witch-craze; background and impact;
  b   The witch-trials in Finnmark, Norway;
  c   Steilneset Witchcraft Memorial, Vardø, Norway;
  d   The Ibn Rushd-Goethe mosque in Berlin.

Applications and reflections

1   Violence, whether in its physical or epistemic form always affects real bodies that also are marked by gender, race, and sex (amongst other characteristics). Considering religion being a source of violence, try to identify the ideologies pertaining to gender, race, and sexuality in a religion you are familiar with. In what ways do these ideologies speak to questions of religious normativity? Can these ideologies be imagined differently? If yes, how do you think the project of re-imagining ideologies of gender, race, and sexuality would affect religious normativity?

2   Using religion as a resource in violent situations can provide healing and empowerment to individuals and collectives whose bodies are being violated or threatened in some way. Identify 3–4 aspects of religious traditions – the stuff that religions are made up of – for example, *salah* (worship), the Earth Mother, chants, etc. and think through the empowering meanings they might carry for religious individuals and/or collectives. Why do you think the aspects that you've identified serve empowering functions? What work do they do (for individuals and/or collectives)?

3   Identify 2–3 historical or contemporary events (perhaps events you consider to be "watershed moments") that situate religion as an accessory to violence. Reflect on the ways in which these events also affect real bodies in terms of race, gender, and sexuality.

4   Consider a religious tradition you are familiar with in terms of its materiality (for example, its aesthetics, food, clothing, spatiality, buildings, memorial sites, pilgrimage trails etc.). Reflect on the ways in which your chosen example may reveal processes of othering, differentiation, and targeting. Also, what are the ways in which your example relates to real bodies and sexualities?

5   Are there other registers or forms of violence you can think of (more than what we presented in this chapter)? If so, what are the different ways in which they relate to religion, bodies, and sexualities?

Resources for further study

Crouch, Melissa (ed.). *Islam and the State in Myanmar: Muslim-Buddhist Relations and the Politics of Belonging*. New Delhi: Oxford University Press, 2016.

Hayes, Kelly E. *Holy Harlots: Femininity, Sexuality & Black Magic in Brazil*. Berkeley, CA: University of California Press, 2011.

Kugle, Scott Sirajal-Haqq. *Living Out Islam: Voices of Gay, Lesbian, and Transgender Muslims*. New York, NY: New York University Press, 2014.

McGuire, Meredith B. "Chapter 6: Embodied Practices for Healing and Wholeness." In *Lived Religion: Faith and Practice in Everyday Life*. Oxford: Oxford University Press, 2008: 119–158.

Merchant, Carolyn. *Radical Ecology: The Search for a Livable World*. New York, NY: Routledge, 2005.

Smith, Andrea. *Conquest: Sexual Violence and American Indian Genocide*. Durham, NC: Duke University Press, 2015 [c2005].

Trafzer, Clifford E., Jean A. Keller, and Lorene Sisquoc (eds.). *Boarding School Blues: Revisiting American Indian Educational Experiences*. Lincoln, NE and London: University of Nebraska Press, 2006.

5 Innovation

Case study 1

In 1970s Japan, some **spiritualists** – people who specialize in contacting the dead – began to advertise their services for a ritual called *mizuko kuyō*. The ritual wasn't entirely new, but it also wasn't very common, and the way they explained it gave it new meaning. Its name, translated literally, means "water baby rites" (Hardacre 1997), and although the historical meaning of *mizuko* has at times included everything from fetuses to young children, the new ads made it clear that these were rites for fetuses. More specifically, they were rituals for fetuses that had been aborted. The ads claimed that these fetuses, now spirits, were angry at their parents – mostly their mothers – for aborting them, and that they would carry out vengeance if not properly honored and memorialized. That promised vengeance, as religious studies scholar Helen Hardacre points out, took forms that threatened or undermined a woman's status as a mother: she might experience any number of symptoms that are associated with menopause, implying that she would never be able to get pregnant again; she might lose the favor and sexual interest of her husband and thereby lose any chance at a socially condoned pregnancy; or she might experience difficulty with her own children's behavior, undermining her reputation as a "good" mother.

Although it never really took off in Japan, *mizuko kuyō* drew a noticeable number of women and men to request the ritual not only from spiritualists but from a number of other religious practitioners. Typically, they asked their own religious leader to conduct the ritual. By the time interest in *mizuko kuyō* began to fade in the mid-1990s, a major religious group in Japan (Jōdo Shinshū) had banned its priests from conducting the rites but many others, across Japan's various religious groups and traditions, had introduced them. These groups didn't take up advertising like the spiritualists; instead, they were responding to requests from members of their congregation or temple. The spiritualists may have begun the practice, but individual Japanese people continued it. And where the spiritualists redefined an older and rather obscure ritual, these individual practitioners redefined the ritual presented by the spiritualists. Some did indeed sponsor a *mizuko kuyō* ceremony out of a fear of fetal wrath, but many others felt neither fear nor shame. Having terminated a pregnancy that they could not afford to bring to term sometimes decades before the rite, they sought simply to honor and perhaps grieve for the fetus and to ritualize a difficult, often ambivalent practice that had become the focus not of religion but of medicine since the late nineteenth century.

Many human cultures regard the human body's capacity to reproduce, and the female body's capacity to develop and give birth to new life, as sacred. Historically, quite a few cultures have had important rituals surrounding reproductive sex, pregnancy, and birth. In many of those cultures, though, such rituals have increasingly faded out as pregnancy care and childbirth have become the province of allopathic medicine, a practice that often keeps religion at arm's length. Although abortion has not historically been considered morally suspect in Japan, in large part because of a belief that a fetus is part of a pregnant person's body and only becomes a human being upon birth, the rise of allopathic approaches to reproduction, pregnancy, and birth seems to have created a need for the reintroduction of such rituals. Both abortion and contraception were legalized in Japan shortly after the end of World War II, but contraception was a newer idea and was initially difficult to practice due to low supplies. Abortion, then, became for a time the main option for addressing unwanted pregnancy. When spiritualists began promoting *mizuko kuyō* a few decades later, they sparked the interest of people who had gone through the decision and the process of abortion and who were interested in ritualizing it. But because an increase in contraceptive availability and use has resulted in a lower abortion rate, because many people see the need to conduct *mizuko kuyō* only once for any given fetus, and perhaps because younger generations see less need for ritualization of reproductive events, the practice of *mizuko kuyō* had mostly faded out two decades after it began.

Case study 2

In Christianity, books that tell the story of Jesus's life and ministry are called Gospels. Although there are a number of Gospels, only four appear in the Christian Bible. Two of these have very similar versions of the same story. When the story begins, Jesus is speaking with the members of another Jewish sect who disagree with his teaching that the dead will rise again to be in heaven. They challenge his teaching by referencing a Jewish law of the time that required a man whose brother had died to marry his brother's widow, in order to support and protect her and her children in a time when it was nearly impossible for a single woman to support herself. If there were seven brothers, they reason, and each one died, then the widow of the first to die would have been married to seven men by the time that she too passed away. Such a situation would cause great confusion if they were all in heaven together. Jesus replies that once resurrected, people "neither marry nor are given in marriage, but are like angels in heaven" (Mt 22:30, Mk 12:25). In both Gospels the story ends there. Many Christians have wondered: What exactly does this mean? What would that family of brothers and wives actually look like in heaven?

Many Christians believe that historical time will one day come to an end. The Christ, the "Anointed One," will return to earth – an event that Christians call the Second Coming because he already came to earth once in the form of Jesus – and then, either immediately or after a final, lengthy battle with Satan, God will establish an eternal realm of blessedness for the righteous. Someone who thinks that eternal realm is about to take shape, or that it's already in process, really needs to know what that Gospel story means. Likewise, if yours is a world-concept where death marks a bodily transition into heaven, where humans themselves become gods – if the veil between the sacred and the human realms is thin and permeable – then you also really need to know what that story means. Such situations make the interpretation of this biblical passage quite urgent and the stakes quite high.

Historian of U.S. religions Lawrence Foster studied three nineteenth-century new religious movements in the U.S. that were in just this sort of situation (Foster 1991). Fascinatingly, each group came up with a different interpretation of Jesus's words, and as a result their approaches to marriage and sexuality differed radically. The groups were the Shakers, the early Latter-day Saints or Mormons, and the Oneida Perfectionists. Although the Shakers began in England, many of them relocated to the United States in response to persecution, and they were well established in that country through much of the nineteenth century. The Church of Jesus Christ of Latter-day Saints traces its history to the discovery of the Book of Mormon by founder Joseph Smith in upstate (northern) New York in the 1820s. The Oneida community initially took shape in the state of Vermont in 1840, but moved to upstate New York in 1848, also in response to persecution. Each of these Christian new religious movements faced societal disapproval and sometimes even violence because they were radically rethinking social norms with the help of the Bible and, more importantly, because they were living out their novel perspectives. They challenged ideals about gender, the body, health, living arrangements and economics, and marriage. So what, to them, did it mean to be "like the angels"?

The Shakers' interpretation was the most consistent with previous Christian understandings of the holy life. Since in their culture it was considered proper to have sex only when married, and with the person to whom one was married, they thought that neither marrying nor being given in marriage meant that people were celibate in heaven. The Shakers also thought that they were living in the end times. Their logic began with the common belief that humans are created in the image of God. Since they saw both female and male humans around them, they reasoned that God must also be both female and male. And since the first incarnation of God on earth – Jesus – seems to have been male, they expected the second incarnation to be in female form. Many Shakers came to believe that their founder, Mother Ann Lee, was this second incarnation, the long-awaited Second Coming of Christ. And if that were the case – if God had again taken human form to live among God's children – that meant that the eternal realm, the Kingdom of Heaven, was at hand. If in heaven they neither marry nor are given in marriage, in order to emulate this ideal the Shakers, too, needed to neither marry nor be given in marriage. All Shakers, consequently, lived celibate lives. They lived in sex-segregated communal housing; even children who arrived in a Shaker community with new converts stayed with the women or the men and were raised communally.

Mormons, on the other hand, do not believe they are living in the kingdom of heaven, and although they believe that Jesus came to North America to visit his people they also believe that the Second Coming, when he will return to rule the earth, has yet to happen. But to Mormons, heaven is a realm in which righteous humans become gods, and the righteous transition there after death with not only their bodies but all human relationships intact. If in heaven they neither marry nor are given in marriage, for Mormons that's because marriage isn't necessary in heaven: a properly-created marriage between two righteous people transfers seamlessly from the earthly realm to the heavenly one. Such a marriage holds deep religious significance. Consequently, it must be performed only by fairly high-ranking religious leaders and in a Mormon temple, and it may only be performed for two Mormons (one male, one female) who are in good standing with the church. The Mormon interpretation of this Gospel story therefore also has significant consequences for divided families in which some members are Mormon and others are not, or in which some members believe that others aren't acceptably Mormon because of excommunication or because of practices they engage in that are considered heretical or sinful. Many Mormons believe that if they are married to a non-Mormon, to someone who has been officially disfellowshipped (excommunicated), or even to a Mormon whom the spouse believes to be in violation of important church tenets, they will not be married to that person in heaven. This has significant consequences, because unmarried people have a lower heavenly status than married people have. While the latter part of the nineteenth century saw the mainstream LDS church move away from the practice of plural marriage (allowing men who had the resources to support a large family to marry multiple women) that was revealed to Joseph Smith in the early years of the movement, this doctrine also may have reflected early Mormons' understanding of what it meant to become "like the angels." Indeed, some Mormons continue to believe that plural marriage is divinely ordained, and some branches of the movement still follow the practice.

Like the Shakers, the Oneida Perfectionists also believed that the Second Coming of Christ had already taken place. But they didn't think it was happening in their lifetimes. Instead, they thought that Jesus had returned when he predicted he would: approximately in the year 70 CE. After all, most Christian theology holds that Jesus was not just the son of God but also *was* God; would God get a prediction wrong? To the Oneida community, led by the theologian and social reformer John Humphrey Noyes, the realm of God was already in place. That meant at least two things: First, righteous humans could become perfected, like the angels (this belief is why they were called "perfectionists"); and second, like the angels they should neither marry nor be given in marriage. But what did that mean? How should they live? Noyes's answer to this question was radically different from Mother Ann Lee's. Marriage, he reasoned, existed to control human sexuality in a state of imperfection. Perfected humans wouldn't – in fact, couldn't – misuse their sexuality in the ways that marriage had been created to prevent. Therefore, in heaven there was no marriage because it was no longer necessary.

At Oneida, although compulsory heterosexuality was still the order of the day (only a few socialist communes in the nineteenth century were open to same-sex eroticism), any woman could have sex with any man given the consent of the two people involved and the approval of the community leaders. But Oneida was a commune, and like many communes it disapproved of exclusive bonds between two members whether those bonds were emotional bonds of close friendship, physical bonds of sexual exclusivity, or both. If in the blessed realm they neither marry nor are given in marriage, that also means they aren't exclusive. As a result, every single sexual interaction had to be approved by the community leaders, and those who sought out sex with the same person too often would be refused and told to seek other partners. Reproduction was also carefully managed at Oneida. While contraceptives in the mid-nineteenth-century U.S. ranged from unreliable to unavailable, Noyes believed that no woman should be burdened with an unwanted or unplanned pregnancy. Long before founding the Oneida community, he advocated what he called "male continence," or withdrawal prior to ejaculation. That principle allowed the leadership at Oneida to control births. A woman and a man who wished to have a child together also had to seek approval, and eventually this policy led to efforts to produce spiritually superior children by encouraging the people who were considered to be the most spiritually advanced members of the community to bear a child together – a kind of spiritual eugenics.

What does it mean to be like the angels? Attempts to answer this simple question, in the midst of the social changes and cultural refashioning that were so much a part of the nineteenth century U.S., led to three equally innovative, albeit radically different, approaches to marriage and sexuality.

Religious innovation

When religious groups or leaders experiment with innovations related to sexualities and bodies, they're generally offering new answers to one or more of three interrelated questions:

- What bodies belong where?
- What bodies should do what?
- Who gets to say?

In addition to changing the practices of their own followers, when religions experiment with sexualities, bodies, and genders they always do so in conversation with the larger society and sometimes also in conversation with the larger religion or family of religions. So changes in the answers to the three questions above may affect entire societies, especially in the case of religious innovations developed by the dominant religion in that society. When developed by organizations or other subsets of a larger religion, they may affect or attempt to affect entire religions. And the innovations that these religious groups or leaders experiment with often respond to changes in the society around them, or to ongoing circumstances that negatively impact some or all of the religion's members.

These are the three themes of Chapter 5: innovation relative to the larger society, innovation relative to the larger religion or family of religions, and innovation as a response to changes in the larger society. Like each set of chapter themes, these are ideal types that aren't strictly separate. Innovations in the larger religion, for example, may also affect the larger society if the religion is an influential one in the society as a whole, and religious innovations that respond to social changes may affect the entire religion, either immediately or over time. The return of interest in *mizuko kuyō* in late twentieth-century Japan was a response to changes in technology, law, religion, gender, and sexuality that had taken place over the course of a century. Although it didn't become an established or widespread practice, it impacted one of the largest religions in Japan when that religion banned priests from performing the ritual, and it impacted the larger society through its unexpected result of encouraging people who felt no concern or guilt about having had an abortion to ritualize the process, sometimes in retrospect.

The three new religious movements that puzzled over what it meant to be "like the angels" in the nineteenth-century U.S. introduced innovations both to the larger U.S. and to Christianity as a whole. Simply the fact that the Church of Jesus Christ of Latter-day Saints is now among the largest, and certainly is one of the fastest-growing, Christian organizations in the world demonstrates the impact that its various innovations have had. The early LDS practice of plural marriage, following a divine revelation to the prophet Joseph Smith, heavily impacted the society around it – although not by leading the larger U.S. to embrace polygyny. Instead, Mormons defended their religious right to practice plural marriage all the way up to the U.S. Supreme Court in

Reynolds v. United States in 1879. Although they ultimately lost the case and the U.S. continues to refuse to recognize more than one living, legal spouse for any given person, the innovations of celestial marriage and plural marriage had a major impact both on the U.S. and on Christianity. And while the Shakers and the Oneida community are no longer known aside from their crafts – furniture and silverware, respectively – nonetheless their innovations responded to developments in the society around them and played a role in shaping the future of both the U.S. and Christianity. Let's look at some other examples for more detail about how each of these themes works and how they relate to each other.

Innovation relative to the larger society

What bodies belong where, doing what, and who gets to say anyway? In the mid-twentieth-century U.S., the Nation of Islam challenged the ways that Black women and men were portrayed by a white supremacist society. An innovative combination of Black nationalism, Islam, metaphysical religions, and Christianity, the Nation argued that Islam is the ancestral and proper religion for African Americans and it portrayed Black men and women as upstanding, strong, and proud people. Drawing on the work of Black nationalists like Marcus Garvey (1887–1940), the Nation and other similar religions fought back against widespread racist portrayals of Black people that questioned their humanity and demeaned their dignity through claims about their gender and sexuality. Typically, these portrayals fell to one extreme or the other. Black men, racists claimed, were either weak in body and spirit or they were uncontrollably strong, aggressive, and violent. Black women were either sexless and nurturing or they were sexually wild and uncontrollable. All, in these racist images, were unintelligent. In response, and also as an answer to the widespread anti-Black violence they experienced from both white civilians and the police, the Nation of Islam developed the Fruit of Islam, a fraternal order and militia whose members paraded the streets with military precision, neatly uniformed and armed. Women in the Nation were and are presented as upstanding, modest members of the community whose role in raising and educating children is critical to the life of the community. Education is stressed for all. While some women (and some men) have chafed against the conservative and strictly binary gender roles promoted within the Nation and related movements, these groups' challenges to racist depictions of Black sexualities, bodies, and genders are unmistakable. And if governmental opposition to such religions – including widespread FBI investigation, infiltration, and attempted destruction – is any indication, those challenges were powerful enough to make white elites extremely uneasy.

These are the sorts of complicated interventions that religions can make in larger social understandings of and prescriptions for bodies and sexualities. When mainstream U.S. society mandated that Black people did not belong in certain parts of a city, should not be displaying intelligence or pursuing advanced learning, *could* not be modest or self-controlled or disciplined, members of the Nation of Islam came out in the streets to prove otherwise. But religion doesn't only argue for women's access to traditional femininity and propriety, as valuable as that argument may be for at least some women who have been denied access to such roles. Many religions, both culturally dominant and culturally marginal, have challenged gender roles and the treatment of women in the larger societies of which they are a part.

Quite a few societies, and the religions that shape them, have historically created barriers to women's full intellectual and sometimes ritual participation, yet determined women have almost always found ways to create space for their own contributions even within strongly gender-segregated traditions. One example of this phenomenon takes us back to the medieval European Christian mystics. In any religious tradition that understands the divine to be in direct contact with the human world, people whose own contributions are disrespected because of their sex, race, class, gender, age, or other characteristics may receive a much more sympathetic reception when their contributions come directly from the divine. According to U.S. religious historian Catherine Albanese, for instance (Albanese 2007), one reason for the fairly widespread acceptance of spiritualism in the mid-nineteenth-century U.S. was that men hearing the wisdom of the spirits who spoke largely through female spirit mediums couldn't imagine women coming up with such complex ideas on their own!

Medieval Roman Catholic women articulated fine points of Christian theology through explaining in minute detail visions they had received from God. Some of these women, like Hildegard of Bingen, Julian of Norwich, and Christine de Pizan, wrote their insights in lengthy tracts that are still read and studied today. Most of these women were **religious specialists**, people who devote the majority of their time and energy to the practice and study of their religion. In fact, becoming a religious specialist, typically either a nun or a celibate laywoman in a third or **tertiary order**, was often the only way for women in such societies to have access to a literary education and to the time and resources that were necessary for their intellectual work. Much of the writing we have from premodern Christian women, ranging from the women mentioned above to the Mexican philosopher and poet Sor Juana Inés de la Cruz (1651?–1695), comes from nuns and tertiaries. Importantly, most of them took vows of celibacy, which are required for nuns and have often been expected of tertiaries. In these cultures, a woman could either be sexually active or be intellectually active; except in rare cases, there was no option that combined the two.

While the Protestant Reformation that created a new branch of Western Christianity in the sixteenth century abolished celibacy, for the most part it continued to constrain women's involvement and therefore their intellectual and religious leadership in Christian societies. Like their Roman Catholic sisters, though, Protestant women found ways to create a public space for their theological insights and their religious leadership. Also like their Roman Catholic sisters, they found that space in divine inspiration and alternative forms of family. While Protestantism had no renunciant option to release women from the expectation to become wives and mothers at the cost of their sexual expression, Protestant women who became religious leaders often were divorced or widowed. Some, like Mother Ann Lee, had suffered through the deaths of all of their children; others' children were grown or in the custody of former husbands, and some were raised by friends or family members. Most, from Seventh-Day Adventism founder Ellen Gould White (1827–1915) to famed African American evangelists and activists like Jarena Lee (1783–185?) and Sojourner Truth (1797–1883), experienced visions or a call to preach directly from God. In a society that doubted women's intellectual capacities even when those women were white, and even more so if they were Black, at least for some people the word of God superseded the sexism and racism of the day.

Religions also innovate in terms of men's roles. Among white evangelical Protestants in the U.S., for instance, movements to reclaim men's place in the church have arisen in reaction against the successes of feminism. In the early twentieth century the most prominent such organization was the Men and Religion Forward Movement, which promoted what leaders termed "muscular Christianity" led by Jesus the brawny carpenter. In the late twentieth century the most prominent organization was called the Promise Keepers; it promoted the need for Christian men to honor their "promise" to serve as the benevolent patriarchs of their homes and families. But while these movements innovated by looking back to what they considered an ideal gendered past, others promoted more novel approaches to masculinity. One movement, founded in the U.S. but now present in many European and European-derived cultures, is the Radical Faeries.

Taking their inspiration from the writings and the leadership of prominent gay rights activist Harry Hay (1912–2002), the Radical Faeries were founded at a gathering of gay men in September 1979. Persuaded by Hay's idea that men, and gay men especially, should recognize and embrace their own femininity, the Radical Faeries came together and continue to gather in order to honor gay men's bodies, sexualities, and genders – especially their male femininity – and to honor the earth and the divine in many and multigendered forms. Appropriate attire for a Faerie ritual can range from nothing at all, through mud or body paint, to jeans, to dresses. Hay himself, known fondly in Faerie circles as "The Duchess," was often seen in a skirt and blouse, a large, floppy hat, and pearls. While the Faeries have not managed to alter the mainstream standards for masculinity in any country in which they are or have been active, they have responded to and supported both an interest in gender fluidity among gay and bisexual men and their allies and a profound need to honor the bodies and the sexualities of same sex attracted men as sacred in the midst of cultures that are intent on demeaning them as profane.

Some religious innovations have introduced widespread changes that have profoundly affected the society around them. One case in point is Islam. At the time of the revelation of the Qur'an to the Prophet Mohammed in 610 CE, the Arabian Peninsula was home to a number of polytheistic indigenous traditions. Jews and Christians lived there too, and others came through regularly on trading routes. Particularly in the polytheistic religions as they were practiced at the time, women had very few rights and were treated with little respect or dignity. The Qur'an and the **hadith** (the sayings and actions of the Prophet) markedly improved the status of women. Mohammed's interactions with his wives and his input to his early followers – both women and men – on the place of women in society raised women's status, increased their access to and inclusion in many social institutions, including religious scholarship, and gave them rights within marriage as well, including the right to sexual fulfillment. Indeed, although like many religions Islam can still be interpreted in patriarchal and misogynist ways, many Muslim feminists argue that the Qur'an has more resources for feminist interpretation than do the Hebrew Bible and the Christian New Testament. As Islam spread throughout the Arabian Peninsula and far beyond, it has often brought with it greater rights and dignity for women in the societies that have adopted the religion on a large scale.

Christianity, too, challenged gender roles in the Roman society in which it took shape. In fact, traces of those challenges and the persecution they engendered can be found in some of the writings from the early church, especially the letters of the apostle Paul. While Paul admonishes the church in Corinth to disallow women from speaking up in church (1 Cor. 14:34–35), his advice is evidence that women *were* being vocal in church. Paul himself often traveled to visit churches and to teach these young congregations together with a female teacher named Thecla. Many of the earliest Christian churches were "house churches," where congregants met in the home of a well-to-do member; these early supporters were often women, since Roman women ran their family households. Some scholars, such as historian Karen Torjesen (1993), have even demonstrated that women served as priests in the earliest churches. And non-Christian Romans were so concerned about the mixing of men and women in these early congregations that they started rumors that Christian worship was really just a cover for sexual orgies. Those rumors were false, of course, but societies that are uncomfortable with new religions in their midst often accuse those religions of sexual impropriety. The nineteenth century wasn't the first time that Christians upset the larger social order in terms of gender and sexuality, then, and it also wasn't the last. Groups like the Unification Church, which became famous for its mass wedding ceremonies and its practice of having the founder and his wife, seen by followers as the new Adam and Eve, arrange spiritually appropriate matches, upset many Christians from more mainstream branches of the religion and sparked similar rumors of sexual misconduct. The Children of God, now known as the Family, went more in the direction of the Oneida community by encouraging women members to use sexual allure to attract men to the group and by experimenting with free love as an explicitly Christian practice. It, too, suffered numerous and largely unfounded accusations of sexual impropriety, leading to repeated government harassment of Family communities in a number of countries in the latter part of the twentieth century.

Even changes in the prevalence or uses of celibacy can be an innovation relative to the larger society. As we saw in Chapter 1, the early Buddhist community in India developed within a culture that already understood celibacy as a potent tool for the development of highly advanced religious practices. Yet the new religion introduced two innovations in the religious practice of celibacy that came to have profound influence in majority Buddhist societies. First, it restructured celibacy from a practice pursued by lone renunciants to one shared by communities of renunciants, and second, it opened the practice to women. As Buddhism became widely practiced across much of Asia, Japanese Buddhist communities introduced another innovation when they created the new, noncelibate role of priest for male religious specialists. More recently, there has been institutional resistance to the spread or re-creation of some Buddhist nuns' orders, particularly in Southeast Asia. These various changes, in addition to impacting entire societies, also involved forms of innovation within the larger religion.

Innovation relative to the larger religion

In 1994 in South Africa, the scholar and feminist theologian Amina Wadud did something that few modern women have ever done: she led a public, mixed-gender, Islamic prayer service. While this specific act was and still is relatively rare, resisting religious restrictions on specific sorts of bodies and identities through simply refusing those restrictions has a long, global, and multireligious history. Religions abound with stories of women and members of other oppressed classes or groups who were barred from a religious activity but engaged in it anyway.

Amina Wadud had good company, for example, among those Roman Catholics who believe that women should be allowed access to ordination. Even some members of the Roman Catholic hierarchy are working to make this belief a reality by ordaining women in secret, officially conferring on them the rights and abilities of a priest even though the

Church as a whole will not acknowledge or honor their status. Also within Roman Catholicism, the members of the organization Dignity proudly claim their identities as Roman Catholics in good standing with God *and* as openly transgender people and sexually active lesbians, gay men, and bisexuals in relationships with members of the same sex. The Roman Catholic Church currently teaches that although experiencing same sex desire is not in itself sinful, such desire is a temptation to sin and must not be acted upon. Likewise, although the Church has been slow to recognize the existence of living transgender people despite having canonized (designated as a saint) at least one gender-variant person – Joan of Arc – in earlier years, statements by Pope Francis indicate his perspective that transgender people are simply an imperialist construction of powerful global North countries.

The history of the relationship between religion, gender variance, and same sex desire is a complicated one. As we saw in the Introduction, it was only in certain scientific circles of mid-nineteenth-century Europe that the linking of same sex desire with gender variance as an indicator of a broader pattern of innate qualities came into being. There was no such thing as a "homosexual" before this time, or elsewhere in the world until these European ideas were actively marketed to, and sometimes eagerly adopted in, cultures outside of Europe. Certainly there was same sex desire, and certainly people acted on that desire. Likewise, there was gender variance, sometimes paired with same-sex eroticism and sometimes separate from it. Different religions, in different time periods and different regions, defined these actions and identities as anything from deeply sacred to deeply sacrilegious, and considered them anything from a minor advantage or infraction to a major sin or blessing. But to put gender variance and same sex desire together and create the concept of a being called a "homosexual" who also had other predictable traits such as mental instability – that was a nineteenth-century European innovation. At first it was specifically a scientific innovation, but as historian Heather White explains (2015), in the early decades of the twentieth century Protestant ministers began to wonder how they could better support their parishioners who had what were coming to be known as mental illnesses. They were concerned about all sorts of mental disorders, which they also considered to be spiritual problems, but among these was the newly-invented category of homosexuality, classed at that time as a neurosis. It was because of the efforts of these concerned pastors that the word "homosexuality" first appeared in an English translation of the Bible in 1946. Not only was this soon-to-be-popular translation anachronistic, since the concept of homosexuality was less than a century old at that time and therefore could not have been referenced in texts written nearly two millennia earlier, but it was used to translate concepts that most scholars agree referred neither to same-sex eroticism nor to gender variance but to gluttony and over-indulgence of a variety of sorts.

Certainly in past centuries Christianity had at times avidly persecuted people who were same sex attracted and/or gender variant, but at other times in the religion's history it considered these to be minor concerns. The same can be said for Islam, Judaism, and Buddhism. Hinduism has deities who change sex and gender, making it difficult to tell at times when sexual activities between two deities should be considered same-sex or different-sex eroticism. Furthermore, many cultures have traditional roles for gender-variant people, who may or may not engage in same-sex eroticism; these roles were often enshrined in indigenous traditions and accommodated by new traditions that were created in or brought to these societies. So, within certain historical boundaries, we can say that contemporary forms of religious homophobia and transphobia were themselves innovations that impacted an entire religion; today's LGBTIQ+ people who refuse to be banned from their own religions, no matter how socially conservative, are engaging in turn in innovation that often impacts the religion as a whole. Sometimes that impact takes the shape of increasing intensity and frequency of homophobic and transphobic statements; this has been the overall historical arc of both Roman Catholicism and Eastern Orthodox Christianity since the 1960s. At other times the impact is that of increasing inclusion, as is the case with liberal branches of Judaism such as Reconstructing and Reform Judaism, both of which now ordain LGBTIQ+ rabbis and have done so for some time; the more centrist Conservative branch of Judaism also began ordaining lesbian, bisexual, and gay rabbis in 2007.

Although such movements are less widespread in Islam as of this writing, prominent imams have argued for the full and open inclusion of LGBTIQ+ people as the will of God. In Cape Town, South Africa, openly gay imam Muhsin Hendricks has been working for years to create greater openness and understanding toward LGBTIQ+ Muslims; he is a key figure in The Inner Circle, an organization for LGBTIQ+ Muslims, and he provides a variety of inclusive religious services such as officiating at Islamic same-sex weddings. Recent years have also seen a significant expansion of LGBTIQ+-friendly mosques. The first such mosque may well have been The People's Mosque in Cape Town, South Africa, which was founded by Imam Hendricks but is not active as of this writing. Others include the Toronto Unity Mosque, organized in 2009 by Imam El-Farouk Khaki, Laury Silvers, and Troy Jackson; Masjid Nur Al-Isslaah, organized in Washington, D.C. by Imam Daayiee Abdullah in 2011; the Paris mosque organized in 2012 by Ludovic-Mohamed Zahed; and Masjid Ibn Rushd-Goethe in Berlin, which formed a few years later. The Toronto Unity Mosque has organized a network of inclusive mosques called the El-Tawhid Juma Circle, which as of a 2015 blog post had six member congregations in Toronto, Montreal, Halifax, Calgary, Vancouver, and Boston. Likewise, Masjid Ibn Rushd-Goethe was supported in its organization by Ludovic-Mohamed Zahed, who together with the Berlin mosque's founder Seyran Ates is working to create a network of inclusive mosques in Europe. Like many other queer and transgender religious organizations, these inclusive mosques not only welcome queer and transgender people; they also practice inclusive forms of worship by integrating genders during services and having women as well as men lead prayers.

Another area of religious practice that has seen extensive recent innovation is celibacy. Again the example of Christianity is instructive. In several regions of the globe, some Roman Catholics have raised the question of whether priests should be required to be celibate. Roman Catholicism is, after all, the only major branch of Christianity that requires celibacy of all its ordained clergy; while other major branches of the church, most notably the Eastern Orthodox churches and the Anglican Church, provide for celibate renunciant roles through monastic and tertiary orders, they allow priests to marry and to be sexually active within marriage. Movements encouraging the Roman Catholic Church to allow married priests thus introduce innovation into Roman Catholicism and also respond to more established patterns of celibacy and marriage among religious specialists.

Protestantism, as we've discussed above, rejected celibacy entirely when it split from Roman Catholicism. Yet among some Protestant evangelicals, a movement for temporary celibacy has developed in recent years. Conservative evangelicals generally prefer to refrain from sexual activity before marriage, but as the age of marriage increases in many countries this policy creates almost by default a cohort of celibate young adults. Some of them are choosing to live communally, often directing their daily lives toward ministering or evangelizing in their neighborhoods or towns. With their commitment to celibacy, even if temporary, and their communal lifestyle, these evangelical Christian communes are, in effect, monastic communities. Thus, even as some Roman Catholics are urging the Church to move away from celibacy, some evangelicals are moving toward the practice. Both are innovating in the context of their own branch of Christianity even as they're drawing on more established practices elsewhere in the larger religion.

Bringing this section full circle and back to the topic of innovation through creating space in existing religions for women, LGBTIQ+ people, and people of color is the work of three contemporary artists in the U.S. All three use their visual art to challenge traditional exclusions enacted by Christianity. Yolanda Lopez and Alma Lopez, both Chicanas from Roman Catholic backgrounds, engage in their art with the image of the Virgin of Guadalupe, the form in which the Virgin Mary, mother of Jesus first appeared to an indigenous man named Juan Diego in Mexico in the sixteenth century. Guadalupe, who is often considered the model of proper femininity for Mexican and Chicana women and for Latinas more broadly, is typically portrayed as she appeared in an image divinely imprinted on Juan Diego's cape. She is clothed in a loose robe that shows little of her body aside from her hands and face; she is still and composed; and she is looking down. In 1978 Yolanda Lopez set out to reimagine this iconic image in ways that reflected the lives and realities of individual women. She created a triptych – a set of three related works of visual art – in which Guadalupe was portrayed as Lopez herself, her mother, and her grandmother. Instead of standing quietly and looking down, these images of Guadalupe embodied by real women showed her active and looking at the viewer; Lopez was running, her mother was sewing, and her grandmother was sitting quietly but holding the skin of a snake and the knife she used to skin it.

Over 20 later, in 1999, digital artist Alma Lopez offered a similar reimagining of the Virgin of Guadalupe. Like Yolanda Lopez, she was thinking about the challenges that Mexican and Chicana women face in responding to Guadalupe as a role model, and especially about Guadalupe's embodiment. How can human women take her as a model for how to live, Lopez wondered, when human women are embodied and experience their embodiment in complex ways whereas Guadalupe's body is almost entirely hidden from view? Seeking to envision Guadalupe as an embodied human woman, Lopez produced the artwork "Our Lady," which pictured Guadalupe as a young Chicana wearing only a bikini of roses and flanked by prominent Aztec symbols, emphasizing her close relationship to ancient goddesses. Like much religious innovation, the work was controversial among those who were content with the more traditional image; however, many viewers who were seeking greater inclusion in the Church found it inspiring.

Like Yolanda Lopez and Alma Lopez, photographer Renée Cox has used her art to challenge common depictions of sacred figures in Christianity, especially depictions that have directly or indirectly supported racism and sexism. Also like the other two artists, Cox has reimagined an image of the Virgin Mary. Using herself and her young son as models, in her 1994 "Yo Mamadonna and Child" she offered an image of the Madonna (the Virgin Mary) as a strong African woman, gazing directly at the camera. A 1996 work entitled "Yo Mama's Pietà" showed Cox in the role of the grieving Mary, holding the body of Jesus after he has been taken down from the cross. A naked, young Black man is here cast in the role of Jesus – crucified, one imagines, not by anti-Semitic

Romans but by anti–Black Americans. And while re-envisioning Jesus as a Black man has been popular for several decades, Cox's "Yo Mama's Last Supper" (1999) goes one step further. In this reimagining of Leonardo da Vinci's classic painting of the meal Jesus shared with his disciples before his crucifixion, Cox is Jesus, standing naked at the table in the center of the image. Surrounding her are Black disciples, with one exception: Judas, who betrayed Jesus to the authorities, is white.

Each of these artists represents one individual voice speaking to a larger desire to innovate around the questions of which bodies belong where, what they should be doing, and who has the right to say. Women's bodies, their work forcefully claims, belong in sacred stories and sacred images. They belong there uncovered and in front, sexually and reproductively active, looking the viewer in the eye and taking up space. Chicana and Black women's bodies belong not only in religion but in the sacred itself. So do queer bodies. Who gets to say? No one but themselves.

Innovation as a response to changes in the larger society

While religious innovation around sexualities and bodies may have as its goal or its result changes in the larger society or changes in the larger religion, and at times both, in many cases such innovation responds to changes that are taking place in the society or to existing situations that need to be changed. Some changes relate directly to religion and sexuality, such as changing attitudes toward and practices around marriage and reproduction or the changing social, legal, and religious status of women, of transgender people (including transgender women, for whom both of these categories are important), and of lesbians, gay men, bisexuals, and pansexuals. Others are rooted in larger social changes, but they nevertheless have consequences for sexualities, bodies, and religions. Two of the most important sources of change that impact bodies, religions, and sexualities are the economy and technology.

Economic changes played a role in both of this chapter's case studies, because a changing economic structure often leads to wider social changes in such areas as gender roles, ideas about proper and improper sexuality, reproduction, and living arrangements. *Mizuko kuyō*, for instance, gained prominence in the wake of Japan's pronounced economic growth in the mid-twentieth century. As more jobs became available and social norms around gender roles shifted, women became more likely to pursue advanced education and career paths. The time between sexual maturity and marriage lengthened for both men and women, while the social stigma of becoming pregnant while single remained in place for women. When contraception was difficult to practice or when it failed, producing an unwanted pregnancy, women and sometimes men (with or without the woman's free and full consent) turned to abortion. Some women saw no ethical difficulty in terminating a pregnancy, although certainly the procedure is unpleasant and some women grieved the loss of the fetus; however, more conservative social forces thought that the rise in teenage abortions during this time period indicated a rise in teen sexual activity. A cultural backlash began in some parts of Japanese society, and Hardacre argues that this backlash was partly responsible for the marketing of images of the angry, destructive aborted fetus. Of course, spiritualists marketing such rituals for the purpose of financial gain is also an economic factor in the brief life of this ritual.

Although the economic changes in the nineteenth-century U.S. were markedly different from those in twentieth-century Japan, nonetheless they had their own impact on religious innovation with regard to bodies and sexualities. Also as in Japan, such economic changes cannot entirely be separated from related political changes that were taking place at the same time. In the U.S. as in Europe, the nineteenth century witnessed a rapid and widespread shift in modes of economic production with the Industrial Revolution and the rise of industrial capitalism. Where in the late eighteenth century most goods and services were still produced by individual proprietors or small, family-owned businesses, by a century later most production of goods and services had been consolidated into large, assembly-line factories and corporate offices. Far fewer people worked in their homes any longer; most went to work at the office or on the factory floor and came home again at the end of the day. But this pattern was also affected by gender, race, and class. For instance, it was commonly assumed that women's role in this economy should be to birth, raise, and teach children; economic analysts like Karl Marx and Friedrich Engels pointed out that women were thereby tasked with producing the future laborers who would grow up and produce new products. But this expectation did not apply to working-class women of any race, or to people of color of any class; these socially non-dominant women had to work like the men even as their work outside the home was denigrated as unfeminine, improper, and sexually inappropriate.

At the same time, political changes were developing throughout the nineteenth century that challenged the newly-founded United States to live up to the ideals of equality that were expressed in its Declaration of Independence. How could a government claim to be "of the people, by the people, and for the people," activists asked, when some of those people were enslaved and only a relatively small portion of the people living in the country had the right to vote? These economic and political changes, along with the upheavals of the U.S. and French revolutions, led some to suspect that the end of time was coming and led others to explore new modes of living and relating with one another. Both sparked the religious innovation that resulted in the differing Mormon, Shaker, and Oneida Perfectionist interpretations of gender roles, sexuality, and marriage. They also led these groups, and quite a few others, to explore communal living and to create their own communities.

Indeed, it was economic factors that led to the religious innovation of enslaving, owning, and even breeding human beings in the first place. As the transatlantic slave trade grew and increasingly racialized politics in the British colonies of North America made Black and Native American slaves a more reliable and more lucrative choice for unpaid labor than white indentured servants, entire colonies came to rely on slavery for their economic growth and wealth. A capitalist system, which offers the greatest reward to the person who can produce the largest amount of a high-priced, desirable product like tobacco or cotton or dye at the lowest cost, drove the search for ever-cheaper labor to its logical conclusion: free labor through slavery. Slaveholding Christian leaders, for their part, focused on the presence of slavery in the Bible and the multiple references in the early Christian writings of the New Testament to slaves obeying their masters.

To reach even farther back in history, an earlier form of religious innovation in India has somewhat unclear origins but eventually became a response to the intertwined social and economic status system known as caste. Although the practice was not itself an innovation, those who were involved in it seem to have created innovative adaptations in its meanings and practice that made it easier for them to survive as Dalits, those so low in the social order that they had no caste at all. The practice is that of marrying daughters, and sometimes sons, to a goddess, thereby initiating them into the group most commonly known as *devadasis*.

In the traditional Indian system, caste is inherited. Like some societies' understandings of class as a hereditary trait, caste limits a person's options for occupation as well as the person's place in society; unlike some hereditary class systems, though, caste specifies precisely what a person's occupation will be. While some higher-status castes may be less wealthy or have less earning power than castes with a lower status, in general higher caste leads to greater economic and political security. Low-caste people, then, often struggle more than those in the higher castes, and poverty is rampant among the lowest castes and among those traditionally defined as "outcaste," so low that they had no caste at all. Since its independence from British rule India has been working to undo the caste system, but as with all long-standing systems of social inequality it has proven difficult to eradicate social differences based on caste. This is especially true in a capitalist system, where poverty is often self-reproducing. People from lower-class and outcaste backgrounds entered into a capitalist system in poverty; many have not escaped the cycle of poverty even after generations. Furthermore, caste is also gendered; the roles and occupations delineated by caste membership are different for women than for men.

In light of these constraints, anthropologist Lucinda Ramberg (2014) argues that becoming formally dedicated to a goddess as a devadasi opens up new possibilities for economic survival. We might interpret these possibilities as another example of religious innovation. For more than a century, women's rights reformers and Hindu traditionalists alike have criticized the practice of dedication, and particularly the dedication of girls as children, saying that it exploits women and in particular poor women. This is because both female and male devadasis generally support themselves financially through sexual relationships with men – working in brothels if they live in urban areas, or in rural areas being supported by a male patron whose economic assistance is repaid in sexual favors. In response to these concerns, both government agencies and non-governmental organizations (NGOs) have turned persistent attention on devadasis in recent years, attempting to eradicate the institution through methods ranging from outright bans on new dedications to offering female (and generally not male) devadasis other sources of income. Neither has been successful. Why?

If the social institution of devadasis arose as a religious innovation in response to a social circumstance, perhaps the social issues it addresses aren't really remedied by the solutions that governments and NGOs offer. If a practice is filling a need, banning it is unlikely to make it stop. A ban simply causes the practice to go underground. It can also exacerbate the problem. If a practice is lessening poverty, for instance, and the act of carrying out that practice is punishable by fines or jail time, then not only will a ban on the practice increase poverty but those violating the ban will become even poorer through being forced to pay fines or being incarcerated. Likewise, if dedicating children to the goddess is addressing a complex set of needs in Dalit communities then teaching women a different, often poorly paid, profession will not adequately address those needs. This is precisely Ramberg's argument.

Devadasis are dedicated to, and often called by, independent goddesses who are not themselves tied to a man through marriage and who are not opposed to disrupting traditional arrangements of sexuality and gender. These goddesses call women out of marriages that are traditionally expected to be lifelong, providing an escape route from abusive or confining marriages in much the same way as nuns' orders have historically done for some Buddhist and Christian women. The goddesses call males to become women and forego sex with the women who have become their sisters, preferring instead hetero-gendered sex with men; these males thereby relinquish their duties to marry and provide descendants for the family, as sons must do. The goddesses likewise call some females to dress and live as men. All of those whom they call become religious specialists, respected in the circles that still revere these independent goddesses.

Because they are married to a goddess, Ramberg tells us, female women who are dedicated as devadasis also have a unique role within their families. While they continue to be recognized as women, they take roles commonly associated with fathers and sons. In Indian tradition, when a woman marries she becomes a part of her husband's family. Therefore, she does not inherit property from her parents, nor can she manage her birth family's finances. But as someone married to a goddess, she is able to do both of these things. For people in poverty, this gender flexibility offers another route for economic survival. In a family with no sons, for instance, a daughter married to a goddess can function as a son, supporting the other daughters and their children and inheriting and maintaining the family's lands so that everyone who needs a place to live and land on which to grow food has that need fulfilled. If a woman's parents die young, as a devadasi she can act as a father, preventing her unmarried siblings from being orphaned. In the role of father she can negotiate marriages, maintain the family's lands until her siblings are old enough to take over their part of the inheritance, and provide for her siblings and their children. In a culture with specific traditional roles for men that are critical to individual and family survival, it comes in handy when female sons and female fathers can step into those roles as needed. No wonder, then, that banning this religious innovation has been ineffective; no wonder that offering devadasis alternative ways of earning money also has not been wildly successful.

Ramberg writes of kinship as a kind of **technology**, a tool that humans use to interact with the world around us. More tangible forms of technology also shape, and drive, religious innovation. As with movements to outlaw abortion in many Christian cultures, for instance, the advertising campaign that attempted to drum up business for spiritualists who performed *mizuko kuyō* made use of new imaging technology to help potential clients see their fetuses as babies. Using images of late-term fetuses, enlarging them, and turning them upside down (because late-term fetuses typically are positioned head-down in the uterus in preparation for birth), these promotional campaigns blurred the conceptual line between a fetus and a baby, making more believable the claim that abortion is infanticide. The fetuses that are removed or expelled when a pregnancy is terminated, either biologically through miscarriage or technologically through abortion, typically look nothing like these images. Advancements in fetal imaging, then, produced these religious innovations in which religious revulsion (in the case of anti-abortion movements) or religious fear (in the case of *mizuko kuyō*) were aroused visually.

More recently, the development of the Internet has led to quite a bit of religious innovation. Every development in communication technology, it seems, leads to such innovation; after all, the invention of the printing press, which made it possible to produce Bibles at a rapid rate in many different languages, supported the Protestant Reformation's focus on each individual person's ability to read and interpret the Bible for themselves. Radio and television, especially when they were relatively new, broadcast religious opinions and religious services and in the process changed even those religious services that weren't being broadcast.

The Internet has taken us from television broadcasts of religious services to interactive religious experiences. Online, one can tour an existing temple or even a long-destroyed one, such as the great Jewish temple in Jerusalem that was destroyed for the second time in 70 CE. One can participate in rituals through chat rooms or multi-user videoconferencing services. One can access religious services and resources at a distance, for instance when living in an area that does not have a congregation or a ritual leader of that specific religion. One can also find resources specific to one's needs, such as an inclusive mosque or a series of discussions on the status of gay men in Orthodox Judaism, and if necessary one can find those resources without sharing with anyone (except perhaps the government) what one is seeking.

Smart phones and other devices, along with the Internet, have also brought us religiously-specific resources for sex. A Muslim looking to date another Muslim, for instance, might look on Minder (the "Muslim Tinder"), an online dating website and app for Muslims. Socially conservative Christians can find sexual advice in a format that does not violate their strict religious standards on looking at the naked body of anyone to whom they are not married. And observant, or *frum*, Orthodox Jews in search of sexual stimulation can seek out frum pornography. Religious innovation, then, is ever-present and ongoing.

Conclusion

Many people think of religion as traditional, unchanging, and socially conservative in two senses: conserving prior practices, that is, resistant to change, and leaning to the right on the political spectrum. But religion is often a powerful force in both larger societies and smaller subcultures, and it can be and has been targeted in many different directions. Religious innovation is an excellent example of religion's ability to respond to social circumstances in varied and creative ways. At times those innovations are conservative, tightening restrictions on certain groups of people or promoting a return to or a re-entrenchment of older practices, but at other times they instigate or support radical change in the religion or the society. Responding to the questions of which bodies belong where, what they should be doing, and who gets to say, religious experimentation and religious innovation have immense power to change or reinforce social structures – for good or for ill.

Review: chapter highlights

- Case study 1: *Mizuko kuyō*;
- Case study 2: What does it mean to be like the angels? The Shakers, the Latter-day Saints, and the Oneida Perfectionists;
- Religious innovation;

   a   What bodies belong where?
   b   What bodies should do what?
   c   Who gets to say?

- Innovation relative to the larger society;

   a   Race and gender in the Nation of Islam;
   b   Women, divine inspiration, and intellectual authority in Christianity;
   c   Men's roles: the Men and Religion Forward Movement, the Promise Keepers, and the Radical Faeries;
   d   Islam and the status of women;
   e   Early Christianity and gender roles;
   f   Early Buddhism, gender, and the uses of celibacy;

- Innovation relative to the larger religion;

  a   Amina Wadud leads public prayers;
  b   Female Roman Catholic priests;
  c   LGBTIQ+ inclusion;

  - Dignity;
  - Putting "homosexuality" in the Bible;
  - LGBTIQ+ people creating inclusive religious spaces;

  d   Innovations in celibacy;

  - The movement for married priests in Roman Catholicism;
  - Celibate evangelical Protestant communities;

  e   Innovation through art;

  - Yolanda Lopez's Guadalupe series;
  - Alma Lopez's "Our Lady";
  - Renée Cox's Yo Mama series;

- Innovation as a response to changes in the larger society;

  a   Economic and political factors;

  - *Mizuko kuyō*;
  - The Shakers, the Latter-day Saints, and the Oneida Perfectionists;
  - Devadasis;

  b   Technologies;

  - Fetal imaging and religious responses to abortion;
  - The Internet;
  - Online practice and education;
  - Anonymous access to resources;
  - Religious dating: Minder;
  - Religious sex education;
  - Religious sexual stimulation: frum porn;
  - Conclusion.

Applications and reflections

1   Many of the religious innovations discussed in this chapter were focused on creating greater inclusion for marginalized groups. Pick one of the examples in the book to explore further. Using the archives at your local library, history books or published collections of archival materials, old media such as early films, or online resources such as digital archives, explore the mainstream culture's and/or religion's portrayal of the minoritized group in question. How were they depicted? Why do you think they were depicted this way? (Hint: "Because that's what they were like" is probably too simple an answer.) Then consider the religious innovation. In what ways did it address the depictions you've just studied? How did it respond to them? Why do you think this was the response that seemed best to the people who developed it?

2   Religious innovation, particularly when it involves bodies and sexualities, always has critics. As we've seen, the religious innovations covered in this chapter have faced a range of social, cultural, legal, and government opposition, ranging from false accusations to murderous violence. Why do you think religious innovation upsets its opponents so much? Is the innovation itself the most likely source of concern? Is it the fact that it's *religious* innovation? Does it have more to do with the fact that it's innovation involving bodies and sexualities? What arguments and evidence support your conclusions?

3   Religious innovation is all around us. What forms exist near you? Has anyone in your family, including yourself, been involved in religious innovation related to bodies and/or sexualities? What about people you know? If so, spend a little time talking with these people, or reflect on your own experiences. What made the innovation important for these people? How did they get involved? Did they ever face resistance, and if so, what form(s) did it take? What can you learn from these conversations and reflections about religious innovation more broadly?

4   How has technology changed around you in the past decade or so, and how has it driven religious innovation? What about the economy, or politics – have changes in those systems sparked religious innovation having to do with bodies and sexualities? Of what type? Why do you think this innovation arose, and why do you think it's taken the forms that it has? What needs is it fulfilling? If technology, politics, and the economy have changed but you've seen no religious innovation, ponder why that is. Has there been no need for it, or has there been active opposition that might have prevented it from arising? Or is there another explanation entirely?

Resources for further study

Burke, Kelsy. *Christians Under Covers: Evangelicals and Sexual Pleasure on the Internet.* Berkeley, CA: University of California Press, 2016.

Herrick, Tirzah Miller. *Desire and Duty at Oneida: Tirzah Miller's Intimate Memoir.* Bloomington, IN: Indiana University Press, 2000.

Jeffries, Bayyinah S. *A Nation Can Rise No Higher than its Women: African American Muslim Women in the Movement for Black Self-Determination, 1950–1975.* Lanham, MD: Lexington, 2014.

Ramberg, Lucinda. *Given to the Goddess: South Indian Devadasis and the Sexuality of Religion.* Durham, NC: Duke University Press, 2014.

Theobald, Simon. "'It's a Tefillin Date': Alternative Narratives of Orthodox Jewish Sexuality in the Digital Age." In Stephen J. Hunt and Andrew K.T. Yip (eds.) *The Ashgate Research Companion in Contemporary Religion and Sexuality.* Burlington, VT: Ashgate, 2012: 289–304.

6 Instrumentalization

Case study 1

In South Sulawesi, Indonesia, *bissu* have played an important ritual role for centuries. Traditionally, they served the royal courts by guarding regalia, arranging marriages, and attending births; they even had a hand in the origin of the world, bringing beauty and the creative arts and "making the world blossom" (Davies 2010, 71). Since the abolition of Indonesian royal courts in the mid-twentieth century, *bissu* have struggled without the support of their high-placed patrons but they have also come to serve people across the spectrum of social statuses, conducting ritual blessings for a wide variety of people and situations. Though they receive their powers through the approval of traditional deities, many *bissu* today are Muslim like the majority of Indonesia's population. Unwilling either to forego their religion or to turn down what they see as a divine and innate calling, they blend traditions that predate Islam's presence in their region with a commitment to Islam that extends, for some, to repeated performances of the *hajj*, the pilgrimage to Mecca.

Bissu obtain their religious abilities through their purity and through the ambiguity of their bodies; they are both male and female, together in one bodily form. For some *bissu*, explains anthropologist Sharyn Davies, the combination is embodied in a sharp lateral division, with one side of a *bissu*'s body being male and the other female. Such people may grow facial hair only on one side, for instance, and dress and adorn one half of their bodies in masculine ways and the other half in feminine ways. For others, maleness and femaleness are more blended; they may wear a woman's outfit with a man's hat and bear masculine regalia, for instance. Some are intersex; others were born male or female but are reproductively inactive. Females who have passed menopause sometimes become *bissu*, as do some males who do not experience erections. Traditionally, male *bissu* seem to have been castrated in order to properly carry out their duties. All are expected to be celibate, although this expectation is not enforced severely, and all are expected to be pure in other ways as well. *Bissu* should be focused on the sacred realm, unencumbered by desire for anything of the human world, whether it be sexual pleasures, delicious foods, or luxury goods.

This purity and ambiguity allowed traditional *bissu* to be possessed by deities during rituals; as Muslims, many *bissu* today understand those beings who possess them as benevolent, if powerful, spirits rather than deities. *Bissu* demonstrate their possession, and their acceptance by the spirits, during rituals when they perform *ma'giri'*, attempting to stab themselves with a ritual knife. Skilled *bissu* who have been possessed by the spirits emerge from this ritual unharmed. What gives *bissu* their powers is their ambiguous embodiment. Whether as intersex people, post-menopausal females, or males who don't experience erections and/or who have been castrated, *bissu* challenge the norm of binary sexes and genders. This in-between, multiple nature allows them to navigate other in-between spaces: in between women and men in marriage, in between promise and life in birth, in between human and divine in possession, in between life and death in healing. Their ambiguously sexed and gendered, sexually inactive bodies serve as religious *instruments*, or tools, for their communities.

Case study 2

For more than a millennium, male South Asian ritual practitioners known as Tantrikas have developed spiritual and bodily powers through sexual intercourse with goddesses embodied by human women. As demonstrated in great detail by Hinduism scholar David Gordon White, the powers that Tantrikas develop through ritual sex stem from sexual fluids (White 2003). In some classic texts, power comes through an exchange of sexual fluids with goddesses who are often not only powerful but dangerous and hungry. Propitiated with the ultimate food offering – semen – they reciprocate by offering their menstrual blood and vaginal fluids to their sexual partners. Some practitioners imbibe these fluids orally, lapping them up directly from the vagina of the woman embodying the goddess or collecting them in a bowl designed for food sacrifices before consuming them. Others pursue a more esoteric method of taking in the "divine nectar" of sexual fluids: through special forms of mental concentration and highly developed spiritual skills, they draw the fluids up through their urethras into their bodies. In a version that developed later but did not replace the ritual imbibing of sexual fluids, the male practitioners understood their female sexual partners to be embodying less unrestrained, more domesticated goddesses and therefore had no need to make offerings of semen. Likewise, they received no gifts of vaginal fluids or menstrual blood. Instead, they practiced the retention of their semen, directing their sexual arousal and their sexual fluids upward within their bodies to create intense spiritual powers and astoundingly superhuman abilities.

   In many of the Tantric practices that are followed by certain groups of Hindus and Buddhists, a key element is the ritual inversion or violation of social norms that practitioners typically respect in all other aspects of their lives. Rituals may take place in cremation grounds, which are considered highly polluting and certainly aren't places that would usually be appropriate for sacred practices. The use of sexual intercourse in rituals is another example of such challenging of social norms, and drinking semen and menstrual blood is normally considered extremely polluting. Likewise, many Tantrikas have traditionally sought out socially inappropriate women for their sexual rites. Most practitioners of **Tantra** have been male and elite; the women with whom they practice these rituals may be revered when they are embodying a goddess, but they generally come from scorned social groups. Often, explains historian Hugh Urban, Tantrikas selected their sexual partners specifically because they were people with whom an elite man was not supposed to have sex, such as low-caste or outcaste women and sex workers (Urban 2006). Venerated when a goddess was believed to be inhabiting her body, such a woman was often disregarded once the ritual had ended. When the goddess left, so too did the Tantrika. Who, or what, is being instrumentalized here? There may be more than one answer.

In the nineteenth century, the British colonization of India and colonial fantasies about the mysterious "Orient" with its glamorous past and gritty present led European scholars to begin investigating ancient religious texts in South Asia. They found them quite confusing at first, and not only were the earliest English translations of these ancient texts garbled but their readers and sometimes their translators struggled to tell the difference between the religions they came to call Hinduism, Buddhism, and Jainism. Among these texts that were arriving in garbled form, and being adapted to uniquely Western uses, were **Tantras** – the ritual texts of the Tantrikas.

Many nineteenth-century Westerners were fascinated with the spirit world and with Asia. Some of them were interested in learning how to better interact with the spirits, even control them, and how to use spiritual powers for earthly benefits. They found the Tantras intriguing, and wove their limited understanding of the texts into their own mystical and magical traditions. Sex had power in Western traditions too, sometimes negative and sometimes positive, so discovering rituals that harnessed these powers was less a source of surprise than one of excitement. These Western practitioners, typically men as the Tantrikas have been, began to experiment with using sex to affect the world around them. Some sought earthly powers – in fact, a famous Italian fascist, Julius Evola, was intensely interested in the potential he saw in Tantra – while others pursued spiritual bliss (Urban 2006). By the late twentieth century, "tantric sex" was all the rage in the West. Variously marketed – but *always* marketed in some way – as a new source of intensified sexual pleasure and as a way of making sex spiritual and spirituality sexy, today's tantric sex classes, books, videos, and gurus literally capitalize on – that is, turn into capital – the ongoing Western conviction that Asia is the source of all good things both erotic and spiritual. "Tantric sex" would be unrecognizable, even laughable, to Tantrikas. Tantric sex also engages instrumentalization differently; unlike traditional Tantra or the rituals of the celibate *bissu*, both of which instrumentalized bodies and sex for the sake of religion, tantric sex instrumentalizes religion for the sake of sex.

Instrumentalizing bodies, sex, and religion

Instrumentalizing something, as we noted above, means making it into a tool – an instrument – that you can use to accomplish a particular goal. Instrumentalization is one of the ways in which bodies, sexualities, genders, and religions can be related, and it takes place in four key ways that form the themes of this chapter: through sexual acts, through sexualized bodies and parts of bodies, through non-conforming bodies, and through traditionally gendered bodies. When reading the chapter, consider whether there are other themes in the religions you're familiar with.

As we've seen in the case studies, sexualized and gendered bodies can be instrumentalized for the sake of religion, such as for the goal of conducting a successful ritual or developing specific spiritual or earthly powers through religion. On the other hand, religion can be instrumentalized for the sake of specific goals around bodies, sexualities, and genders, such as in the use of Western tantric sex practices to enhance sexual pleasure or sexual prowess. These frameworks – instrumentalizing bodies for religion and religion for bodies – weave through each of the themes in this chapter. They also stand on their own, though, and we could just as easily have structured the chapter around these two themes, each subdivided by the four themes we discuss below. Each set of themes, in other words, exists within the other set. Watch for these intersections as you continue reading.

Sexual acts

Examples of the instrumentalization of sex for religion and the instrumentalization of religion for sex can be found around the globe and across history. Think, for example, of how important it is in some religious traditions for a person to be sexually active in the correct ways at the correct times, or to avoid sexual activity entirely, since celibacy is also a way of instrumentalizing sex for religious goals. Think, too, of religious rites that make sexual activity appropriate or inappropriate, or that have as their goal the promotion or inhibition of fertility. It turns out that sex and religion have a strongly instrumental relationship. A closer look at the history of modern sex magic in the West offers an instructive range of examples of such instrumentalization.

Christianity has long instrumentalized sexuality – and vice versa – through the practice of celibacy and through the ritual of marriage, which makes sexual activities between two people permissible and even sacred while it also, in some branches of the religion, designates those sexual activities as intended solely for the purpose of procreation. In Roman Catholic and Eastern Orthodox Christianity marriage is considered a sacrament, a sign of the blessings and grace of God. Although both of these traditions officially allow marriage to take place only between a man who was assigned male at birth and a woman who was assigned female at birth, gender variant and same sex attracted practitioners of these traditions also take their marriages very seriously. Some priests will even bless such unions, albeit away from the watchful gaze of their leadership.

Likewise, Judaism has long instrumentalized sex – and been instrumentalized for sexual purposes. Although the mainstream of this religion has never revered the practice of celibacy as Christianity has done, and indeed the early Jesus movement and the sect of Judaism that influenced it were among the few offshoots of Judaism to recommend celibacy to their practitioners, Judaism has important rituals surrounding the practice of sexuality. The most important of these, in Judaism as in Christianity, is marriage. Other important rituals, as we've seen in earlier chapters, surround the preparation of the body for sex, particularly for observant Jews who follow *niddah* laws that proscribe sexual relations or even physical contact between married couples during and near the time of a woman's menstruation. When engaged in appropriately, though, with the right partner under the right conditions, sex is widely regarded in Judaism as a blessing. Given that many of the more socially liberal branches of the religion today also have more expansive views on which bodies may properly be engaged in sex with each other, in what bodily states, and when, there is significant opportunity within Judaism for a wide range of instrumental connections between religion and sex.

During the medieval period in Europe, the mystical Jewish tradition known as Kabbalah rose to prominence. Because many of its central metaphors for the relationship between God, Torah, and humanity were images of lovers or spouses, some thinkers in this tradition expanded the metaphors into practices, finding sanctity in the union of spouses on the Sabbath. Later Europeans and European-influenced thinkers and practitioners, whether Jewish or not, would be drawn to these esoteric ideas about the connections between sexuality and God. Likewise, Renaissance forms of magic and **alchemy** – a mystical and early form of chemistry – whether practiced by Christians, Jews, or those of other religious traditions, perceived powerful connections between sexual love and magic. Some alchemists even became interested in the possibility of creating spiritually perfected beings through the correct, mystical use of sexuality. Through the seventeenth and eighteenth centuries, and into the Romantic period of the nineteenth century, where some people reacted against the scientific neglect of the spirit world by attempting to fuse science and religion, mystics explored the spiritual magic that could be generated through the sexual union of two properly prepared, religiously approved bodies – always one male, one female, and married.

With Judaism and Christianity forming the most central religious influences in Western cultures, we might ask not only about their effects in creating positive instrumental connections between sexual activity and religion but also their impact on the negative connections between these two. After all, while both traditions have rituals that make certain forms of sexual activity legitimate and even blessed, these same rituals reinforce a perspective that other forms of sex – between certain kinds of bodies, in certain bodily conditions, at certain times, in certain places or on certain occasions, and so on – are illegitimate. And as the Tantrikas knew, social illegitimacy can be very powerful. Historically, both Jews and Christians have associated some of the sexual activities that they considered illegitimate with dangerous superhuman beings, such as demons. Perhaps predictably, those within their societies who were less firmly committed to mainstream religious perspectives on sex became curious about the powers attributed to socially illegitimate sex.

European interest in the power of ritual for sex, and possibly the power of sex for ritual, appears to date back before the rise of Christianity. While much of the literature that has come down to us today from ancient and medieval Europe demonstrates more fear of the theoretical power of socially illegitimate sex than interest in or tools for harnessing that power, by the end of the nineteenth century several factors had come together to encourage exploration of the latter. For one thing, the rise of mechanistic understandings of science over the course of the past few centuries had culminated in the Industrial Revolution. Machines were everywhere, and everything could be thought of as a machine, including the human body. If everything was a potential machine, that also meant that everything was a potential tool; everything could be instrumentalized. To many people at the time, machines and tools were morally and religiously neutral. They could not be judged as good or bad in themselves, but only as making good-quality or poor-quality products, or as being more effective or less effective. In a time when some people came to think of religion as a spiritual form of science and to apply scientific principles to the study of paranormal phenomena, such as séances in which the dead reappeared in the world of the living, it wasn't that big a stretch to suggest that sex could have scientifically provable results in the world beyond the human and that those results could, in turn, create profound change in the human world. This was the beginning of the socially transgressive forms of sex magic within modern Western cultures (see Urban 2006).

The Austrian chemist and mystic Carl Kellner and fellow European Theodor Reuss, co-founders of the esoteric organization known as the Ordo Templi Orientis or OTO, were among the earliest people to attempt to draw together Western interpretations of Tantric practices with Western magical, Kabbalistic, and alchemical ideas about the ritual uses of sex. At a time when the discovery and harnessing of electricity was creating profound changes in the world around them, these two thinkers described the spiritual capacities of sex through an electrical metaphor that's still with us today: energy. Energy, to Reuss, was gendered – or perhaps better, sexed – in ways that were rooted in the oppositions that he believed existed between male and female bodies. Like other nineteenth-century thinkers, such as leading Spiritualists, Reuss understood these physical, energetic differences to function similarly to electrical poles, with both being necessary for current to flow. Through a flamboyant member of the OTO, Aleister Crowley, and Crowley's student Gerald Gardner, these ideas about the electrical or energetic polarity of male and female bodies would survive all the way into the twenty-first century in some forms of Neopaganism.

For the OTO, for Crowley, and for their various mystical and esoteric descendants, the most powerful generator of spiritual energy was sexuality. And unlike their predecessors, who focused on the divine power and blessings of socially approved sex, these magicians saw much greater potential – in the electrical sense as well as the metaphorical sense – in socially transgressive sex. At a time when same-sex eroticism was being named, categorized, and pathologized as "inversion" or "homosexuality" in Europe and its settler colonies, there are indications that the early OTO experimented with same-sex sexual magic. Certainly Crowley, who was the most flagrant practitioner of transgressive sexual magic, made use of same-sex eroticism as a source of magical power. Through the latter half of the twentieth century and into the twenty-first, organizations descended from Crowley have applied his ideas about sex magic in a number of different ways. The Church of Satan, a movement founded in opposition to what it sees as the moral prudery and shaming condoned by Christianity, generally considers Satan to be a symbol of the antithesis of those values rather than an actual superhuman being. In working to resist such prudery, Satanists often instrumentalize sex in dramatic and sometimes wryly parodic forms, drawing great amusement as well as frustration from the intense condemnation and terror they encounter in those for whom Satan is a very real and eternally destructive force in the world.

Through Gerald Gardner's influence, Wiccans and by connection a number of other Neopagan groups also value the role that erotic energies or even sexual acts can play in ritual. Gardner, who claimed to have been initiated by a hereditary coven of witches descended from practitioners of European pre-Christian traditions, taught that a priestess and a priest (Gardner was opposed to same-sex eroticism) could embody the Great Goddess and the Great God in a sexual ritual he called the Great Rite. While the Great Rite is more discussed than practiced in most Neopagan circles, those discussions have taken interesting forms as Neopaganism has changed and developed. Separatist feminist Zsuzsanna Budapest, founder of the women-born-women-only Dianic branch of Wicca, advocated a lesbian Great Rite that would affirm women's sacred connection to each other. Starhawk, co-founder and prominent theologian of Reclaiming Wicca, studied with Budapest for a time but sought a more inclusive form of Wiccan practice; although Reclaiming still has roots in a binary polarity model of gender and sex, as it has become increasingly inclusive of LGBTIQ+ people its own understandings of the ritual powers of sexuality have also diversified. For the Radical Faeries, influenced by the philosophy of gay activist Harry Hay, by the Jungian psychology of co-founder Mitch Walker, and by the Neopagan interests of author and activist Arthur Evans, among others, consensual sexual contact between men in a ritual space is an affirmation of the sacredness of their bodies, their spirits, and their sex itself.

Sexual activity, then, can be instrumentalized by religion for causes ranging from the creation of spiritually perfect heterosexuals to the generation of world-altering energies. Likewise, religion can be instrumentalized for sexual purposes such as affirming various forms of sexual desire and gender identity, creating a bond through which new life can be created, or – as in many if not all cultures – drawing the attention of a beloved. After all, love charms too are very much a part of the instrumentalization of religion and sex.

Sexualized bodies and parts of bodies

Several of our examples so far have involved the instrumentalization of *sexualized* bodies – those bodies that are viewed by social and cultural norms as particularly sexual. In many cultures women's bodies are sexualized; because they are defined as intrinsically sexual, women in such cultures are under greater expectations than are men to cover their bodies and keep them from sight. To whatever extent a culture considers public sexual expression inappropriate, that culture will also mandate the control, covering, and even public invisibility or eradication of sexualized bodies, such as those of women, sex workers, same-sex attracted and gender-variant people, and the like.

But on another level, anyone's body can be sexualized – interpreted in specifically sexual ways – if attention is drawn to sexualized parts of that person's body. While secondary sexual characteristics such as breasts or body hair, and gendered features such as hair length and style, are sexualized in different ways by different cultures, genitalia are nearly always sexualized. For that reason, they play an important role in the instrumentalization of bodies, religions, and sexuality.

There is clear evidence in the Torah that the patrilineal, patriarchal (male-led) ancient Israelites instrumentalized male genitalia as a central part of their cultural and legal practices. In a number of instances, the biblical text describes one man placing his hands on the "loins" of a powerful leader, often an elder relative, to swear an oath. Such a vow, sworn in fact on the man's testicles, may have been meant as a promise to the family's descendants. In a culture that understood semen as the most important substance for human reproduction, to swear on a man's testes was to make a deeply binding oath.

Male genitalia are instrumentalized in other religious ways, too; one of the most common is circumcision. Removing the foreskin of the penis is not always a religious act; there are ongoing conversations in medical communities, for example, about the health benefits of circumcision, and some medical communities circumcise newborn males routinely unless a parent requests that the child not be circumcised. There are also anti-circumcision movements whose followers consider male circumcision inappropriate, unnecessary, and unethical. But circumcision has long been a marker of both Jewish and Muslim identity for males. In Judaism, in particular, ritual circumcision is part of welcoming a male into the Jewish community either as a newborn or as an adult. Male adult converts to Judaism who are not already circumcised typically undergo circumcision, and those who are already circumcised undergo a symbolic shedding of blood from the penis. Transgender men have developed meaningful ways to engage in such traditions when they convert to Judaism as adults or when they transition to living as men. In Muslim communities, there is debate among scholars as to whether male converts to Islam should be circumcised if they have not been already, but males born into Muslim families are typically circumcised.

While the centrality of circumcision as an identity marker and an important religious ritual constitutes one way in which the penis – specifically, the foreskin – can be instrumentalized for religious purposes, this is a fairly benign and often even celebrated instrumentalization of genitalia. As we saw in the chapter on violence, though, bodies can be instrumentalized in the pursuit of religiously-based violence, and genitalia are often a key target of such instrumentalization. In 1947, for instance, the country of Pakistan was formed by splitting off the northwestern portion of India; what is now Bangladesh was also split off, originally as East Pakistan. This separation is known as the partition of India, and it was based on religious definitions of citizenship: Pakistan and East Pakistan were to be Muslim countries, and India, though remaining multi-religious, would be by default a Hindu nation. The chaos that resulted from the partition was dominated by extreme violence on all sides that some have termed ethnic cleansing. While much of the violence against men resulted in death, it was also sexualized violence. Living or dead, Hindu and Sikh men were forcibly circumcised, effectively engraving Islam on their bodies, while some men on all sides of the struggle were castrated, literally removing their ability to expand their populations. As with most instances of violent confrontation, and particularly in religio-ethnic conflicts, men on all sides also raped other men.

But like in many cases of ethnic cleansing, particularly those cases involving *religio-*ethnic violence, the most common targets of sexual violence during India's partition were women. Many authors have pointed out that rape and other forms of sexual violence are crimes not of lust but of power, and in the case of ethnic cleansing the symbolism of sexual violence against women and girls is especially potent. As child-bearers, whether in the past, in the present, or in potential, female-bodied people are often represented symbolically as embodying the future of their nation or ethnic group. Men may rape women and girls of the "enemy" religio-ethnic group with the intent of impregnating them, making their wombs, as Stasa Zajovic says in the case of the Bosnian War, into "occupied territory" (Zajovic 1994, qtd. in Menon and Bhasin 1998, 44). Men from a woman's own religio-ethnic group may force her to abort a fetus conceived during occupation, or they may shun her and her children because she had sex with the enemy, even though it was against her will. And as with the castration of male bodies, much of the sexualized violence against women in religio-ethnic conflicts directly attacks their reproductive capacities. In addition to rape, men involved in such conflicts often slash or stab the vaginas and uteruses of "enemy" women and girls. It is this high incidence of sexual violence against women in war that led the early rabbis to break with the patrilineal tradition of ancient Israel and of the Torah; recognizing the frequency with which their small and often oppressed people experienced violence at the hands of colonizers or warring factions, they declared that Jewish descent was determined by the mother, not the father, of a child.

Although it might sound at first like a parallel to the positive religious symbolism of male circumcision, what is variously called "female circumcision," "female genital cutting," and "female genital mutilation" is a religious and cultural practice that has been widely criticized by women's rights activists. The practice varies, but it always involves the removal of some part of a girl's external genitalia. In some cases the labia are removed, in some cases also the highly sensitive and erotogenic clitoris. In the most severe cases, a girl's vulva may be cut and stitched together, resulting in a scar that makes the opening too small to be penetrated by a penis. This small opening must be widened again when she becomes sexually active, and it can cause serious complications when a woman menstruates or gives birth. In some cultures a woman is considered sexually unclean or even immoral if she is not cut, so attempts to simply ban female genital cutting run the risk of damaging an uncut woman's status in her community and her ability to survive economically. Activists in the parts of Africa where female genital cutting is considered traditional are therefore working to change public perceptions of the practice and of uncut women.

Many cultures that are horrified by the idea of female genital cutting nonetheless instrumentalize women's bodies in other religious ways; often, these connect to the value these cultures place on women's sexual "purity." While religious emphases on purity today are commonly cast as concerns over women's modesty as a reflection of their piety, such concerns – especially given the fact that they always focus more intensely on women than on men – stem from millennia-old needs to control women's offspring in cultures where wealth, status, and lineage are passed through men. Prior to the availability of genetic testing, the only way for a man to determine that he was actually the genetic father of a child was to ensure that no other man had been sexually active with the child's mother. While some forms of female genital cutting seek to ensure this restricted sexual access by making a woman incapable of being penetrated by a penis prior to marriage, most other religions that stress women's purity (and not all do) have focused intensely instead on the hymen, also called today the vaginal corona. A thin, often folded membrane present in the cervix of many girls and young women, the hymen can be detected by digital examination, and quite a few religions have traditionally required women and girls to submit to such an examination prior to marriage. When the hymen stretches or tears it often bleeds slightly, so other religions make a practice or even a celebratory ritual out of looking for blood on the bedsheets the morning after a wedding. Since the presence of a hymen continues to be important for marriage in some religious cultures and surgical techniques are becoming ever more advanced, there is a thriving industry in so-called "hymen repair" for girls and women who never had a hymen to begin with or whose hymen has been torn through tampon use, masturbation, sexual activity with another person, or intense physical activity.

All of this religious violence against and control of sexualized bodies, all of this instrumentalization of genitalia and reproductive organs as the targets of religio-ethnic cleansing, might make you think that the instrumentalization of sexualized bodies and parts of bodies is largely a negative thing. But for millennia, such bodies have also been revered. Ancient Mediterranean figurines, presumed or in some cases known to be fertility goddesses, sometimes bear multiple breasts; fertility-related figures carved on ancient Celtic churches open their vulvas to the sharp-eyed viewer who can spot them in the stonework. And in India, both literal and metaphorical fertility is venerated through carved phallic and vulvic forms known as lingams and yonis. Worshipped separately but also often together, with the lingam seated inside the yoni, these representations of Shiva and Shakti are often bathed in milk that visually symbolizes both ejaculation and breastfeeding.

So far, we've discussed at some length the ways in which sexualized bodies and sexualized parts of bodies can be instrumentalized for religious purposes. There are many more examples, but it's also worth considering how religion might serve as an instrument for sexualized bodies. One particularly intriguing case in this regard comes from medieval Japanese Buddhism.

As we've seen in previous chapters, celibacy is important to the history of Buddhism and is still practiced by Buddhist monastics. But also as we've seen, what appears to be a straightforward ban often becomes quite complex in practice, because in order to practice celibacy one must be certain what constitutes sex. Presuming that celibacy for monks meant avoiding sex with women, some abbots have traditionally forbidden women's presence in Buddhist monasteries, and quite a few classical Buddhist texts describe the restrictions monks must follow in regard to interactions with women. Few, however, mention men. While a male-bodied, gender variant, same sex attracted type of person called a *pandaka* appears in some texts, either as a warning against the *pandaka*'s seductive ways or occasionally in praise for the accomplishments of a renunciant *pandaka*, in general sex between men in the monastery seems not to have been among the main concerns of these classical Buddhist authors. In fact, tales from medieval Japan indicate that certain forms of male–male sex may even have been valorized: according to literary historian Paul Gordon Schalow (1992), legends abound in Japanese history that the practice of male pederastic love was brought to Japan by the founder of the esoteric Shingon branch of Buddhism, Kūkai.

Pederasty refers to age-differentiated sexual relationships between adult and teenage men. Certainly, age-differentiated relationships between older men and teenage women also have been and are common practice in many cultures, but they are generally considered so unremarkable as to need no other name than "marriage." Similarly, sex between women brings up in many cultures the question of whether an activity counts as sex if no penis is involved; as a consequence both of the importance of penises to the definition of sex and of the relative invisibility of women in the historical record, sex between women rarely has a name at all, much less different names for different types of partnerings. Pederasty, on the other hand, has been the subject of artistic and literary celebration in cultures ranging from ancient Greece to the Ottoman Empire to medieval and early modern Japan. Like many mainstream sexual norms, pederasty has traditionally been structured by specific expectations about the roles of the sexual partners. The partner from the socially dominant group – the older man, in a pederastic relationship – is expected to be the lover, the one who woos, seduces, and eventually penetrates the beloved. The younger man, the beloved, is often described as coy, or shy, just as women are often expected to be in different-sex relationships. He may play hard to get, toying with the older man's feelings, and he is generally believed (again like women in the social norms of many cultures) to enjoy the actual sex act less, as the receptive partner. For the beloved in a pederastic relationship, the rewards are believed to lie elsewhere, such as in the attentions and patronage of the lover. Typically, in cultures that celebrate pederasty, the beloved is expected to become a lover as he matures, pursuing rather than being pursued and penetrating another, younger man rather than being penetrated. Unlike women in these cultures, men are expected to play the role of the demure and sexually receptive partner only until they grow up.

Pederasty was widely practiced in the traditional Japanese samurai culture, but numerous texts in praise of pederasty attribute its origins as an institution in Japan to a famous Buddhist monk named Kūkai. These references are intriguing, not only because of the requirement of celibacy for Buddhist monks – which again raises the question of what counts as sex – but especially because the branch of Japanese Buddhism that Kūkai founded bore clear indications of connection to Tantric practices. While there is little evidence directly from Buddhist monastic sources indicating that pederasty was a widely accepted monastic practice in Japan, tales of sexual relationships between monks and their acolytes were present in Japanese literature for several hundred years. Certainly it is quite possible that the country which developed a married Buddhist priesthood also defined celibacy as the avoidance specifically of male-female sex, but for the lay (non-ordained), probably male readers of this literature the stories celebrating Kūkai's advocacy of pederasty in Buddhist terms offered an opportunity to instrumentalize religion in a way that infused their own sexual practices with sacred meaning.

Non-conforming bodies

Religious traditions, like many aspects of human culture, have a tendency to assign special meaning to unusual phenomena. Sometimes those phenomena are astrological, like eclipses and comets; sometimes they're geological, such as unusually-shaped features of the earth. And sometimes they're biological, including less-common aspects of human bodies, minds, and behaviors.

We saw in the first case study for this chapter that intersex and gender-variant people are instrumentalized in South Sulawesi as the ritual specialists known as *bissu*. People who are perceived as "in between" genders and "in between" sexes are sometimes regarded as having special capacities to be in between other aspects of human experience, and are therefore considered to be innately capable of performing certain types of ritual functions. Across the Pacific from South Sulawesi, a number of Native traditions in the Americas also regard gender variance as indicating innate ritual skills. In other Native traditions, people who are female and perform men's tasks and those who are male and perform women's tasks are simply another gender – perhaps special because they are rarer than females who perform women's tasks and males who perform men's tasks, but not special in a specific ritual way.

However, difference is perceived in some traditions as dangerous. Early Spanish colonial texts tell of the *conquistadores* slaughtering indigenous Central American men who are referred to in these texts as "sodomites." Christians have used the terms "sodomy" and "sodomite" in various ways over the centuries, often vaguely referring to a wide variety of sins and sometimes to a wide variety of specifically sexual sins such as sex outside of marriage or the use of forbidden sexual positions; only in the modern period did these words come to be associated specifically with the newly-invented "homosexual" person or with anal sex. But images and descriptions of this colonial slaughter seem to indicate that those being killed – torn apart by dogs, actually – were males who lived as women, and Native Two-Spirit people today consider the victims of this war crime to be among their ancestors (Driskill 2016).

Just as the difference of being gender variant can be perceived as either a blessing or a curse by one's tradition, so too with being intersex. In some traditions, intersex people are simply a recognized part of the culture; for instance, in Navajo tradition they are one of five genders (Thomas 1997). In some traditions they are valued, like the Greek god Hermaphroditus or like intersex *bissu*. In others, such as in late-nineteenth and early-twentieth century Iran, people whose intersex status manifests at puberty are considered to be the result of divine miracles. But in other traditions, rare and unusual embodiments are considered dangerous and intersex infants may be killed or abandoned. A similar variety of attitudes exists toward multiple births; the birth of twins and triplets (larger numbers of multiples have been exceedingly rare in human history until the development of modern assisted reproductive technologies) have traditionally been viewed in some religions as a bad omen and in others as a blessing or even as a sign that the parent or parents are under the protection of a specific deity. The Yoruba and African diasporic figure of Changó (also Shango, Xangó), for instance, is associated with twinning. Albinism is another case that may lead to reverence or revulsion on the part of one's tradition.

People with disabilities face similar reactions from their religious and cultural traditions. Most people who are perceptibly different from what is considered "normal" in their cultures have to deal with being defined in ways that are often out of their control. Not everyone, after all, wants to be considered a special sign from God, just as most people wouldn't want to be considered demonic or a bad omen. But whether positive or negative, these cultural evaluations are generally out of the control of the people they target. In some traditions, people with disabilities may be barred from particular kinds of religious or cultural participation. The Torah, for instance, forbids a man whose testicles have been crushed or whose penis has been cut off from certain activities among the ancient Israelites (Deut. 23:1) – a ban that has caused much discussion among transgender Jews and their allies. In the context of religions that believe one's current incarnation to be a direct consequence of one's actions in previous lives, disabilities may be taken as a sign of poor choices in an earlier incarnation. Having made mistakes in a previous life, this argument suggests, the person accrued negative karma and was therefore born with greater physical limitations in the current life. Such an interpretation makes the assumption that having a disability is automatically and entirely a negative thing in and of itself, whereas many disability theorists and activists have pointed out that the limitations arising from disability often exist because of the built environment; that is, they are not intrinsic to the disability but rather are caused by failures of design and architecture. After all, many people who transport themselves in wheelchairs can move much more quickly than those who transport themselves on feet – until there are stairs.

Another important intersection between religion and disability – or, as literature scholar Chris Mounsey puts it, variability – has to do with neurology and neurochemistry. A minority of people in every culture perceive things that most people around them do not perceive. They hear voices others don't hear, feel things on their skin that others don't feel, see things that others don't see, speak in ways that others can't speak, and sometimes do things that they can't remember later. Sometimes these experiences come along with bodily changes such as convulsions or immobility. While modern neuroscience and psychiatry consider such phenomena to be caused by mental illness and other neurological disorders, many religions have traditionally considered them to be evidence of contact with the spirit world. As with other bodily differences, these too can be presumed to be divine or demonic, prophetic or cursed. Sometimes, too, different traditions' interpretations clash in ways that can harm both the person experiencing unusual perceptions and the community around them.

During the middle of the twentieth century, many Hmong people fled from violence in Southeast Asia and settled in the United States, where Hmong understandings of seizures came into serious conflict with Western allopathic medical understandings. In Hmong tradition, someone who experiences seizures has been chosen for special communication by the spirits. The effects of the seizures may be treated and managed with traditional medicine, but to eradicate the seizures through Western allopathic treatments would be to refuse the spirits' gift. This would be improper, and more importantly it could cause harm to the chosen person – far more harm than the seizures themselves, as long as they are properly managed. In the case of one Hmong family whose story is recounted by medical anthropologist Anne Fadiman (1997), repeated failures of translation and miscommunications at their small, rural hospital in California led to their young daughter's declining health, her being taken from her parents by the state and placed in foster care because neither her doctors nor the Child Protective Services staff were willing to understand Hmong approaches to seizure disorders, and eventually to her brain death at the age of four (the rest of her body died twenty-six years later). While this case, made famous by Fadiman's book, has become a rallying cry for greater cultural competence on the part of physicians, it also points to the severe consequences of the often insurmountable differences between those who view neuroatypicality as a spiritual gift that should be nurtured and those who view it as a defect that should be eradicated.

As U.S. religious historian Robert Orsi points out (2005), people with both mental and physical disabilities may also be placed on religious pedestals. This is particularly true in Christianity because of the importance of suffering in the sacred stories of that religion. Most Christians believe that Jesus was the son of God and sacrificed himself to atone for the sins of humanity; for this reason, in much of Christian theology suffering is seen as divine. People with disabilities are often presumed to be suffering by those who are temporarily fully-abled, so in Christian contexts this suffering (whether perceived or actual) can lead to people with disabilities being seen as Christ-like. Although it may sound nice to be compared to a deity, most people who've had this experience will tell you that the expectation of patient, pious suffering gets old pretty quickly. Whether they prefer to honor or downplay their differences from fully abled people, and while it may at times be better to be placed on a pedestal than to be scorned for misbehavior in a past life, most people with disabilities would prefer not to be cast either as saints or as sinners, but rather to be treated as equals. There is a growing field of study focused on disability and religion that seeks to understand and change both the practice of religiously condemning people with disabilities and the practice of placing them on religious pedestals.

While there are many examples of non-conforming bodies being instrumentalized for religious purposes, often against their will, religion can also be instrumentalized for the goals of people with non-conforming bodies. One excellent example of this takes us back to the topic of transgender Jews. Gender transition is a deeply important and meaningful process for transgender people. Whether it involves aligning their bodies with their sense of self, presenting themselves to the world in ways that are true to that sense of self, or some combination of the two, the change from living in what to many people feels like drag or a costume to living in ways that feel less hidden and, to some people, more authentic is often a profound life event. As with all meaningful life events, most people seek to mark or celebrate their gender transition in some way. Since transitioning is a process, different people choose different points – and sometimes more than one – to mark. And because religious traditions are such a key source for life cycle rituals, some people mark their transitions religiously. In the edited collection *Balancing on the Mechitza: Transgender in the Jewish Community* (Dzmura 2010), a number of transgender Jews share their experiences with ritual in a religion and a language (Hebrew) in which gender and sex have traditionally been both important and binary. The rituals to mark gender transition are all new creations; there are no traditional Jewish rituals of this sort. But these new creations draw on Jewish tradition in both profound and innovative ways. One man, for instance, asked his wife and her community to develop a ritual for him. They held it outside, at a bridge, with the women standing on one side of the bridge, the men on the other, and their rabbi in the middle. Having lived as a woman up to this point in his life, he began on the women's side of the bridge and received their blessings. His wife went with him partway up the arched bridge, then returned to the other women while he proceeded alone to the top where the rabbi awaited. The rabbi blew the shofar, a ram's horn traditionally used in ritual, proclaimed the man's new name, and welcomed him to the community of men to which the rabbi also belonged. They then went together to the waiting men on the far side of the bridge, who welcomed and congratulated him. The use of Jewish traditions – the shofar, blessings and songs in Hebrew, the presence of the rabbi – all made the ritual deeply meaningful not only to this man and his wife but also, he writes, to their larger community (Devor 2010).

Another ritual included in this collection was co-authored by a literature scholar and a liturgist, someone who studies and develops rituals, for the literature scholar's gender transition (Madsen and Ladin 2010). It, too, uses imagery of leaving one gender behind and being welcomed into a new gender, but rather than make use of a bridge as its main symbol it centers on traditional rituals for death and mourning, followed by a traditional prayer offering praise for divine revival of the dead. In the case of this transition ritual, a person who was assigned male at birth offers a traditional men's prayer in order to grieve that she was not born as a woman. She laments her suffering using traditional biblical texts such as Psalms and the book of Job, then lies down. The witnesses present respond as though she has died, and say kaddish – prayers for the dead – in which the person transitioning also participates. Water is poured over her body as though it were a corpse undergoing ritual preparation for burial. She then rises, leaves the room, and changes from men's clothes into women's clothes. Aspects of mourning are removed from the ritual space, and new blessings offered. She announces her name, offers praise, and is welcomed by the witnesses.

Although this latter ritual involves water and the person transitioning is instructed to prepare as though for immersion in a ritual bath called a mikveh, it is clear from the text that the ritual is not expected to take place in a mikveh. This is because most such spaces are gender-segregated. Which mikveh – the men's or the women's – would someone use to transition from living as a man to living as a woman? Additionally, most mikvaot (the plural of mikveh) are unwelcoming to transgender people. But religious studies scholar S.J. Crasnow (2017) writes of an egalitarian mikveh in Boston where LGBTIQ+ people are welcomed, genders are not segregated, one of the baths is wheelchair-accessible and another is equipped for an infant, and transgender people seeking a Jewish transition ritual can find resources and a safe space. Other egalitarian mikvaot do exist, and as one of the participants in Crasnow's study explained, Jewish law also allows for natural bodies of water to serve this purpose. Even though the mikveh has for some time been considered a more conservative, traditional ritual space and has not held much relevance for more liberal Jews, clearly it can play an important role in marking gender transition for some transgender Jews and their families and communities regardless of which branch of the religion they are part of. In this way, religion is instrumentalized to honor, name, and celebrate people whose non-conforming bodies and genders are more commonly denigrated and shunned by the society – and, at times, the religion – around them.

Traditionally gendered and sexed bodies

Part of the reason why religion can be so effectively instrumentalized to mark gender transition, and part of the reason why such rituals can be so important to both the person transitioning and their family and community, is that most religions are already instruments of gender formation. Sacred stories tell us a great deal about traditional gender roles in a community, whether they're stories of revered ancestors or cautionary tales about people who've followed the wrong path. Philosophies and theologies can also be illuminating; for instance, some historians are fond of pointing out that at one point in Christian history there was heated debate between male Church leaders over whether women had souls. Of course, not all entities in the spirit world are presumed to be role models for humans; Roman Catholic girls are sometimes dissuaded from choosing the gender variant warrior Joan of Arc as their patron saint, and despite the reverence many Hindus have for Kṛṣṇa, only in very specific ritual circumstances does one find Hindu men dressing as women in imitation of the god's disguised foray among the gopis, or cow-herding women.

But maybe even more than role models in the spirit world, many religious rituals induct children into their socially-assigned gender roles and reinforce those gender roles for adults. One way to understand how this process works is through the concept of performativity. This concept, developed by gender theorist Judith Butler (1990), suggests that our enactment of gender *forms* our identity rather than expresses it. Enacting gender also reinforces the existing gender systems in our societies and cultures. For example, in a society in which girls and women are the ones tasked with raising children, a parent who gives a little girl a doll to play with may believe that they are offering the girl an opportunity to express her innate qualities of nurturance. People who believe that gender is socially constructed would say instead that by choosing to give the little girl a doll rather than a toy truck this parent is teaching the child that girls are supposed to care for babies and not drive trucks. The theory of performativity adds to this interpretation the idea that when she plays obediently with the doll, this little girl is in fact learning to see herself *as* a girl; as she develops a sense for who she is, that sense will include "I am a girl" and "I like to nurture things." Later on, the adult woman may look back and think "I've always liked to nurture things; that's innate in me as a woman." And she may give her own daughter a doll – and the cycle continues.

But not all children are obedient, nor are all adults. The theory of performativity isn't a gendered brainwashing scare. In fact, Butler herself points out that although people in a gendered society don't have much choice about enacting *some* sort of gender, or at least being perceived by others in a gendered way, they do have choices in terms of whether to enact gender in an obedient or resistant way. Say, for instance, that little girl took her doll over to her brother's toy truck, put the doll behind the steering wheel, and proceeded to drive over to a toy construction set and build a sky-scraper. Or maybe she put on her toy doctor's kit and conducted brain surgery on the doll. In playing these games with her doll, she might be learning that being a girl means building things, driving trucks, and being a neurosurgeon. Or she might be starting to understand herself as a boy – some transgender children identify as young as three – and might be using the doll in resistant ways that challenge not the gender "girl" but a little boy's assignment to that gender.

Where does religion come in here? Nearly anywhere that children are involved in rituals. Many traditions have rituals to welcome and often to name a new baby, and it's not uncommon for those rituals to be gendered. Although the new baby prob-ably isn't thinking, "Oh, I get it, I'm a boy!" in the middle of a Catholic christening or a Jewish bris, the ways in which such rituals are gendered can reinforce the family's and the community's understanding of sex, gender, and the relationships between them. The very act of choosing a name for a child reflects the family's ideas about gender, because many cultures believe that a child's name can contribute to shaping their personal qualities and even their future, through inspiration if nothing else. And most names are gendered, so naming a baby is one step toward assigning a gender to that child, which they may come to accept, reject, complicate, or – fol-lowing Butler – subvert later in life.

Coming of age ceremonies are also often gendered. Some traditions, both secular and religious, have coming of age ceremonies only for boys becoming men or for girls becoming women. Even in a tradition where both young women and young men have such a ritual, even when they have the same one, most such rituals are designed not only to welcome new adults into the community but to welcome new *men* and *women*. Sometimes the gendered aspects of this welcome are subtle, such as when a religious leader speaks glowingly of the future contributions of all the young adults being honored but makes assumptions about the kinds of contributions they will make, or when traditional celebratory gifts are gendered. At other times they're much more blatant, with young men taking different roles in the ceremony than young women or with the two having different ceremonies altogether.

To point out that religious rituals are part of the performative construction of gender is not necessarily to say that this is bad. Religious studies scholar Inés Talamantez, for instance, writes of the importance of 'Isánáklésh Gotal*, the traditional coming of age ceremony for young Apache women, in fighting back against the ongoing ravages of settler colonialism, racism, and misogyny that Apache girls and women face, in giving young women the strength they will need to go through the world and the knowledge they need to help keep their traditions alive and thriving (Talamantez 2000). Similarly, the practice of allowing Jewish girls to have a bat mitzvah just as boys have traditionally had a bar mitzvah is profoundly meaningful to many Jewish parents, family members, community members, and rabbis, as well as to the girls themselves. Like all Jewish ritual, much of a bat mitzvah is conducted in Hebrew, which is a gendered language. The ritual itself, then, is subtly changed when a girl partakes in it, and opening this important life cycle event to girls has had a deep and positive impact on the communities that have chosen to do so. Further questions arise, though, about how gender-variant youth can participate in such important yet gendered rituals – and these questions return us to points such as the ritual innovations of transgender Jews. Religion, then, plays an important role in the performative construction of gender. This, in itself, is neither purely beneficial nor purely harmful; instead, the impact varies depending on how different communities and individuals within those communities enact, subvert, and enforce sex and gender norms.

Just as religion can serve as a tool for the creation, shaping, re-creation, and resistance of traditionally gendered and sexed bodies, such bodies can also serve as instruments for religion. Part of the reason for the refusal of the Roman Catholic and Eastern Orthodox churches to ordain women as priests, for instance, is the Christian belief that a priest is God's and, by extension, Jesus' representative on earth. In Christianity as in many theistic religions, a priest is a go-between who connects the human to the divine. And in Christianity, the majority of traditional images of the divine are male. To some Christian groups, this alone is argument enough that women should not be ordained: God cannot be properly represented, they say, by the body of a woman.

In a completely different religious context, we see a similar argument about excluding people from religious leadership because their bodies don't represent someone's idea of the divine. The founder of modern Wicca, Gerald Gardner, wrote that because the divine is manifested in both the Great Goddess and the Great God, every coven should have both a high priestess and a high priest. In certain rituals, these two leaders became not just the representatives but the actual embodiments of the divine. For this reason, Gardner cautioned, a high priestess should take good care of her body and should have the grace and good sense to step down when advancing age or other changes in her body make her incapable of embodying the Goddess's beauty. Perhaps predictably, given this ageist and sexist remark – and perhaps also because of his own religious leadership and advancing age – Gardner had no similar recommendation for the high priest. For Gardner, it seems, the Great God could be envisioned at all ages, while the Great Goddess could only be young and nubile.

Traditionally gendered bodies can also be a soul's route to the divine. Bodies are always involved in religious rituals, whether they simply sit, listen, or watch, whether they are intensely physically active, or whether their endurance becomes a test or evidence of a person's religious prowess. In the mystical Sufi tradition of Islam, practitioners known as dervishes – traditionally men, although women are allowed at times to practice separately – use a stately spinning or whirling motion as a meditative practice to bring them closer to unification with God. This deep desire for union with God, a spiritual and sometimes physical yearning experienced by mystics across a number of religions, makes up part of what we might call the erotics of religion. Different from but not divorced from physical sexuality, the erotic refers to love, desire, and fulfillment that are experienced sensually, in the emotions as well as in physical sensation. It may be this kind of mystical eroticism that has led so many mystics to teach about connection with the divine using terms that seem sensual, physical, and even sexual. It is this eroticism that, when the longing for union is fulfilled, can lead to the religious ecstasies that are the topic of the following chapter.

Conclusion

Religions and bodies can be instrumentalized, can become tools, to help fulfill each other's goals. In this chapter we've seen that religion can be instrumentalized for purposes related to genders, sexual activities, and bodies, and that genders, sexual activities, and bodies can be instrumentalized for religious purposes. Sexual activities can produce religiously efficacious results, and religion can be mobilized in support of sexual goals. Sexualized bodies and especially sexualized parts of the body such as genitalia can become religious tools in both positive and destructive ways, and religion can in turn support access to sexualized bodies such as those of Japanese male youth. Non-conforming bodies, those that are perceptibly "different" in some way, are especially important religious tools, often but not always in positive ways, and religion can become a tool for affirming and blessing non-conforming bodies and genders in the face of larger communities and cultures that reject them. Finally, religion is one important tool in the performative construction of gender, and traditionally gendered bodies can serve as routes to the divine through rituals as wide-ranging as the Wiccan Great Rite and the traditional whirling meditation of Sufi dervishes.

Review: chapter highlights

- Case study 1: *bissu* in South Sulawesi;
- Case study 2: classical Indian Tantra and contemporary Western tantric sex;
- Instrumentalizing bodies, sex, and religion;

  a   What is instrumentalization?
  b   Additional sub-themes: bodies, genders, sexual activities instrumentalized for religious purposes; religion instrumentalized for the purposes of bodies, genders, sexual activities;
  c   Introduction to the themes;

- Sexual acts;

  a   Instrumentalizing sex;

      - Sex and religious power;

- Dangerous sex;
- Proper sex;
- Transgressive sex;
- Sex magic;

b   Instrumentalizing religion (interwoven in this section with instrumentalizing sex);

- Rituals making sex permissible (e.g., marriage);
- Rituals affirming non-dominant sexualities;
- Love charms;

- Sexualized bodies and parts of bodies;

a   Instrumentalizing bodies;

- Sexualized bodies;
- Testicles, penises, and foreskins;
- Vulvas, wombs, clitorises, and hymens;
- Sexual body parts: lingams, yonis, and milk baths;

b   Instrumentalizing religion;

- Medieval Japanese Buddhism and traditions of pederasty;

- Non-conforming bodies;

a   Instrumentalizing non–conforming bodies;

- Intersex and gender-variant people;
- People with disabilities;
- Neuroatypical people;

b   Instrumentalizing religion;

- Jewish gender transition rituals;

- Traditionally gendered and sexed bodies;

a   Instrumentalizing religion;

- Gender performativity in religious rites of passage;

b   Instrumentalizing gendered and sexed bodies;

- Representing the divine: theology and sexism;
- Desiring the divine: Sufi Muslim dervishes and religious ecstasy;

- Conclusion.

Applications and reflections

1   Reflect on a religion you're familiar with – perhaps your own, or one practiced by a close friend or family member. What roles do bodies play in that religion? In what ways are they instrumentalized? In what ways are sexual activities, or lack thereof, instrumentalized? What about gender? Conversely, in what ways is the religion

instrumentalized for the purposes of bodies, genders, or sexual activities? Can you find other themes that we haven't discussed here, or other instances of our themes?

2   Whether or not you're convinced by the theory of performativity, applying it to an analysis can help you understand its principles. Think back to a time in your own life when you learned about the gender you were expected to perform. What did you learn about your gender during that event? How did you learn it? What did "performing" your gender – carrying it out, really, not like a theatrical performance – look like? What were you supposed to actually do? What were you not supposed to do? Was this a positive experience? A negative one? Somewhere in between? Did you enact your assigned gender the way you were supposed to? In a resistant way? Did you refuse to enact it at all? How could the theory of performativity explain this event and your experiences with it?

3   How are people with non-conforming bodies approached in the religion you're most familiar with? In what ways are intersex and gender-variant people, people with disabilities, and neuroatypical people regarded? Are they seen as different in religiously relevant ways? If so, are those differences considered positive or negative? How do the people who are thereby defined as different experience their place in this religion? Do you know of innovations through which the religion is instrumentalized to support people with non-conforming bodies? If so, what are they? If not, do you think this is because such rituals don't exist, because they're not made public, or for some other reason? Why might this be?

Resources for further study

Butler, Judith. "Performative Acts and Gender Constitution: An Essay in Phenomenology and Feminist Theory." In Carole R. McCann and Seung-kyung Kim (eds.) *Feminist Theory Reader: Local and Global Perspectives*, 3rd ed. New York, NY: Routledge, 2013: 462–473.

Crasnow, S.J. "On Transition: Normative Judaism and Trans Innovation." *Journal of Contemporary Religion* 32, no. 3 (2017): 403–415.

Dzmura, Noach (ed.). *Balancing on the Mechitza: Transgender in the Jewish Community*. Berkeley, CA: North Atlantic Books, 2010.

Orsi, Robert A. "'Mildred, is it Fun to be a Cripple?' The Culture of Suffering in Twentieth-Century American Catholicism." In *Between Heaven and Earth: The Religious Worlds People Make and the Scholars Who Study Them*. Princeton, NJ: Princeton University Press, 2005: 19–47.

Schumm, Darla, and Michael Stoltzfus (eds.). *Disability and World Religions: An Introduction*. Waco, TX: Baylor University Press, 2016.

Talamantez, Inés. "The Presence of Isanaklesh: A Native American Goddess and the Path of Pollen." In Nancy Auer Falk and Rita M. Gross (eds.) *Unspoken Worlds: Women's Religious Lives*, 3rd ed. Belmont, CA: Wadsworth Press, 2000: 290–300.

7 Ecstasy

Case study 1

In the Catholic church of Santa Maria della Vittoria in Rome, Italy, one can see a masterpiece sculpted in white marble by Gian Lorenzo Bernini called L'Estasi di Santa Teresa (*Saint Teresa in Ecstasy*). This Baroque sculpture depicts Teresa of Avila, a sixteenth century Spanish cloistered Carmelite nun, with her head rolled back in ecstasy while a smiling male youth lifts her garment, spear in hand. Saint Teresa wrote of being pierced by the spear of an angelic youth in her autobiography, *The Life of Teresa of Jesus*. Teresa described the delicious pain that this youth caused her with his iron-pointed spear in this way:

> In his hands I saw a long golden spear, and at end of the iron tip I seemed to see a point of fire. With this he seemed to pierce my heart several times so that it penetrated my entrails. When he drew it out, I thought he was drawing them out with it and he left me completely afire with a great love of God. The pain was so sharp it made me moan several moans; and so excessive was the sweetness caused by this intense pain that one can never wish to lose it nor will one's soul be content with anything less than God.
>
> (Peers 1957, 192–193)

St. Teresa gives us insight into key themes of this chapter. In the passage just quoted from her autobiography, Teresa gives a vivid depiction of the profound feelings involved in an intimate relationship with a divine being like Jesus or an angel. She also suggests that an intimate relationship with such a being could be interpreted as painful and pleasurable at the same time. The spear that pierces her goes deep inside her in a way that suggests sexual penetration and the pleasure that entails. The spear also seems to pull her entrails out in a way that suggests a painful wounding, language that suggests the profound psychic and physical disturbances that can arise from deep visionary experiences.

The term ecstasy comes to us from a Western context. The word comes into the English language from Greek roots (*ekstasis*) meaning to be displaced or removed from the proper place (Simpson and Weiner, s.v. ecstasy). The term suggests what it feels like when a person is so deeply engaged in a vision of divine realities that ordinary awareness is suspended. In this altered state of consciousness, one has a reduced awareness of external objects and an expanded mental awareness. One feels transported outside oneself, being in state of rapture in which the body is not capable of ordinary sensation.

In her writings, Teresa gives us the metaphor of being shot from a gun as a way to understand the state of ecstasy. In her 1557 theological treatise on mystical experiences, *El Castillo Interior* (*The Interior Castle*, in English), Saint Teresa uses the metaphor of a bullet flying away from a gun (6.5.9). In this passage, she describes her soul taking an interior flight away from the limits of the body. Flying like a bullet, her soul travels far and sees amazing things. Great things are shown to the soul, and great benefits result. Once the senses return and a person comes down to earth, everyday things can seem worthless by comparison.

Mystical experiences of ecstasy can take many forms. Saints who offered up their lives in devotional and ascetic practices were said to gain visions of realities beyond what the rest of us can experience. We have already encountered the visionary experiences of the thirteenth-century Flemish writer Hadewijch. Like other medieval Christian mystics, Hadewijch experienced extremely physical visions of Jesus as a being of flesh and blood. Historian Caroline Walker Bynum tells us that Hadewijch described many visions of Jesus in which she relates to him as a physical being. In some, she consumes the sacrament of his body as one does in Mass. In others, she united with his body sexually. Some visions combine both forms of intimacy, as in this passage translated by Bynum (1988, 156):

> He came in the form and clothing of a Man, as he was on the day when he gave his Body for the first time … he gave himself to me in the shape of the Sacrament, in its outward form … and then he gave me to drink from the chalice … . After that he came himself to me, took me entirely in his arms, and pressed me to him; and all my members felt his in full felicity, in accordance with the desire of my heart and my humanity. So I was outwardly satisfied and fully transported.

As with Teresa, the visions of Hadewijch sometimes involve pain. Erotic bliss and torment go hand in hand, as in this vision where the saint reports desire so intense that it is bone-breaking (McGinn 2006, 103):

> One Pentecost at dawn I had a vision. Matins were being sung in the church and I was there. And my heart and my veins and all my limbs trembled and shuddered with desire. And I was in such a state as I had been so many times before, so passionate and so terribly unnerved that I thought I should not satisfy my Lover and my Lover not fully gratify me, then I would have to desire while dying and die while desiring. At that time I was so terribly unnerved with passionate love and in such pain that I imagined all my limbs breaking one by one and all my veins were separately in tortuous pain.

Sexual intimacy with divine beings appears with some frequency in the history of religions. It is an enduring theme in medieval Christianity, especially in the writings of women saints. In some scholarly circles, the term "bridal mysticism" is used to classify such erotic visions of God. Elizabeth Clark explains how bridal mysticism developed in Christian practice as the religion developed from a religious counterculture to a religion more in harmony with the dominant culture. Celibacy made sense in the early years of the Jesus movement, a time when it seemed that Jesus would return at any moment. Investing in marriage made no sense in those years, given the belief that the world as we know it would soon be replaced by a very different world once Jesus returned to earth.

As time went on, however, expectation of the imminent return of Jesus fell away. Hope began to focus on the afterlife, not on a transformed life here on earth. Thus marriage to Jesus came to be seen as a heavenly reward. Jesus was the spiritual bridegroom that a girl or woman would win by her self-control in practicing celibacy. It is said that she would stand before the throne of judgment at death and that the throne room would resolve into a bridal chamber where the celibate girl or woman would join with her divine bridegroom. Such a belief forms the basis for the ecstatic visions of Teresa of Avila, Hadewijch, and many other saintly women whose visions can be described as varieties of bridal mysticism.

Case study 2

The Indian region of Bengal gave birth to a vibrant sect of Hinduism centered around devotion to the youthful god Kṛṣṇa and the erotic circle of his blissful play. This sect is known as Bengali Vaiṣṇavism since it falls within the Vaiṣṇava branch of Hinduism, a branch that includes worshippers of various earthly incarnations (*avatars*) of the sustainer god Vishnu (Sanskrit,Viṣṇu; pronounced "Vish-noo"). This sect of Hindu devotional religion developed in the region of Bengal, in eastern India, hence it is called in English **Bengali Vaiṣṇavism**. The god Kṛṣṇa, described as a dark-skinned, enchantingly beautiful earthly incarnation of the sustainer god, is the sole focus of this group.

For medieval Bengali Vaishanavas, Kṛṣṇa is not just an incarnation among other incarnations. Kṛṣṇa is the supreme being, the creator of the universe. Kṛṣṇa incarnates himself in this world in order to enjoy the expression of his creative powers. When he incarnates, he brings down to earth a complete replica of his heavenly realm, a place of ecstatic bliss where he makes love to a bevy of young women. Devotees of Kṛṣṇa focus their devotion on the god's divine lovemaking in the blissful realm of Vṛndāvana. In Vṛndāvana, Kṛṣṇa dances and frolics with rustic cow-herding women called *gopīs*. The gopīs excel at singing and dancing. With whirling bracelets and earrings, they express their adoration of Kṛṣṇa through dance, song, and passionate lovemaking. They play with him in solitary groves, on riverbanks, in mountain caves, and other bucolic locations. Bengali Vaishnavas celebrate the ecstatic bliss of Kṛṣṇa's self-expression. In devotional practices such as singing and the repetition of holy names in temples and in public gathering places, the goal is to cultivate an ecstatic mood of holy erotic passion as the highest expression of devotion to and intimacy with Kṛṣṇa. The feverish erotic love of the cow-herding women for Kṛṣṇa is understood as the love of the soul that longs for its creator. As in Christianity, sexual ecstasy is one way to imagine the relationship between the soul and the divine. Devotees seek liberation from the cycle of birth and death through the power of this erotic love for the divine. Devotees kindle this passion in order to see Kṛṣṇa in a vision while living and to dwell with him in his heavenly realm after death. In the cultivation of intimacy with the creator, it is common for devotees to imagine themselves as a particular gopī named Rādhā, said to be Kṛṣṇa's favorite gopī. Kṛṣṇa satisfies all his forest lovers by creating physical multiples of himself, but poems and dramas celebrate the breathless nature of the special erotic bond that draws Kṛṣṇa and Rādhā together. Some theologians say that Rādhā is a particularly apt representation of the way that Kṛṣṇa draws souls to him because Rādhā is actually a married woman who is compelled by Kṛṣṇa's charms to leave her household at night and make love to the god. Such is the compelling power of the divine: we cannot resist, even though our training tells us that we should. Like the soul drawn to the divine, Rādhā is so smitten by the charismatic young Kṛṣṇa that she behaves like one who is not bound by the constraints of marriage. As Kṛṣṇa plays his flute in the forests at night, the sounds of his flute compel Rādhā to flee to the forest even while in the middle of mundane tasks like making dinner for her family.

The sixteenth-century Saint **Caitanya** is a highly influential for figure for Bengali Vaiṣṇavas. It is said that this saint incarnated both Kṛṣṇa and Rādhā in one body. Caitanya's fair complexion is said to come from Rādhā. Caitanya began life as a scholar but eventually found a path of devotional practice more to his liking. He identified with Rādhā as a way to experience complete submersion in Kṛṣṇa's love. Caitanya is particularly famous for his ecstasies, and it's said that during the last part of Caitanya's life his consciousness was often sunk deeply in the divine world of Kṛṣṇa's love play. In taking the role of Rādhā, Caitanya exemplifies Bengali Vaiṣṇavism's core religious practice of developing an inner spiritual identity as one of the characters in Kṛṣṇa's erotic circle. One can adopt the spiritual role of any of the villagers in Kṛṣṇa's circle, but the most powerful ecstatic states come from taking on the identity of Rādhā or one of Rādhā's attendants who help her to meet up with Kṛṣṇa in hidden-away nocturnal locations. Female roles give the devotee the greatest purchase on intimacy with the youthful god. It is said that Caitanya was so identified with his role as Rādhā that he often fainted, and much of the time he couldn't walk without support from companions. He would often gaze into space and ask about Kṛṣṇa's whereabouts, complaining about how Kṛṣṇa could be so cruel as to abandon him.

Caitanya practiced celibacy and had little interest in human women. To him, such worldly associations would distract him from Kṛṣṇa. Caitanya criticized some of his disciples for being too friendly with women. But there were some people in Caitanya's set of associates who felt that women offered a key means of achieving salvation. Caitanya's disciples formed a number of lineages, including one that was deeply influenced by **Tantrism** and the instrumental use of sexuality for achieving religious goals. Inspired by the religious ecstasies of Caitanya but taking the practice of ecstasy from celibate ecstasy to sexually active ecstasy, a group that focused on the sexual union of Rādhā and Kṛṣṇa as a way to unite divine male and divine female principles emerged. Called Sahajiyā, this group flourished for about three centuries after Caitanya's death. Sahajiyā exponents taught a monistic philosophy that proclaims that all things in the cosmos are in essence one thing – the supreme being. Humans are microcosms or miniature expressions of the supreme being, and as such they contain divine male and divine female principles within themselves just as the supreme being does. But humans are not aware of their true natures. In order to realize divine potential, sexual union is needed. Women and men should join together sexually in order to realize the union of female and male divine principles. In women, the aspect of Rādhā predominates; in men, the aspect of Kṛṣṇa predominates. After getting initiated by a guru and being trained in the requisite chants and other rituals, practitioners of Sahajiyā practiced ritualized sex in the personas of Rādhā and Kṛṣṇa.

In prior chapters we have seen the instrumental use of bodies for the sake of religious insight or enlightenment. In line with premodern South Asian Tantric practices, Sahajiyā practitioners used sex as an instrument for enhanced spiritual power. Using sex for religion in this way, sexual pleasure was not the goal. In men, ejaculation was discouraged. Since semen is thought in Tantric circles to be a source of spiritual power, sexual practices that result in the shedding of semen are thought to cause spiritual debilitation in the male practitioner. The path of the Sahajiyā is thus considerably different from the way of contemporary Western consumers who partake of marketed forms of Tantric sex that instrumentalize religion for the sake of enhanced sexual pleasure.

Ecstasy, sex, and religion

We see several important themes in these case studies. Some ecstatically inclined persons are celibate (such as Hadewijch, Saint Teresa, and Caitanya) where some are sexually active (such as Sahajiyā practitioners). Some ecstasies involve engagement with other humans (Sahajiyā practitioners) while in other cases the ecstasies involve the divine sphere only (Hadewijch, Saint Teresa, and Caitanya). Some ecstasies are collective (such as group worship of Kṛṣṇa) where others involve individuals only (Hadewijch, Saint Teresa). The ecstasies analyzed thus far can be characterized as productive, as states that bring positive things such as insight and liberation. But not all ecstasies are productive. Some, as we shall see, are destructive and socially disruptive.

Dionysus and the ecstatic rituals associated with him

One of the more fascinating religious practices of classical antiquity is that associated with the Greek god of wine and fertility **Dionysus** (Bacchus in Roman mythology). The worship rituals that went on in honor of this god are not entirely clear to scholars. If we wish to know all about the worship of Dionysus, we have the problem of limited sources. Much of what we know is derived from literary accounts that have their own agenda. But this much is clear: the worship of Dionysus was ecstatic, could be highly destructive, and was particularly attractive to women. Myths about Dionysus depict him as frenzied or mad. His female followers partake of the same qualities. The name given to the women worshippers of Dionysus, the **Maenad**s, suggests this connection. It translates as "raving ones." Ross Kraemer (1979) suggests that women in classical antiquity were attracted to the worship of Dionysus because it gave them permission to participate in activities not normally permitted women of the time, particularly in Greece where restrictions on women's movement and behavior made women's lives extremely circumscribed and narrow. Restricted to staying at home much of the time, women in ancient Greece might have gained relief from the boredom of their daily lives by participating in the exciting worship of this mad god. And because Dionysus was thought to compel his worshippers and draw them out into the forest against their will, no moral judgment would have been attached to the nocturnal ecstasies in which women were released from domestic restrictions. As raving Maenads, they were thought to act in accordance with the will of the god, not their own wills.

Spirit possession

In her analysis of how the worship of Dionysus appealed to women of classical antiquity, Kramer draws on the work of anthropologist I.M. Lewis, whose exploration of African and Caribbean spirit possession found a connection between spirit possession and powerlessness. Lewis argued in his classic work on the topic, *Ecstatic Religion: An Anthropological Study of Spirit Possession and Shamanism*, that being subject to spirit possession gives the weak and downtrodden an indirect way to acquire liberties and redress grievances. When women and low-status men on the periphery of society are possessed by spirits, they are able to vent frustrations in a socially acceptable way. It is often said that the possessing spirit afflicts the person possessed with an illness. The spirit demands certain gifts and offerings in order to leave the afflicted person. Those around the possessed person do what they can to placate the spirit and provide for the afflicted person, who is seen as morally blameless. The afflicted person is thus in a position of special privilege and is allowed many liberties not normally available. But there is no direct confrontation, no demand for power on the part of the powerless. Thus the system is not threatening to those in positions of dominance, such as men who are empowered by patriarchal systems. Spirit possession gives those on the margins of such unequal systems some breathing room and some scope for personal expression while enabling hierarchical systems to continue.

The worship of Dionysus involved ecstatic dancing to loud, beat-driven music: cymbals crashed and drums beat frenetically. Dancers spun around wildly and cried out. The Maenads dressed in fawn skins and wore snakes around their heads. Filled with the spirit of Dionysus, Maenads ran through the forests in a frenzy. Intoxicated by the god of intoxication, Maenads drew honey, wine, and other life-giving substances from nature. Touching the earth with their staffs, wine bubbled up. Scratching the ground, milk appeared. The rituals came to a crescendo with a bloody sacrament: the flesh of a bull, symbol of the god Dionysus, was pulled apart by hand and eaten raw. By this act, the worshippers of Dionysus achieved a union with or internalization of their god.

In Euripides' play *The Bacchae*, the destructive side of the cult is stressed. The female followers of Dionysus who live in Thebes kill Pentheus, the ruler of the city, after Pentheus bans the worship of Dionysus, saying that it causes madness among the women of the city. Pentheus is lured into the woods at night where the rites are celebrated. He attempts to hide in a tree to observe the Maenads unseen. But the women spy him there. Their powers of perception altered by the influence of Dionysus, the Maenads take Pentheus to be a mountain lion. They tear him limb from limb. Pentheus's own mother, not recognizing her son, mounts his head on a pike and takes it away as a trophy. In this play, we have a literary depiction that is stark and unflinching in its evocation of the powerful, unstoppable aspects of the worship of Dionysus. One could see in the play a depiction of the two sides of human nature: the rational side, associated with Pentheus, and the emotional or instinctive side, as represented by Dionysus and the Maenads. Both sides demand expression. If one attempts to suppress the Dionysian side, the result will be disruptive to the ordered world.

Sexual ecstasies that involve pain

Another aspect that emerges from studies of ecstatic religion such as the worship of Dionysus is the prominence of pain mixed with pleasure as a theme of the rituals. The ecstatic rites of the Maenads make them insensible to the pain that they inflict. One could even say that for the Maenads, painful things can be experienced as pleasurable. Likewise, one sees in the activities of contemporary practitioners of BDSM (bondage, discipline, dominance, submission, sadism, and masochism) a penchant for finding pleasure in pain. One can find segments of the BDSM community that regard their play as a form of religious expression and occasions where BDSM practitioners utilize ritual forms taken from sacred settings. Such is the case when examples of the pain that Jesus suffered as an embodied human are reenacted by the BDSM community in ritualized forms. I heard about a fascinating example of this sort of interweaving of the sexual and the spiritual at an event at the Michigan Women's Music Festival in 1994. At this women-only festival, I encountered flyers indicating that at midnight on one particular night of the festival, there was to be a BDSM-themed celebration of the **fourteen stations of the cross**. Widely known to Roman Catholics, the stations of the cross are a series of images and accompanying prayers that depict Jesus on the day of his crucifixion. The object of the stations is to give Christians the opportunity to make a spiritual journey of identification with the suffering of Jesus. At one station, for example, Jesus is stripped of his clothes. At another, he is nailed to the cross. For someone who belongs to a community of people who practice BDSM play, the stations of the cross would offer the opportunity to harness the religious power of suffering to the pursuit of sexual pleasure. It might seem like an odd combination to some. But journalist and LGBTIQ+ activist Dan Savage observes that the high esteem given to pain and torment in religious discourse begins when we are young and our sexualities are developing. Reflecting on his own Catholic upbringing, Savage writes (2013, 117–118) of schoolchildren being told to "worship a man who was tortured to death. And what do we call His grisly execution? Oh that's right: the Passion. Catholic schoolchildren kneel in front of life-size representations – some highly realistic – of a ripped dude in a loincloth nailed to a cross with a look of ecstasy on his face." Savage goes on in this passage to describe how he learned as a young man that pain and suffering were gifts from God, signs of God's favor. God permits us to suffer "to test the depths of our love for Him" (118). Given the strong association between suffering and divine favor, perhaps it is not so strange that the BDSM community would choose to leverage the power of religious symbols for the sake of sexual enhancement.

Gnostic sexual rituals

Gnosticism, a movement that flourished within early Christianity but was eventually declared heretical, included sexual rituals that attempted to set right what in the created world had become distorted. A number of different strands of religious practice fall under the category of Gnosticism. They have in common a religiosity that takes a negative view of the universe and human existence while promising that a person can know God in a profound way by learning secret teachings that Jesus gave only to his more advanced disciples (among whom, it must be noted, are women such as Mary Magdalene). Spiritual reality is hard to know, for what we typically know pertains only to lower spheres of reality. Rituals attributed to some Gnostic groups attempt to subvert the norms that Gnostics generally associated with the created material order of existence, deemed a lower order of reality than the higher realms that Gnostics sought to experience. Constituted by mere matter, the inferior lower order of existence was created by a jealous demiurge who wished to entrap enlightened spiritual beings in mortal bodies. The demiurge is a mere creator who has profound limitations. For Gnostics, the true deity is a God beyond all other gods. Because the demiurge has captured a divine spiritual essence in an inferior physical body, ritual interventions are necessary to free the soul and set things right. For certain Gnostic groups, one form of ritual intervention was sexual. There are several different sexual practices thought to have been part of the religious life of some Gnostics, practices that aimed to harmonize the human and divine worlds. One is the sanctification of married sex as a reflection of the joining of male and female principles at the most subtle, refined level of existence. Another ritual attributed to some Gnostics involves semen and other sexual fluids. Worshippers were said to drink ejaculated sperm as ritual act. This act of a male inseminator drinking his own sperm is attributed to Jesus in one narrative. It's said that Jesus takes Mary Magdalene up into the mountains, creates a female from his side, begins to have sex with her, and then partakes of his own sexual fluids, explaining "Thus we must do, that we may live." (Epiphanius 1987, 26).

What we know of these sexual rituals, however, is limited and must be read with critical assessment of motives. Like other aspects of Gnostic practice, such rituals are often described by writers who are decrying heresies in the early church. But even if the accusations of heresy-fighters leave us with puzzles, there are some things that we can know. For example, the idea that sex would be used by some Gnostics as a ritual to unite on earth the male and female principles that are conjoined at the highest order of existence – this idea resonates with some known Gnostic texts. For example, in one text the highest Gnostic deity proclaims that he/she copulates with him/herself. The divine Barbelo describes him/herself in this way, in the Gnostic text known as the *Trimorphic Protennoia* 45:2–8:

> I am androgynous. I am Mother (and) I am Father, since I copulate with myself. I copulated with myself and with those who love me, and it is through me alone that the All stands firm. I am the Womb that gives shape to the All by giving birth to the Light that shines in splendor.
>
> (Turner 1996, 24)

Gnosticism was eventually stamped out, its adherents forced to give up practices that more orthodox Christians found threatening. But from the texts that remain, we can see that the beginnings of Christianity were fertile years that offered a range of practices and attitudes toward sexuality and its place in religious life.

Sexuality and the messianic heresy of Sabbatai Zevi

Another fascinating example of a group found to be heretical that is associated with sexual indulgence is the mystical Jewish messianic movement that focused on the controversial figure of Sabbatai Zevi (1626–1676), who lived in Turkey. Jewish messianic movements are oriented to the idea that the Savior, promised in the Hebrew Bible as a future Jewish king who will rule during an era of peace and prosperity, has been born and is about to inaugurate the events that will restore to the righteous their proper place. Sabbatai Zevi made a number of proclamations and behaved in ways that indicated his identity as the messiah. He would dress in the style of a king and behave extravagantly. He proclaimed that he had come to liberate his people from the Old Law and to implement the New Law. Where the Old Law was dominated by notions of sin and restriction, the New Law offered freedom and salvation. Antinomian elements abounded in the life of the group that surrounded Sabbatai Zevi. Conventional gender roles, for example, were challenged. Where women had been subject to pain in childbirth and the requirement to be obedient to their husbands as a result of the fall that occurred in the Garden of Eden, now women were told that the dawning of the messianic era brought new norms for them. It appears that the group's tendency to challenge conventions and rules increased as a result of persecution. After keeping their eye on this figure and his following for a while, state authorities eventually brought their power to bear on the supposed messiah and his group. Sabbatai Zevi was taken into custody and given a stark choice: he could either accept a death sentence for his apostasy or convert to Islam. He chose the latter. After this, the group carried on with even greater transgressive tendencies. Ritual transgression of sexual prohibitions were introduced. It is said that sexual norms were flaunted at ceremonies in which lights were turned off and congregants were told to find sexual partners other than their spouses.

Charismatic Christians slain in the spirit

Charismatic Christians emphasize what they call the gifts of the Holy Spirit in their worship services. This movement within (largely Protestant) Christianity takes its name ("charismatic") from the Greek term *charisma*, meaning a divinely conferred power. Drawing on passages in the New Testament such as 1 Corinthians 12:8–10, Charismatic Christians understand spiritual gifts such as speaking in tongues, healing, handling poisonous snakes, and prophecy as capacities that are given by God to assist congregations by providing encouragement and comfort. Just as the Holy Spirit descended on members of the early church as described in the New Testament, so too Charismatic Christians expect that today the Holy Spirit can work through individual members of a congregation to benefit the entire group. Being **slain in the spirit** is an expression used when a person falls under the power of the Holy Spirit. Often the spirit descends in group settings such as church services or other collective gatherings such as prayer meetings. As the Holy Spirit descends, the person affected enters a state of religious ecstasy that makes it difficult to remain standing. Often, other members of the congregation rush to assist a person slain in the spirit as their energy fades and they collapse, helping the person to lay down on the floor without doing themselves bodily harm. Sometimes those who are slain in the spirit also experience other charismatic gifts such as speaking in tongues. Those who have reported on such experiences to researchers often indicate that after the experience is over, a state of tranquility and peacefulness results.

Vodou possession – Papa Gede

Vodou religion, practiced in Haiti and parts of the world where Haitians have migrated, offers fascinating examples of religious ecstasy. Spirits who serve as intermediaries between humans and the Supreme Creator play an important role in worship. With roots in West African religions, Vodou came about in dialogue with Catholicism, and many of the spirits in Vodou religion have counterparts in Catholic saints. Accessible to humans in ways that the Supreme Creator is not, Vodou spirits are grouped into a number of different nations and families. They are said to give assistance to the human world by speaking and acting through individuals in the course of all-night services. During the course of a night-long Vodou service, a variety of spirits might visit. When a spirit enters a person, the person is said to be "mounted" like a horse. As different spirits appear and make themselves known to the assembled worshippers, different people enter into a state of trance characterized by special ways of eating and drinking, stylized dances, physical feats, and other forms of behavior unusual for the person in question. As a particular spirit is recognized in the behavior a human who brings the spirit into the gathering, that spirit is greeted by worshippers present and encouraged to provide assistance to those assembled. The spirit proceeds to give advice, interpretations of events, and cures to those who ask for assistance.

Eroticism is associated in Vodou with a family of spirits who govern the realms of fertility and death. Known as the gede (or ghede) family, these spirits are important in healing rituals and in helping to mediate between the living and the dead. One particular spirit who plays a key role in the realms of life, death, and fertility in vodou is **Papa Gede**, said to be a master of sex, death, and humor. A trickster figure, Papa Gede uses humor to guide people through tough situations in life. In Karen McCarthy Brown's account of a Vodou priestess who lives in Brooklyn named Mama Lola, Papa Gede plays a key role as the main spirit that Mama Lola serves. Mama Lola brings the wisdom and sometimes crass humor of Papa Gede to bear on a variety of situations that arise in her community in Brooklyn. McCathy Brown describes Papa Gede in this way:

> Through his randy, playful, childish, and childlike personality Gede raises life energy and redefines the most painful situations – even death itself – as one worth a good laugh. Gede is a transformation artist … . He is horny and predatory with women, like a young man with raging hormones. Like a favorite uncle, he hunkers down with the faithful and listens with genuine care to the most homely of their complaints – an abscess on the buttocks, a disrespectful child, a car with a malfunctioning heater.
>
> (2001, 330, 360)

For Mama Lola's community, Papa Gede is a key figure who puts things in perspective for people struggling to manage difficult situations. He always shows up at the end of a long night of spirit work as a presence both entertaining and profound: he helps people to make the transition from the deep drama of Vodou spirit work to reenter their daily lives as workers and family members struggling with the intractable materiality of ordinary life. His farcical, randy presence helps people to put things in perspective. His invocation of sexuality also heats things up in a way that helps people overcome fatigue, intensify their energy, and reenter the world of work and everyday conflicts with renewed energy.

Conclusion

We see several important themes in this chapter. Some ecstatically inclined persons are celibate (such as that of Hadewijch, Saint Teresa, and Caitanya) where some are sexually active (such as Sahajiyā practitioners). Some ecstasies involve engagement with other humans (Sahajiyā practitioners) while in other cases the ecstasies involve the divine sphere only (Hadewijch, Saint Teresa, and Caitanya). Some ecstasies are collective (such as group worship of Kṛṣṇa, Vodou spirit work, Gnostic rituals, and rituals associated with the Jewish messiah, Sabbatai Zevi). In other cases, ecstasies involve individuals only (for example Hadewijch and Saint Teresa). We have explored ecstasies that arise in the context of pain. This was the case with the deliberate infliction of pain in a religiously marked BDSM performance at a women's music festival. We have examined ecstasies that could be characterized as productive, such as Vodou spirit work, with its accent on healing and solving concrete problems. We have also encountered destructive ecstasies. With the worship of Dionysus in antiquity, destructive currents prevail: the ecstatic worship of the Maenads worshipping Dionysus is often described as violent and bloody. Such ecstatic rituals, it is suggested, may have productive effects nonetheless. The cult of Dionysus may have given women an outlet in a society that was particularly oppressive to them in the various ways that their freedom was limited. Several other ecstatic sexual practices discussed here may also have been emancipatory for women. From what we can discern from scriptures attributed to this group, Gnosticism gave women a more powerful role than other forms of early Christian practice. Likewise, the group that formed around the early modern Jewish messiah Sabbatai Zevi was invested in helping women to break out of the limitations traditionally imposed on them. Like the Gnostics, they gave women a voice and authority that their more conventional counterparts denied them. In this sense, one might look on ecstatic religiosity as a mechanism for creativity and innovation. New realities are glimpsed in such radically altered states of mind and new social forms invented. Given the exalted state of mind of the person undergoing ecstasy, novelties that might ordinarily be ignored are taken more seriously and given a chance to take root. The religious traditions that emerge in the context of ecstatic states sometimes break away (or are pushed away) from their orthodox counterparts, and some of these traditions are no longer being practiced. But even when, as with Gnosticism, some of these traditions are of limited historical duration, they offer a great deal of food for thought for both scholars and religious practitioners.

Review: chapter highlights

- Case study 1: medieval women mystics;
- Case study 2:medieval Hindu mystics;
- Ecstasy, sex, and religion;

  a   Cross-cutting themes: celibate ecstasies versus sexually active ecstasies, ecstasies with other humans versus ecstasies with the divine, individual versus collective ecstasies, productive vs. destructive ecstasies;

- Dionysus and the ecstatic rituals associated with him;
- Spirit possession;
- Sexual ecstasies that involve pain;
- Gnostic sexual rituals;
- Sexuality and the messianic heresy of Sabbatai Zevi;
- Charismatic Christians slain in the spirit;
- Vodou – Papa Gede;
- Conclusion.

Applications and reflections

1   Have you ever experienced an ecstatic state? Was it a solo experience or one that involved a group? If it was a group experience, how would you describe the makeup of the group in terms of gender and social status? What did you learn from the experience? Was it a positive or a negative experience for you?

2   Consider the ways that people gain authority in the religions that you know best. Does the experience of ecstatic visions enhance a person's authority or undermine his or her stature in the community?

3   We have suggested a distinction between productive and destructive ecstasies. But some of the ecstatic experiences discussed in this chapter have life-changing consequences that make them difficult to classify unambiguously. How would you classify the ecstatic experiences of the Hindu saint Caitanya? Were his ecstasies productive, destructive, or perhaps in a grey area in between the two?

4   How might ecstasy be linked with healing? Does ecstasy bring some of the kinds of emotions needed to bring about physical and emotional growth?

Resources for further study

Clark, Elizabeth A. "The Celibate Bridegroom and His Virginal Brides: Metaphor and the Marriage of Jesus in Early Christian Ascetic Exegesis." *Church History* 77, no. 1 (2008): 1–25.
Hansen, Ron. *Mariette in Ecstasy*. New York, NY: E. Burlingame Books, 1991.
Kraemer, Ross S. "Ecstasy and Possession: The Attraction of Women to the Cult of Dionysus." *The Harvard Theological Review* 72, no. 1 (1979): 55–80.

Glossary

969 A Burmese nationalist movement; the number 969 signifies the nine attributes of the Buddha, the six attributes of his teachings, and the nine attributes of the Sangha, or monastic order.

'Awrah *Lit.* Nakedness.

Ahimsa Non-violence.

Alchemy A mystical and early form of chemistry.

Anthropocene The current geological age where human activity has constituted the dominant influence on climate and the environment.

Apartheid A system of institutionalized racial segregation and hierarchy (white supremacy) that existed in South Africa from 1948 until the early 1990s.

Bengali Vaiṣṇavism A branch of Hinduism that developed in the region of Bengal, in eastern India.

Bhakti A Hindu tradition of passionate devotion to a personal god.

Caitanya A sixteenth-century saint who is highly influential for Bengali Vaishnavas. It is said that this saint incarnated both Kṛṣṇa and Rādhā in one body.

Celibate Sexually inactive.

Cisgender Identifying with the gender one was assigned at birth.

Clash of civilizations Samuel P. Huntington hypothesized in his book *The Clash of Civilizations* that the main source of conflict in the post-Cold War era would be religious identities and singled out Islamic extremism as the primary threat to world peace.

Compulsory heterosexuality The cultural expectation that all humans are naturally heterosexual.

Co-religionist Someone who follows the same religion.

Corrective rape Also referred to as curative or homophobic rape; is a hate crime in which one or more people are raped due to their (perceived) sexual orientation or gender identity with the aim that the person will become heterosexual or conform to society's gender norms.

Creed A statement of belief.

Demonology The study of demons or beliefs about/in demons.

Dhamma flag A Buddhist flag commonly symbolizing faith and peace, used throughout the Buddhist world.

Dionysus A Greco-Roman god who is associated with wine and life-giving fluids.

Divination The process by which a religious specialist determines something otherwise unknown and unknowable.

Durgā-Taleju A female deity who is associated with state rule in Nepal.

Ecstasy   An expansive state of mind that takes one outside one's normal limited awareness.

Emic   Local or indigenous, pertaining to a concept or term; stemming from the culture to which it is applied; the opposite of etic.

Epistemic violence   A term used by scholar Gayatri Spivak and others to denote violence that is caused through discourse.

Epoché   Suspension; specifically, the suspension of one's own world-concept in order to better comprehend another world-concept.

Evangelical Christianity   A movement within Protestant Christianity that teaches that the core of the Gospel is the doctrine of salvation through faith alone.

Fatwa   An authoritative legal opinion or ruling pertaining to Islamic law made by a qualified jurist or mufti.

Favela   A slum or shanty town in Brazil.

Fourteen stations of the cross   A series of images and accompanying prayers that depict Jesus on the day of his crucifixion.

Gender   Social identities, expressions, and roles that some societies assign based on assigned sex.

Gender segregation   The practice of dividing homes and other spaces into areas designated for woman and children that are separate from areas designated for adult men.

Gnosticism   A heretical movement of the early Christian Church, influenced by pre-Christian philosophies.

Guerilla performance   The staging of an unannounced concert, commonly performed in a non-traditional setting.

Hadith   The sayings of the Prophet Muhammad, initially related as oral history and later recorded in writing.

Heresy   False belief.

Hijra   A gender-fluid person with a distinct religious role in Indian culture. Hijras celebrate the birth of babies by visiting the parents and seeking gifts in exchange for giving their blessing to the family and the baby. The lives of hijras are regulated by a combination of Hindu and Muslim conventions.

Hindutva   Hindu nationalism.

Hjell   A wooden rack used to dry stockfish, especially cod.

Ideal type   A conceptual category that's useful for comparative study.

Instrumentalizing   Making something into a tool that you can use to accomplish a particular goal.

Intersectionality   The concept that different axes of social power affect each other, such that no single one can be studied accurately without taking the others into account.

Intersex   Someone with male and female physical traits.

Invert   A nineteenth-century European sexological concept that both named and explained gender-variant, same sex attracted people.

Jihad   *lit.* "striving," "exertion," or "effort in the direction of a certain goal." There is a basic distinction between two forms of *jihad*: the "great" *jihad* and the "small" *jihad*. The "great" *jihad* denotes an effort imposed upon oneself to achieve moral and religious perfection, whereas the "small" *jihad* refers to the duty to do battle against an outside enemy.

Khutbah   Friday sermon.

Kṛṣṇa   One of the major gods of Hinduism. Kṛṣṇa is one of the incarnations of the god Vishnu, the protector.

Kufr   An Arabic term used to refer to a person who has rejected God, often translated as "disbeliever" or "infidel."

Kumārī   Living incarnations of the Hindu goddess Durgā/Taleju.

Lived religion   The ways in which people live out their religions in practice and belief.

Maenad   A female worshipper of the Greek god Dionysus, god of wine and life-giving fluids.

Mikveh   A Jewish ritual bath.

Mitzvah   A commandment that Jews consider an obligation to do good.

Monasticism   An institution for those who wish to devote themselves to religious pursuits such as scholarship and meditation.

Mystic   A person who has religious experiences that transcend human understanding.

Niqab   A veil covering the face.

Orientalism, Orientalist   A nineteenth-century Western mode of art and scholarship that promoted specific stereotypes of Asian and Middle Eastern people and cultures; the application of those same stereotypes today.

Orthopraxis   Correct conduct.

Papa Gede   Chief figure in a class of spirits in Vodou religious practices of the Afro-Caribbean world that is associated with death, fertility, and satire.

Pass laws   During apartheid South Africa, an internal passport used as a means to control the population.

Pederasty   Age-differentiated sexual relationships between adult and teenage men.

Polygyny   A practice that allows a man to marry and to be married to more than one woman.

Pomba Gira   Female spirit being.

Profane   Not sacred; everyday; mundane.

Religious specialists   People who devote the majority of their time and energy to the practice and study of their religion.

Renunciant   A person who renounce the pleasures and comforts of everyday life, usually for religious purposes.

Sami   Indigenous peoples inhabiting Norway, Sweden, Finland, and parts of Russia.

Shakti   Divine energy regarded by Hindus as the animating power behind all things.

Shari'ah law   Moral and ethical principles set out in the Qur'an.

Shiva   One of the major gods of Hinduism. Shiva is known for his powers of yogic self-control and his cosmic task of destroying the universe when chaos has come to prevail and life is unlivable, thus wiping the slate clean so that the world can be created anew.

Slain in the spirit   A term used by evangelical Christians to describe falling to the floor while in a state of religious ecstasy induced by the Holy Spirit. People often assist those slain in the spirit so that they do not harm themselves in falling down.

Social construct   An idea, concept, or perspective that receives its meanings from society.

Social construction   The process by which a social construct is developed.

Spirit possession   An altered state of consciousness in which a person is believed to become a vehicle for a spirit or deity to appear in the human world.

Spiritualists   People who specialize in contacting the dead.

Stigmata Manifestation of wounds on the body that resemble the wounds inflicted on the body of Jesus Christ when he was crucified.

Stole A Liturgical vestment worn in many Christian denominations.

Tantras The ritual and esoteric texts of classical Indian tantra.

Tantrism A form of religious practice with origins in South Asia in which the ritual manipulation of sexual fluids is said to increase spiritual power.

Technology Tools that humans use to interact with the world around us.

Tertiary order A renunciant group for laypeople, typically women, who do not take full monastic vows but nonetheless dedicate their lives to religious practice.

Transgender A person who identifies with a gender other than the one they were assigned at birth.

Transsexual A person who has medically altered some or all aspects of their biological sex.

Ubuntu A state of being that contributes to the well-being of others and of community.

Ulama Religious clergy in Islam.

Vishnu One of the key gods of Hinduism, known as the sustainer god who protects the world from dark forces.

Visionary experience Religious experiences that offer a person a glimpse of realities beyond those of ordinary daily life, often said to transcend human understanding.

Vodou A type of religion practiced mainly in Haiti and the Haitian diaspora that emphasizes the idea of practitioners serving the spirits and in turn receiving protection and knowledge from them.

World-concept A way of understanding the world around one.

Zelador A caretaker, custodian.

Resources for teaching

Introduction

A useful resource for teaching the social construction of gender is the short film *The Happiest Day of His Life*, directed by Ursula Burton. The film tells a stereotypical white, middle-class American "white wedding" story from engagement to wedding reception, with all the gender roles swapped (the woman proposes, the man swoons over the ring, the mother of the groom gets drunk and boorish at the wedding while the father is maudlin, and so on). While the full film may be increasingly difficult to obtain, a trailer is still available online that can be effectively used as a conversation-starter in the classroom. See http://fivesistersproductions.com/the-happiest-day-of-his-life/.

Chapter 1

Assign a documentary on evangelical Christian abstinence pledges and their ceremonial expression in what are known as Purity Balls (such as *Purity Balls: Lifting the Veil on Special Ceremony*, produced by ABC News in 2014) combined with an essay by a feminist who once took an abstinence pledge such as Shelby Knox ("Abstinence is the New Feminism and Other Things I Learned at Harvard," Huffpost, May 25, 2011) to show different perspectives on the contemporary trend of teenage women taking pledges to remain celibate until marriage (some also pledge to reserve their first kiss for their husbands). One could assign a book on the idealization of virginity in women such as Jessica Valenti's 2010 book *The Purity Myth* to expose students to a wide range of arguments against the Christian abstinence movement. If one were to follow such an assignment with a reading by Elizabeth Clark ("Ascetic Renunciation and Feminine Advancement: A Paradox of Late Ancient Christianity") on the ways that celibacy empowered girls and women of late antiquity, this would offer students the opportunity to see how celibacy can work in various contexts, offering enhanced agency in some contexts and submission to patriarchal authority figures in other contexts.

Chapter 2

McCarthy, Julie. "The Very Strange Life of Nepal's Child Goddess." National Public Radio. May 28, 2015. https://www.npr.org/sections/parallels/2015/05/28/410074105/the-very-strange-life-of-nepals-child-goddess. Accessed Aug. 15, 2018.

Wilson, Liz. "Embodiments of Shakti: Cosmic Power Displayed by Kumārīs, Incarnate Goddesses of Nepal." In Jeanine E. Viau and Otto von Busch (eds.) *Silhouettes of the Soul: Meditations on*

Fashion, Religion, and Subjectivity. London: Bloomsbury Press, Dress Cultures series, edited by Reina Lewis and Elizabeth Wilson. Forthcoming.

Further exploration of Case Study 2 on gender variant people and governmental support for gender reassignment surgery in Iran could lead to useful discussion about the ways that we tend to endow certain ethnicities and religions with an aura of backwardness in the arena of sexuality. Many Americans are Islamophobic due to the consumption of biased mass media images of what life is like in Muslim majority countries. And scholarly sources are not always better than mass media: the Orientalist history in which Muslims have been studied makes practices like polygamy, child marriage, and honor killings highly legible in scholarly Western representations of Islam. So to correct this imbalance, we included Case Study 2 as a way of thinking differently about life in Muslim majority countries like Iran. The discussion might start with the question of the extent to which culturally dominant Islamophobic prejudices make it difficult to approach topics like state support for same sex surgery in Iran with a spirit of empathic understanding or suspension of one's own world-concept (*epoché*). Students might think about what it is like to have the government offering monetary support for an operation that might be prohibitively expensive, were one relying only on personal savings and donations from family members. Students might also imagine what it is like for a person assigned the male gender at birth and raised as a male person to dress as a female after surgery. As will be explained in Chapter 3, many girls and women in Muslim majority countries dress modestly when in the presence of men outside their families. While in some countries, modest dress means wearing a scarf to cover the hair or a shawl over the shoulders, Iran has highly specific state regulations about female dress that those raised as men might well find difficult. This process can be observed in the You Tube video "Transgender in Iran: Arsham's Story," a three minute video funded by Radio Free Europe/Radio Liberty: https://www.youtube.com/watch?v=agr2ZkbRghs. As a next step, it might be useful to ask how fruitful it is to separate out how gender variant people are treated in Iran against the background of how same sex attracted people are treated. For showing how the two themes are often fused together in the way that the topic of sex change surgery in Iran is framed, there is a film that follows the stories of some patients at a Tehran clinic:

Eshaghian, Tanaz, dir. *Be Like Others: Transsexual in Iran*, 2008. 74 min. https://www.documentarystorm.com/like-others-transsexual-iran/.

Chapter 3

Pussy Riot: A Punk Prayer, 2013 (Roast Beef Production, dir. Mike Lerner and Maksim Pozdorovkin).

The documentary showcases the punk group Pussy Riot. Focus is on their "guerrilla performances" and footage of the court proceedings, which also includes interviews with families of band members.

Music Videos

Naima Bouteldja and Fatima Ali (producers), *Thriller in Paris*, 2010, https://vimeo.com/18616413. Madonna, *Like a Prayer*, 1989, https://www.youtube.com/watch?v=79fzeNUqQbQ.

Pussy Riot, *Punk Prayer: Mother of God Drive Putin Away*, 2012, https://www.youtube.com/watch?v=lPDkJbTQRCY.

Pussy Riot, *Make America Great Again*, 2016, https://www.youtube.com/watch?v=s-bKFo30o2o.

Tooji, *Father*, 2015, https://www.youtube.com/watch?v=kiVOtUpSA8w.

Exhibitions

Ecce Homo by Elisabeth Ohlson Wallin, https://web.archive.org/web/20071213010136/http://www.ohlson.se:80/utstallningar_ecce.htm.

Chapter 4

Hayes, Kelly E., and Catherine Crouch, dir. *Slaves of the Saints*. 2010. 64 min.

> This ethnographic documentary about Afro-Brazilian religions can accompany the book *Holy Harlots* by Kelly E. Hayes. The documentary focuses on a range of spiritual beings who are active, and embody, human beings. Particularly, we get acquainted with the Pomba Giras, unruly spirits, who are commonly associated with black magic. The documentary shows the important ways in which the Pomba Giras function in the lives of devotees on the margins of society.

Summer, Red, dir. *Al Nisa: Muslim Women in Atlanta's Gay Mecca*. 2013. 63 min.

> This documentary explores what it means to be Black, Muslim and lesbian, and to live in the "Gay Mecca" of Atlanta. Participants in the documentary discuss Muslim belonging and faith commitments and how these relate to and are complicated by racialized and queer embodiment.

McCarthy, Tom, dir. *Spotlight*. 2015. 129 min.

> American biographical drama that follows The Boston Globe's "Spotlight" team in their investigation to uncover systemic child sexual abuse by Roman Catholic priests.

Mullan, Peter, dir. *The Magdalena Sisters*. 2002. 119 min.

> Irish-British drama that unravels the history of the very real Magdalene Asylums, homes where teenage girls who were considered "fallen" or "immoral" by their families or society were sent to be disciplined and become redeemed. The drama documents the abuses that took place at the Magdalene Asylums.

Lorentzen, Nefise Özkal, dir. *A Trilogy on Gender and Islam*. 2015.

> *Gender Me*, 52 min.

> The documentary explores the questions of faith and gender in Islam, with a special focus on the stories of Muslim queers.

> *A Balloon for Allah*, 58 min.

> The documentary sets out to unravel the mysteries surrounding women in Islam and includes interviews with well-known scholars of Islam and women such as Asma Barlas.

> *Manislam*, 58 min.

This film examines the burdens of manhood within Islamic cultures. The main characters share deeply personal memories and experiences in their effort to high-light and question the role of men in contemporary Islam.

Chapter 5

More information on many of the movements mentioned in this chapter can be found online. Be careful, however, to pre-screen such resources or equip students with tools for thinking critically about them, since they are often slanted toward mainstream perspec-tives on these forms of innovation. Evaluating a biased source can be an excellent exer-cise, though. Some films also contain violent or explicit scenes and bigoted verbal condemnation that students might wish to be forewarned about. A few films that are useful for teaching this topic:

Harris, Sarah, dir. *Prostitutes of God*. *Vice Magazine*, 2012. 28 mins. https://www.you-tube.com/watch?v=2GFaN9-1iz0.

> This is a teachably biased film. From the start it's clear that Harris is seeking to tell a story of devadasis as oppressed sex workers. She visits both male and female devadasis, and one after another they all refuse her story line. The film ends when she finds two former devadasis who do tell the story that Harris wants to hear. This film works really well with class discussion about critical media consumption; it can also be paired with an excerpt from Ramberg's (2014) excellent and nuanced book.

Osder, Jason, dir. *Let the Fire Burn*. New York: Zeitgeist Films, 2014. 95 mins.

> This is a documentary on the clashes between MOVE, a Black nationalist, nature-focused new religious movement in Philadelphia, and the Philadelphia police – clashes that involved clear incidents of racist police brutality and anti-NRM bias, and that ended in the destruction by fire of several square blocks of a predominantly Black neighborhood. Since MOVE was communal and the members preferred to live nude, it's a clear example of religious innovation around bodies and sexualities, of mainstream resistance to such innovation, and of the complicated intersections between anti-NRM bias and white supremacy. A good case to discuss with students, since its links to sexuality aren't always obvious. This film contains vivid scenes of police brutality against Black people, particularly Black men.

Sharma, Parvez, dir. *A Jihad for Love*. New York: First Run Features, 2007. 81 min.

> This film focuses on LGBTIQ+ Muslims, and includes significant coverage of Imam Muhsin Hendricks. There is some discussion with Muslims who oppose LGBTIQ+ welcoming perspectives within Islam. Regardless of their own religious background, students from Islamophobic cultures such as the U.S. and much of Europe may need help remembering the examples of contented and self-accepting LGBTIQ+ Muslims in the film; confirmation bias tends to lead them to remember primarily the homo-phobic violence that is also described therein.

Slade, Eric, dir. *Hope Along the Wind: The Life of Harry Hay*. 2002. 57 min.

> This film is useful either in total or in clips. It traces the life of early U.S. gay activist Harry Hay, including but definitely not limited to his work with the Radical Faeries.

Williams, Roger Ross, dir. *God Loves Uganda*. Brooklyn, NY: Full Credit Productions, 2013. 83 min.

> This film can be used to discuss religious innovation in multiple directions. Grounded in the story of an Anglican priest allied with the Ugandan LGBTIQ+ community, the film explores the complex dynamics of colonialism that are present in white U.S. evangelical efforts to combat "homosexuality" in Uganda, and Ugandan political and religious leaders' efforts to capitalize on the resulting gay scare. There is footage of religious leaders promoting the nearly-pornographic homophobia that prevails in certain conservative evangelical circles in the U.S., and that representatives of such groups have exported to Uganda.

Chapter 6

The Butler article that's listed in the "Resources for further study" section of this chapter is one of Butler's most accessible explanations of performativity. With help, undergraduates at any level who have not been previously exposed to Butler's work can come to understand the basics of her argument through this piece. In teaching this concept, it's often important to help students understand the difference between a performance (which the audience interprets as an act) and performativity (which audiences, and sometimes performers, interpret as an expression of an inner essence or truth). A simple comparison between a friend behaving badly on stage (i.e., as a character) versus in the local coffee shop or dining hall, and the different meanings we might attribute to the same behavior in these two different settings, is often sufficient to clarify the difference and to dissuade students from the idea that performativity means that gender is just something we decide how to act out each day.

Having students explore tantric sex and sex magic resources online, such as the websites, tutorials, books (there's an *Idiot's Guide to Tantric Sex*, among other resources), videos, workshops, and other materials available for purchase or free consumption, can be eye-opening. When turned into a show-and-tell exercise in class, where students show the class examples they found particularly intriguing, this tour of the marketing resources of modern Western tantra and sex magic can lead to generative discussions about the differences from classical Indian tantra and the complexities of appropriation, neoliberal marketing of religion, and the like.

The section on pederasty can spark thoughtful discussion of cultural ideas about childhood, adolescence, and sexuality, if those discussions are well guided by the instructor. In most cultures where this book will be taught, there is little legal delineation between children and adolescents, so pederasty and pedophilia become merged in moral and legal discourse. But often such discourse is also gendered, and sometimes sexualized, especially in cases where the legal age of consent is different for women and men, or for same-sex relations and different-sex relations. All of this can be useful for students to ponder.

Chapter 7

Students who have never been exposed to ecstatic religion could benefit from seeing the 1967 documentary film "The Holy Ghost People." This 52-minute film documents a range of phenomena demonstrated by Pentecostal Christians at the Scrabble Creek Holiness Church, in Scrabble Creek, West Virginia. In the documentary, viewers see faith healing, snake handling, speaking in tongues, and people whose bodies are engaged in convulsive movements while in prayer. At one point in the film, viewers can see young people imitating the movements of adults, suggesting how some of the ritual gestures associated with the gifts of the Holy Spirit are learned by example.

The film is easily accessed as it is in the public domain and available on the internet: https://archive.org/details/HolyGhostPeople_201403.

In the novel *Mariette in Ecstasy* that's listed in the "Resources for further study" section for this chapter, author Ron Hansen presents the spiritual love affair of a bright seventeen-year-old postulant seeking to become a nun in a Benedictine convent in upstate New York at the beginning of the twentieth century. Mariette Baptiste, the novel's protagonist, has a passionate inner life in erotic play with her bridegroom Jesus. Hansen's novel was published 1991 and has stood the test of time. It is a rare depiction of cloistered life that presents religious miracles without sensationalizing what it describes. The novel received critical approval from Roman Catholic conservatives and from secular critics drawn to its spare poetic style. Hansen became a deacon in the Catholic Church in 2007 and so might be considered an insider in the religious community he described in writing *Mariette in Ecstasy*. The presence of Jesus as revealed in the flesh, so ordinary in medieval Christian mysticism, is depicted in the novel with sensitivity and complexity. For example, stigmata appear on Mariette's palms and feet. The wounds that were inflicted on the hands and feet of Jesus during his crucifixion appear on the body of Mariette as mystical gifts of the spirit. When the stigmata appear, the novel shows a range of responses in the characters surrounding Mariette. Mariette's father, a physician, thinks his daughter has been duped. Some girls and women in the convent burn with envy; some are dubious but open to persuasion; some find their capacity for mystical abandon renewed by the example of Mariette's deeply physical relationship with Jesus. Assigning the novel would give students the opportunity to see the complicated sociological dynamic of convent life that closely resembles what might have taken place in medieval Catholic communities.

Bibliography

Abu-Lughod, Lila. *Do Muslim Women Need Saving?* Cambridge, MA: Harvard University Press, 2013.

Albanese, Catherine L. *A Republic of Mind and Spirit: A Cultural History of American Metaphysical Religion*. New Haven, CT: Yale University Press, 2007.

Allen, Michael. *The Cult of Kumārī: Virgin Worship in Nepal*. Kantipath, Kathmandu: Mandala Book Point, 1996.

Althaus-Reid, Marcella. *Indecent Theology. Theological Perversions in Sex, Gender and Politics*. New York, NY: Routledge, 2000.

Andrews, William L. (ed.). *Sisters of the Spirit: Three Black Women's Autobiographies of the Nineteenth Century*. Bloomington and Indianapolis: Indiana University Press, 1986.

Asad, Talal. *Genealogies of Religion: Discipline and Reasons of Power in Christianity and Islam*. Baltimore, MD: Johns Hopkins University Press, 1993.

Atwood, Margaret. *The Handmaid's Tale*. London: Jonathan Cape, 1985.

Berger, Peter. *The Sacred Canopy: Elements of a Sociological Theory of Religion*. New York, NY: Doubleday, 1967.

Biale, David. *Eros and the Jews: From Biblical Israel to Contemporary America*. New York, NY: Basic Books, 1992.

Bly, Robert, Mirabai, and Jane Hirshfield. *Mirabai: Ecstatic Poems*. Boston MA: Beacon Press, 2004.

Boisvert, Mathieu, "Death as Meditation Subject in The Theravada Tradition." *Buddhist Studies Review* 13, no. 1 (1996): 47–50.

Brown, KarenMcCarthy. *Mama Lola: A Vodou Priestess in Brooklyn*. Comparative Studies in Religion and Society: 4. Berkeley, CA: University of California Press, 2001.

Brown, Peter, and Robert Lamont. *The Body and Society: Men, Women, and Sexual Renunciation in Early Christianity*. New York, NY: Columbia University Press, 1988.

Brundage, James. *Law, Sex, and Christian Society in Medieval Europe*. Chicago, IL: University of Chicago Press, 1987.

Bucar, Elizabeth M., and Anne Enke. "Unlikely Sex Change Capitals of the World: Trinidad, United States, and Tehran, Iran, as Twin Yardsticks of Homonormative Liberalism." *Feminist Studies* 37, no. 2 (2011): 301–328.

Bucar, Elizabeth M., and Faegheh Shirazi. "The 'Invention' of Lesbian Acts in Iran: Interpretative Moves, Hidden Assumptions, and Emerging Categories of Sexuality." *Journal of Lesbian Studies* 16, no. 4 (2012): 416–434.

Burke, Kelsy. *Christians Under Covers: Evangelicals and Sexual Pleasure on the Internet*. Berkeley, CA: University of California Press, 2016.

Burrus, Virginia. *The Sex Lives of Saints: An Erotics of Ancient Hagiography*. Philadelphia, PA: University of Pennsylvania Press, 2004.

Butler, Judith. *Gender Trouble: Feminism and the Subversion of Identity*. New York, NY: Routledge, 1990.

Butler, Judith. "Performative Acts and Gender Constitution: An Essay in Phenomenology and Feminist Theory." In Carole R. McCann and Seung-kyung Kim (eds.) *Feminist Theory Reader: Local and Global Perspectives*, 3rd ed. New York, NY: Routledge, 2013: 462–473.

Bynum, CarolineWalker. *Holy Feast and Holy Fast: The Religious Significance of Food to Medieval Women*. Berkeley, CA: University of California Press, 1988.

Cahana, Jonathan. "Dismantling Gender: Between Ancient Gnostic Ritual and Modern Queer BDSM." *Theology & Sexuality* 18, no. 1 (2012): 60–75.

Clark, Elizabeth A. "Ascetic Renunciation and Feminine Advancement: A Paradox of Late Ancient Christianity." *Anglican Theological Review* 63, no. 6 (1981): 240–257.

Clark, Elizabeth A. *St. Augustine on Marriage and Sexuality*. Washington, D.C.: Catholic University of America Press, 1996.

Clark, Elizabeth A. "The Celibate Bridegroom and His Virginal Brides: Metaphor and the Marriage of Jesus in Early Christian Ascetic Exegesis." *Church History* 77, no. 1 (2008): 1–25.

Cohen, David. *Law, Sexuality and Society: The Enforcement of Morals in Classical Athens*. Cambridge: Cambridge University Press, 1991.

Cole, Alan. "Buddhism." In Don S. Browning, M. Christian Green, and JohnWitte, Jr., (eds.) *Sex, Marriage, and Family in World Religions*. New York, NY: Columbia University Press, 2006:299–366.

Collins, Steven. "Monasticism, Utopias and Comparative Social Theory." *Religion* 18 (April1988): 101–135.

Crasnow, S.J. "On Transition: Normative Judaism and Trans Innovation." *Journal of Contemporary Religion* 32, no. 3 (2017): 403–415.

Crenshaw, Kimberlé. "Mapping the Margins: Intersectionality, Identity Politics, and Violence Against Women of Color." *Stanford Law Review* 43, no. 6 (1991): 1241–1299.

Crouch, Melissa (ed.). *Islam and the State in Myanmar: Muslim-Buddhist Relations and the Politics of Belonging*. New Delhi: Oxford University Press, 2016.

Daly, Mary. *Beyond God the Father: Toward a Philosophy of Women's Liberation*. Boston, MA: Beacon Press, 1973.

Daly, Mary, and Jane Caputi. *Webster's First New Intergalactic Wickedary of the English Language*. Boston, MA: Beacon Press, 1987.

Das, Runa. "Encountering." *International Feminist Journal of Politics* 8, no. 3 (2006): 370–393.

Davies, Sharyn Graham. *Gender Diversity in Indonesia: Sexuality, Islam, and Queer Selves*. New York, NY: Routledge, 2010.

de Lauretis, Teresa. "Queer Theory: Lesbian and Gay Sexualities: An Introduction." *differences* 3, no. 2 (1991): iii–xviii.

de Lauretis, Teresa. "Habit Changes." *differences* 6, no. 2–3 (1994): 296–313.

DeConick, April. "The True Mysteries: Sacramentalism in the Gospel of Philip." *Vigilae Christianae* 55 (2001): 225–261.

DeConick, April. "The Great Mystery of Marriage: Sex and Conception in Ancient Valentinian Traditions." *Vigilae Christianae* 57 (2003): 307–342.

Devor, Aaron. "Narrow Bridge." In Noach Dzmura (ed.) *Balancing on the Mechitza: Transgender in the Jewish Community*. Berkeley, CA: North Atlantic Books, 2010: 93–97.

Dimock, Edward C., Jr. *The Place of the Hidden Moon: Erotic Mysticism in the Vaisnava-Sahajiya Cult of Bengal*. Chicago, IL: University of Chicago Press, 1966.

Doniger, Wendy, and Brian K. Smith. *The Laws of Manu*. London: Penguin Books, 1991.

Driskill, Qwo-Li. *Asegi Stories: Cherokee Queer and Two-Spirit Memory*. Tucson, AZ: University of Arizona Press, 2016.

Dzmura, Noach (ed.). *Balancing on the Mechitza: Transgender in Jewish Community*. Berkeley, CA: North Atlantic Books, 2010.

Epiphanius, Saint, Bishop of Constantia in Cyprus. *The Panarion of Epiphanius of Salamis*. Nag Hammadi Studies: 35. Leiden and New York: E.J. Brill, 1987.

Fadiman, Anne. *The Spirit Catches You and You Fall Down: A Hmong Child, Her American Doctors, and the Collision of Two Cultures*. New York, NY: Farrar, Strauss, and Giroux, 1997.

Faure, Bernard. *The Power of Denial: Buddhism, Purity, and Gender*. Princeton, NJ: Princeton University Press, 2003.

Fausto-Sterling, Anne. *Sexing the Body: Gender Politics and the Construction of Sexuality*. New York, NY: Basic Books, 2000.

Feinstein, Eve Levavi. *Sexual Pollution in the Hebrew Bible*. Oxford and New York: Oxford University Press, 2014.

Fine, Cordelia. *Delusions of Gender: How Our Minds, Society, and Neurosexism Create Difference*. New York, NY: Norton, 2011.

Fink, Christina. "Myanmar: Religious Minorities and Constitutional Questions." *Asian Affairs* 49, no. 2 (2018): 259–277, doi:10.1080/03068374.2018.1469860.

Foster, Lawrence. *Women, Family, and Utopia: Communal Experiments of the Shakers, the Oneida Community, and the Mormons*. Syracuse, NY: Syracuse University Press, 1991.

Foucault, Michel, and Richard Sennett. "Sexuality and Solitude." *London Review of Books* 3, no. 9 (1981): 3–7.

Fruzzetti, Lina. *The Gift of a Virgin: Women, Marriage, and Ritual in a Bengali Society*. New Brunswick, NJ: Rutgers University Press, 1982.

Gamieldien, Fahmi. *The History of the Claremont Main Road Mosque, Its People and their Contribution to Islam in South Africa*. Cape Town: Claremont Main Road Mosque, 2004.

Girard, René. *Violence and the Sacred*. Trans. Patrick Gregory. Baltimore, MD: Johns Hopkins University Press, 1977.

Glassman, Hank. "At the Crossroads of Birth and Death: The Blood-Pool Hell and Postmortem Fetal Extraction." In Mariko Walter and Jacqueline Stone (eds.) *Death Rituals and the Afterlife in Japanese Buddhism*. Honolulu, HI: University of Hawaii Press, 2008: 175–206.

Gombrich, Richard. *Theravada Buddhism: As Social History from Ancient Benares to Modern Colombo*. London: Routledge & Kegan Paul, 1988.

Gray, Hillel. "Not Judging by Appearances: The Role of Genotype in Jewish Law on Intersex Conditions." *Shofar: An Interdisciplinary Journal of Jewish Studies* 30, no. 4 (2012): 126–148.

Gray, Hillel. "The Transitioning of Jewish Biomedical Law: Rhetorical and Practical Shifts in Halakhic Discourse on Sex-Change Surgery." *Nashim: A Journal of Jewish Women's Studies and Gender Issues* 29 (2015): 81–107.

Hall, Donald E., and Annamarie Jagose with Andrea Bebell and Susan Potter (eds.). *The Routledge Queer Studies Reader*. New York, NY: Routledge, 2013.

Hammer, Juliane. *American Muslim Women, Religious Authority, and Activism: More than a Prayer*. Austin, TX: University of Texas Press, 2012.

Hansen, Ron. *Mariette in Ecstasy*. New York, NY: E. Burlingame Books, 1991.

Hardacre, Helen. *Marketing the Menacing Fetus in Japan*. Berkeley, CA: University of California Press, 1997.

Hawley, John Stratton, and Mark Juergensmeyer. *Songs of the Saints of India*. London: Oxford University Press, 2004.

Hayes, Glen Alexander. "The Necklace of Immortality: A Seventeenth-Century Vaisnava Sahajiya Text." In David Gordon White (ed.) *Tantra in Practice*. Princeton, NJ: Princeton University Press, 2000: 308–325.

Hayes, Kelly E. *Holy Harlots: Femininity, Sexuality & Black Magic in Brazil*. Berkeley, CA: University of California Press, 2011.

Herrick, Tirzah Miller. *Desire and Duty at Oneida: Tirzah Miller's Intimate Memoir*. Bloomington, IN: Indiana University Press, 2000.

Hoel, Nina. *South African Muslim Women's Experiences: Sexuality and Religious Discourses*. Unpublished PhD thesis. Department of Religious Studies, University of Cape Town, 2010.

Huntington, Samuel P. *The Clash of Civilizations and the Remaking of World Order*. London: Simon & Schuster, 1996.

Jeffries, Bayyinah S. *A Nation Can Rise No Higher than its Women: African American Muslim Women in the Movement for Black Self-Determination, 1950–1975*. Lanham, MD: Lexington, 2014.

Johnson, Luke, and Mark Jordan. *Sex, Marriage, and Family in World Religions.* New York, NY: Columbia University Press, 2006.

Kinsley, David. "Devotion as an Alternative to Marriage in the Lives of Some Hindu Women Devotees." *Journal of Asian and African Studies* 15, no. 1 (January1980): 83–93.

Kraemer, Ross S. "Ecstasy and Possession: The Attraction of Women to the Cult of Dionysus." *The Harvard Theological Review* 72, no. 1 (1979): 55–80.

Kripal, Jeffrey J. *The Serpent's Gift: Gnostic Reflections on the Study of Religion.* Chicago, IL: University of Chicago Press, 2007.

Kugle, Scott Sirajal-Haqq. *Homosexuality in Islam: Critical Reflections on Gay, Lesbian, and Transgender Muslims.* Oxford: Oneworld, 2010.

Kugle, Scott Sirajal-Haqq. *Living Out Islam: Voices of Gay, Lesbian, and Transgender Muslims.* New York, NY: New York University Press, 2014.

Langenberg, Amy Paris. *Birth in Buddhism: The Suffering Fetus and Female Freedom.* London and New York: Routledge, 2017.

Lewis, I.M.1989. *Ecstatic Religion: An Anthropological Study of Spirit Possession and Shamanism.* Harmondsworth, UK: Penguin Press, 1971.

Madsen, Catherine, and Joy Ladin. "Ritual for Gender Transition (Male to Female)." In Noach Dzmura (ed.) *Balancing on the Mechitza: Transgender in the Jewish Community.* Berkeley, CA: North Atlantic Books, 2010: 85–92.

Marriot, McKim. "Hindu Transactions: Diversity Without Dualism." In Bruce Kapferer (ed.) *Transaction and Meaning: Directions in the Anthropology of Exchange and Symbolic Behavior.* Philadelphia, PA: Ishi Press, 1976: 109–142.

Martin, Dale B. "Paul without Passion: On Paul's Rejection of Desire in Sex and Marriage." In Halvor Moxnes (ed.) *Constructing Early Christian Families: Families as Social Reality and Metaphor.* London: Routledge, 1997: 201–215.

Masuzawa, Tomoko. *The Invention of World Religions, or, How European Universalism was Preserved in the Language of Pluralism.* Chicago, IL: University of Chicago Press, 2005.

McCarthy, Julie. "The Very Strange Life of Nepal's Child Goddess." National Public Radio. May 28, 2015. Accessed Aug. 15, 2018. https://www.npr.org/sections/parallels/2015/05/28/410074105/the-very-strange-life-of-nepals-child-goddess.

McGinn, Bernard. *The Essential Writings of Christian Mysticism.* New York, NY: Modern Library, 2006.

McGuire, Meredith B. *Lived Religion: Faith and Practice in Everyday Life.* New York, NY: Oxford University Press, 2008.

Menon, Ritu, and Kamla Bhasin. *Borders and Boundaries: Women in India's Partition.* New Brunswick, NJ: Rutgers University Press, 1998.

Merchant, Carolyn. *Radical Ecology: The Search for a Livable World.* New York, NY: Routledge, 2005.

Mohanty, Chandra Talpade. "Under Western Eyes: Feminist Scholarship and Colonial Discourses." In Chandra T. Mohanty, Ann Russo, and Lourdes Torres (eds.) *Third World Women and the Politics of Feminism.* Bloomington and Indianapolis: Indiana University Press, 1991: 51–80.

Momoko, Takemi. "'Menstruation Sutra' Belief in Japan." *Japanese Journal of Religious Studies* 10, no. 2–3 (1983): 229–246.

Najmabadi, Afsaneh. "Transing and Transpassing Across Sex-Gender Walls In Iran." *Women's Studies Quarterly* 36, no. 3–4 (2008): 23–42.

Nanda, Serena. "The Hijras of India: Cultural and Individual Dimensions of an Institutionalized Third Gender Role." *Journal of Homosexuality* 11 (1986): 35–54.

Nandy, Pritish. *The Songs of Mirabai.* London: Arnold-Heinemann, 1975.

Narozhna, Tanya, and W. Andy Knight. *Female Suicide Bombings: A Critical Gender Approach.* Toronto: University of Toronto Press, 2016.

Orsi, Robert A. *Between Heaven and Earth: The Religious Worlds People Make and the Scholars Who Study Them.* Princeton, NJ: Princeton University Press, 2005.

Otto, Walter Friedrich. *Dionysus, Myth and Cult*. Bloomington, IN: Indiana University Press, 1965.

Peers, E. Allison (ed. and trans.). *Complete Works of Saint Teresa of Jesus*. Vol. 1. London and New York: Sheed and Ward, 1957.

Petro, Anthony. *After the Wrath of God: AIDS, Sexuality, and American Religion*. New York, NY: Oxford University Press, 2015.

Pruitt, William (ed.). *Paramatthadipani: Dhammapala's Commentary on the Therigatha*. London: Pali Text Society, 1893.

Ramaswamy, Vijaya. "Rebels — Conformists? Women Saints in Medieval South India." *Anthropos* 87, no. 1 (1992): 133–146.

Ramberg, Lucinda. *Given to the Goddess: South Indian Devadasis and the Sexuality of Religion*. Durham, NC: Duke University Press, 2014.

Rapoport-Albert, Ada. Translated from the Hebrew by Deborah Greniman. *Women and the Messianic Heresy of Sabbatai Zevi, 1666–1816*. Oxford and Portland: Littman Library of Jewish Civilization, 2015.

Reddy, Gayatri. *With Respect to Sex: Negotiating Hijra Identity in South India*. Chicago, IL: University of Chicago, 2005.

Rich, Adrienne. "Compulsory Heterosexuality and Lesbian Existence." *Signs* 5, no. 4 (1980): 631–660.

Roberts, Rosemary. "'Healing my Body, Healing the Land': Healing as Sociopolitical Activism in Reclaiming Witchcraft." *Ethnologies* 33, no. 1 (2011): 239–256.

Roy, Arundhati. *The Ministry of Utmost Happiness*, 2017.

Ruether, Rosemary Radford (ed.). *Women Healing Earth: Third World Women on Ecology, Feminism, and Religion*. Maryknoll, NY: Orbis Books, 1996.

Salomonsen, Jone, and Sarah Pike. *"Presence and Absence at the Steilneset Witchcraft Memorial,"* paper presented at the AAR2017, Contemporary Pagan Studies Group. 2017.

Salomonsen, Jone. "Reclaiming." In Bron Taylor (ed.) *The Encyclopedia of Religion and Nature*. New York, NY: Continuum, 2005: 1350–1351.

Savage, Dan. *American Savage: Insights, Slights, And Fights On Faith, Sex, Love, And Politics*. New York, NY: Dutton, 2013.

Schalow, Paul Gordon. "Kūkai and the Tradition of Male Love in Japanese Buddhism." In José Ignacio Cabezón (ed.) *Buddhism, Sexuality, and Gender*. Albany, NY: State University of New York Press, 1992: 215–230.

Scholem, Gershom. *Sabbatai Sevi; the Mystical Messiah, 1626–1676*. Bollingen Series: 93. Princeton, NJ: Princeton University Press, 1973.

Schumm, Darla, and Michael Stoltzfus (eds.). *Disability and World Religions: An Introduction*. Waco, TX: Baylor University Press, 2016.

Scott, Joan Wallach. *Sex and Secularism*. Princeton and Oxford: Princeton University Press, 2018.

Sider, Ron. "AIDS: An Evangelical Perspective." *Christian Century* 6, no. 13 (January1989): 11.

Simpson, J.A., and E.S.C. Weiner. *Oxford English Dictionary*. Oxford: Clarendon Press and New York, NY: Oxford University Press, 1993.

Siraj, Asifa. "Isolated, Invisible, and in the Closet: The Life Story of a Scottish Muslim Lesbian." *Journal of Lesbian Studies* 15, no. 1 (2011): 99–121.

Smith, Andrea. *Conquest: Sexual Violence and American Indian Genocide*. Durham, NC: Duke University Press, 2015 [c2005].

"Spiritual Friendship." Accessed Sept. 29, 2018, https://spiritualfriendship.org/.

Spivak, Gayatri. "Can the Subaltern Speak?" In Cary Nelson and Lawrence Grossberg (eds.) *Marxism and the Interpretation of Culture*. London: Macmillan, 1988: 271–313.

Stryker, Susan, and Stephen Whittle. *The Transgender Studies Reader*. New York, NY: Routledge, 2006.

Stryker, Susan, and Aren Z. Aizura (eds.). *The Transgender Studies Reader 2*. New York, NY: Routledge, 2013.

Talamantez, Inés. "The Presence of Isanaklesh: A Native American Goddess and the Path of Pollen." In Nancy Auer Falk and Rita M. Gross (eds.) *Unspoken Worlds: Women's Religious Lives*, 3rd ed. Belmont, CA: Wadsworth Press, 2000: 290–300.

Teresa of Avila, Saint. "General Introduction, Life." In E. Allison Peers (ed. and trans.) *Complete Works of Saint Teresa of Jesus.* Vol. 1: London and New York: Sheed and Ward, 1957.

Teresa of Avila, Saint. *The Interior Castle.* The Classics of Western Spirituality. New York, NY: Paulist Press, 1979.

Theobald, Simon. "'It's a Tefillin Date': Alternative Narratives of Orthodox Jewish Sexuality in the Digital Age." In Stephen J. Hunt and Andrew K.T. Yip (eds.) *The Ashgate Research Companion in Contemporary Religion and Sexuality.* Burlington, VT: Ashgate, 2012: 289–304.

Thomas, Tissy Mariam. *The Clan Culture of Hijras: An Exploration into the Gender Identity and Status of Hijras Inside and Outside of Gharanas.* Bangalore: Centre for Research Projects, Christ University, 2013.

Thomas, Wesley. "Navajo Cultural Constructions of Gender and Sexuality." In Sue-Ellen Jacobs, Wesley Thomas, and Sabine Lang (eds.) *Two Spirit People: Native American Gender Identity, Sexuality, and Spirituality.* Chicago, IL: University of Illinois Press, 1997: 156–173.

Torjesen, Karen Jo. *When Women Were Priests: Women's Leadership in the Early Church and the Scandal of their Subordination in the Rise of Christianity.* San Francisco, CA: Harper San Francisco, 1993.

Trafzer, Clifford E., Jean A. Keller, and Lorene Sisquoc (eds.). *Boarding School Blues: Revisiting American Indian Educational Experiences.* Lincoln, NE and London: University of Nebraska Press, 2006.

Tree, Isabella. *The Living Goddess: A Journey into the Heart of Kathmandu.* New York, NY: Eland Publishing, 2015.

Turner, John D. "Trimorphic Protennoia." In James M. Robinson (ed.) *The Nag Hammadi Library in English.* Leiden and New York: E.J. Brill, 1996: 511–522.

Tushnet, Eve. *Gay and Catholic: Accepting My Sexuality, Finding Community, Living My Faith.* Notre Dame, IN: Ave Maria Press, 2014.

Tushnet, Eve. "Coming Out Christian: How Faithful Homosexuals Are Transforming Our Churches." *The American Conservative* 13, no. 1 (2014b): 20–23.

Urban, Hugh B. *Magia Sexualis: Sex, Magic, and Liberation in Modern Western Esotericism.* Berkeley, CA: University of California Press, 2006.

Valenti, Jessica. *The Purity Myth: How America's Obsession with Virginity Is Hurting Young Women.* Berkeley, CA: Seal Press, 2010.

Van der Leeuw, Gerardus. *Religion in Essence and Manifestation.* Trans. J.E. Turner. Gloucester: Peter Smith, 1967.

van Klinken, Adriaan S. *Transforming Masculinities in African Christianity: Gender Controversies in Times of AIDS.* Surrey: Ashgate, 2013.

Wadud, Amina. *Qur'an and Woman: Rereading the Sacred Text from a Woman's Perspective.* New York and Oxford: Oxford University Press, 1999[c1992].

Wadud, Amina. *Inside the Gender Jihad: Women's Reform in Islam.* Oxford: Oneworld, 2006.

Ward, Sister Benedicta (trans.). *The Wisdom of the Desert Fathers; Apophthegmata Patrum.* Fairacres, Oxford: Fairacres Press, 1975.

Wenger, Tisa. *We Have a Religion: The 1920s Pueblo Indian Dance Controversy and American Religious Freedom.* Chapel Hill, NC: University of North Carolina Press, 2009.

White, David Gordon. *Kiss of the Yoginī: "Tantric Sex" in its South Asian Context.* Chicago, IL: University of Chicago Press, 2003.

White, Heather R. *Reforming Sodom: Protestants and the Rise of Gay Rights.* Chapel Hill, NC: University of North Carolina Press, 2015.

Wilson, Liz. *Charming Cadavers: Horrific Figurations of the Feminine in Indian Buddhist Hagiographic Literature.* Chicago, IL: University of Chicago Press, 1996.

Wilson, Liz. "Buddhism and Gender." In David McMahon (ed.) *Buddhism in the Modern World.* Abingdon: Routledge, 2012: 257–272.

Wilson, Liz. "Buddhism and Family." *Religion Compass* 8, no. 6 (July2014): 188–198. http://religion-compass.com/sections/buddhism/.

Wilson, Liz. "Embodiments of Shakti: Cosmic Power Displayed by Kumārīs, Incarnate Goddesses of Nepal." In Jeanine E. Viau and Otto von Busch (eds.) *Silhouettes of the Soul: Meditations on Fashion, Religion, and Subjectivity*. London: Bloomsbury Press, Dress Cultures series, edited by Reina Lewis and Elizabeth Wilson. Forthcoming.

Yalom, Marilyn. *A History of the Wife*. New York, NY: Harper Perennial, 2002.

Zajovic, Stasa. "Women and Ethnic Cleansing." Trans. Cynthia Cockburn. *Women Against Fundamentalism* 1, no. 5 (1994): 36.

Index

9/11 terrorist attacks 79
969 (Burmese nationalist movement) 85

Abdullah, Daayiee 102
abortion 92–93, 104, 107; anti-abortion
    movements 107; right to abortion 61
Abu-Lughod, Lila 79
academic study of religion 2–8
African Americans 97; religion for 97; women
    preachers 64
age-differentiated relationships 120
agender 12
ahimsa (non-violence) 76
AIDS in United States and in sub-Saharan
    Africa 58–59, 61; God's punishment for
    homosexuals 58; transmission 58
Albanese, Catherine 98
albinism 121
alchemy 114
Ali, Fatima 70
Al-Isslaah, Masjid Nur 102
al-Qaida 79, 86
Andrews, William L. 64
androgynos 9
Ann Lee 98
anthropocene 81
anti-abortion movements 107; *see also* abortion
anti-Black violence 97
anti-circumcision movements 117; *see also*
    circumcision
Anti-Homosexuality Act, Uganda 77–78
Apache girls 126
apartheid 55, 62
Asad, Talal 5
aśubha-bhāvanā 25
Atwood, Margaret 81
Augustus 48
'*awrah* 63

Bacchae, The 135
Bajracharya, Chanira 42
*Balancing on the Mechitza: Transgender in the
    Jewish Community* (Dzmura) 122

BDSM (bondage, discipline, dominance,
    submission, sadism, and masochism) 135, 139
belief 5
Bengali Vaiṣṇavism 132–133
Berger, Peter 8
Beyond God the Father (Daly) 81
bhakti 28
Bharatiya Janata Party (BJP) in India 8,
    83–86
Bharatmata 84
birth 93
bissu in South Sulawesi 111–112, 121
Black: Christians 16; independent churches 64;
    nationalism 97; sexualities 97; women 97
black magic 86
"black night" 41
bleeding corpse 25
Blood Bowl Sutra 48
Bly, Robert 30
bodily impurity 45
Body and Society (Brown) 48
body hair 117
Book of Mormon 94
Bosnian War 118
Bourgeois, Louise 87
Bouteldja, Naima 70
breast milk 46
breasts 117
breeds 9
bridal mysticism 131
British colonization 7
Brown, Peter 25, 48
Bucar, Elizabeth M. 45
Budapest, Zsuzsanna 116
Buddha 23–28
Buddhism 5–7, 23, 100–101; craving 24;
    nirvana 24; nuns and monks 24–27; sexuality
    and 25; suffering 24
Buddhist: meditation manuals 25; menstrual
    blood taboos 48; militancy 86; nationalism
    in Myanmar 84
Burrus, Virginia 31
Bush, Laura 79

Butler, Judith 125
Bynum, Caroline Walker 1, 131

Caitanya, Saint 133–134, 139–140
capitalism 81
capitalist system 105
Carlisle Indian School 74–76
caste stratification 51
caste system: high caste women 51; marriages
    in 50–51
Catherine of Siena 1
Catholicism 5, 65
Catholics 75
celibacy 2, 18, 98, 100, 102–103, 131, 133;
    benefits of 31–32; Buddha 23–28; desirable
    36–37; erotics of 31; female 26–28;
    instrumentalizing sex 114; involuntary
    33–34; Mirabai (Mira) 28–31; nun-like
    existence 29; permanent 33; and sexual
    identity 34–35; social and religious
    regulations 35; social reproduction of
    religion 32; temporary 33; types of 32–34;
    voluntary 33–35
celibate religious persons 32
celibate (sexually inactive) practitioners
    1–2
chastity 31
childbirth 45–46; and ritual impurity 47
child sexual abuse 60
Christ-centered chaste friendships 34
Christian: civilization 86; demonology 87;
    Gospels 6; justice movement 58; morality
    58; mystics 1
Christianity 6, 76–77, 97; celibacy 114; gender
    roles in Roman society 99; instrumentalized
    sexuality 114; ritual of marriage 114
Christianization 76
Christianized European cultures 50
Christine de Pizan 98
Church of Satan 116
circumcision 1, 117
cisgender 13–15
Clark, Elizabeth 31, 131
clash of civilizations 69
class systems 50
Collins, Steven 24
colonialism 81
Common Era 25
compulsory heterosexuality 15, 38, 44, 95
condom-use 58
Confucianism 6
consumerism 81
contemplative practice 25
contraception 61
controversy: AIDS in United States and in
    sub-Saharan Africa 58–59; external to
    religion 65–68; internal to religion 62–65;

Muslim marriages in South Africa 55–57;
    religion and 59–61; religion as cipher 68–70
Convention on the Elimination of all Forms
    of Discrimination against Women
    (CEDAW) 86
Convention on the Rights of the Child 86
Coptic Christians 5
co-religionist 19
corpses, Buddhist contemplation of 25
corrective rape 83
Cox, Renée 103–104
Crasnow, S.J. 124
craving 24
creed 5
critical heterosexuality studies 13, 17
critical race theory 17
Crowley, Aleister 116
Cruz, Sor Juana Inés de la 98
cultural genocide 75
Customary Marriages Act 55
cyberspatial activity 60

Daly, Mary 81
Darwin's theory of natural selection 14
Davies, Sharyn 111
death 45
Declaration of Independence 105
deities 5, 7–8, 48, 111; Hindu 36, 40
demonological treatises 86
demonology 87
Desert Fathers tradition 25
devadasis 105–107
deviance 14
Dhamma flag 85
Dionysus 134–135, 139–140
disability theory 17
disease 45
divine: inspiration 98; nectar of sexual
    fluids 112
divorce 56, 57
domestic abuse 77
Do Muslim Women Need Saving?
    (Abu-Lughod) 79
drinking semen and menstrual blood 112
drugs 73
Duchess, The 99
Durgā, goddess 40, 52, 84
Durgā-Taleju 40–42

earth-healing rituals 82
Eastern Orthodox Christianity 5, 102
ecofeminism 81
ecstasy 19–20, 130; Charismatic Christians slain
    in spirit 138; Dionysus 134; gnostic sexual
    rituals 136–137; medieval Hindu mystics
    132–133; medieval women mystics
    130–132; sex, and religion 134; sexual

ecstasies that involve pain 135–136; sexuality and messianic heresy of Sabbatai Zevi 137; spirit possession 134–135; Vodou possession, Papa Gede 138–139
Ecstatic Religion: An Anthropological Study of Spirit Possession and Shamanism (Lewis) 134
ecstatic union 31
Egyptian Fatwa Council 88
ejaculation 46
Elaw, Zilpha 64–65
El-Tawhid Juma Circle 102
emic 7
empathetic understanding 3
empathy 3
enemy of God 86
Engels, Friedrich 105
English Bengali Vaiṣṇavism 132
epistemic/epistemological violence 77, 80
epoché 3–4, 21
ethnic cleansing 79, 118
European colonization 6
European education 6
Evangelical Christianity 19, 58–61, 103
Evans, Arthur 116
Evola, Julius 112

Fadiman, Anne 122
Father (Tooji Keshtkar) 66–67
fatwa 88
Fausto-Sterling, Anne 10
favelas 73
female: body's capacity 93; celibacy 26; circumcision (*see* female genital mutilation (FGM)); deities of Hinduism 40; divine energy 36; fluids 48; perseverance 80; suicide bombers 79
female genital mutilation (FGM) 60, 79, 118–119
femaleness 111
female sexuality: and male honor 80
feminine men 16
femininity 10–11
feminist theory 17
fertile feminine energy 36
fetuses, rites for 92
Finnmark 86–87
Foote, Julia 64–65
forced castration 79
Foster, Lawrence 94
Foucault, Michel 25
fourteen stations of the cross 135
France 70
Fruit of Islam 97
frum pornography 108

Gardner, Gerald 116
Garvey, Marcus 97

Gay and Catholic: Accepting My Sexuality, Finding Community, Living My Faith (Tushnet) 34
gay and lesbian studies 13, 16
gay men 16, 58, 99; in Orthodox Judaism 108
gender 9–11; multiple understandings 12; roles 10; segregation 35, 51–52; studies 8–13
gender fluid 12, 36
genderqueer 12
gender segregation 51–53; traditions of 98
gender variant 13; roles 12
genitalia 117; male 117
gharana 37
Glassman, Hank 48
gnosticism 136–137, 139
gnostic sexual rituals 136–137
Goddess symbolisms 82
gopīs 132; *see also* Kṛṣṇa
Gospels 93–94
Great Rite 116
guerilla performances 67

Hadewijch 1, 20, 31, 131–132, 134, 139
hadith 43, 99
hajj 111
Handmaid's Tale, The (Atwood) 81
Hardacre, Helen 92
hate crime 83
Hawley, John Stratton 30
Hay, Harry 99, 116
Hayes, Kelly E. 74
Hendricks, Muhsin 102
hereditary class systems 50
heresy (false belief) 5, 86, 137; of Sabbatai Zevi 137
hermaphrodites 9, 14
Hermaphroditos 9
Hermaphroditus 121
hetero-gendered sex 106
heterosexual 15, 59; Black Africans 58
heterosexuality 44, 95
higher-status castes 106
hijra 36–37, 83
Hildegard of Bingen 98
Himalayan Buddhist wedding ceremonies 50
Hindu: goddesses of destruction 84; nationalism 8, 84; wedding ceremonies 50
Hinduism 6–7; high cast girls 51–52
Hindutva 8, 84
Hirschfield, Jane 30
hjell 87
Hmong people 122
Hoel, Nina 56–57
holiness 45–46, 52; code 47
Holy Spirit 138
homophobia 77
Homo religiosus 80

homosexuality 101, 116
homosexuals 15, 44, 101; sexual behavior 58
hooliganism 67
hormones shift 17
house churches 100
human phenomenon 2
human sexuality 1
hymen 119; repair 119
hypergamous marriage 51

Ibn Rushd-Goethe mosque 88
ideal type 20, 77, 96
in-between sex 43
incarnation of God 94
indecent theology 65
independent goddesses 106
Indian boarding schools 77
indigenous peoples 74
Industrial Revolution 115
The Inner Circle 102
innovation: angels in heaven 93; Latter-day
    Saints (Mormons) 94, 96; *Mizuko kuyō*
    92–93; Oneida Perfectionists 94–95; relative
    to larger religion 100–104; relative to larger
    society 97–100; religious innovation 96–97;
    response to changes in larger society
    104–108; Shakers 94–95, 97
Inside the Gender Jihad (Wadud) 62
instrumentalization: *bissu* in South Sulawesi
    111–112; bodies, sex, and religion 113;
    defined 113; of genitalia 117, 119; Judaism
    114; non-conforming bodies 120–124; of
    religion 116; of sex 114; sexual acts
    114–116; sexualized bodies and parts of
    bodies 117–120; tantric sex 112–113;
    tantrikas 112–113; traditionally gendered
    and sexed bodies 124–127
instrumentalizing 113–114, 128
interfaith 61
intergenerational continuity 46
intergenerational trauma 76
Internet 107
intersectionality 16
intersex 9–14, 36, 43–44, 111–112, 121, 129
inversion 116; theory of desire 15
invert 14–16, 18, 22
involuntary celibacy 33–34
'Isánáklésh Gotal 126
ISIS 86
Islam 6–7, 47, 97; polygyny 55; status of
    women 99, 104; women in 79
Islamic law 34
Islamic same-sex weddings 102
Islamic terror 70, 88
Islamophobes 78
Islamophobia 78
Islamophobic current 86

Jackson, Michael 70
Jackson, Troy 102
Jainism 6–7
Jesuits 74
Jesus 94
Jewish law 93
Jewish Torah 6
Jihad 62, 83
Joan of Arc 101
Jōdo Shinshū 92
Joseph Smith 96
Judaism 5–6, 47; instrumentalized sex 114;
    marriage 114
Juergensmeyer, Mark 30
Julian of Norwich 98

Kabbalah 114
Kali, goddess 84
Kellner, Carl 115
Keshtkar, Tooji 66–67
Khaki, El-Farouk 102
Khomeini, Ayatollah 43
khutbah (the Friday sermon) 62–63
Kinsey, Alfred 15
Kinsey reports 15
kosher dietary laws (*kashrut*) 5
Kraemer, Ross 133
Kramer, Heinrich 86
Kṛṣṇa 28–30, 35, 37, 124, 132
Kṛṣṇa-oriented saints 29
kufr bill 56
Kugle, Scott Siraj al-Haqq 83
Kūkai 120
Kumārī-elect 41
kumāri pujā 52
Kumārīs of Nepal's Kathmandu valley 40–42,
    50, 52

labia removal 118
Langenberg, Amy Paris 48
Latinx Christians 16
Latter-day Saints (Mormons) 94, 96
Laws of Manu 47
Lee, Jarena 64–65, 98
Leeuw, Gerardus van der 3
Leopold, Aldo 81
lesbian, gay, bisexual, transgender, intersex, or
    queer+ (LGBTIQ+) 12
L'Estasi di Santa Teresa (*Saint Teresa in
    Ecstasy*) 130
Lewis, I.M. 134
LGBTIQ+ people 61, 68–69, 88, 102–103,
    124, 136; Muslims 102; rabbis 102
Like a Prayer (Madonna) 65–66
lingam 119
Linnaean classification 14
lived religion 19–20

Live to Tell (Madonna) 66
livid corpse 25
Lopez, Alma 103
Lopez, Yolanda 103
love-smitten monk 25–26
low-caste people 106
lust 48

Macey, Joanna 81
Madonna 65; Blond Ambition tour (1990) 66; intimate encounter with the saint 65–66; play on sexual passion 65
Maenads 134–135, 139
magic 5
maiden-gift 50
Make America Great Again (Pussy Riot) 67
male bissu 111
male circumcision 118; *see also* female genital mutilation (FGM)
male continence 95
male–male sex 120
maleness 10, 111
Malleus Maleficarum 86
Mama Lola's community 139
testicles 117
Maria Molambo 73–74
marital bond 49
marriage legitimacy 49
martyrdom 78
Marx, Karl 105
masculinity 10–11; female invert 15; in Islam 79
mass suicide 3
Masuzawa, Tomoko 5
McCarthy, Julie 42
McGuire, Meredith 3, 5
meditation 26, 32; hair-induced 27
Men and Religion Forward Movement 99
men's mikveh 47
menstrual blood 46–47, 53, 112; and afterlives (*Blood Bowl Sutra*) 48; during childbirth 47; ecological circulation 48; miasma of 48
menstrual seclusion 47
menstruating woman 46; Buddhists 47–48; Hindu 47; sex with 47
menstruation 46; and childbirth 47–48
mental concentration 112
metaphysical religions 97
mezuzah 5
mikveh 47, 124
militant nationalism 85
Ministry of Utmost Happiness, The (Roy) 83
Mirabai (Mira) 28–31, 35; bhakti 28; Bhoraj 29; celibacy within marriage 28, 37; songs 30–31
mitzvah 49, 126
Mizuko kuyō 92–93

Mohanty, Chandra Talpade 69
monasticism 24–28, 32–33, 35, 37, 85
monastic life 24, 27
monogamy 49, 59
Mormons 94–95
Mother Ann Lee 94
Mounsey, Chris 122
muscular Christianity 99
"Muslim ban" 69
Muslim Marriages Bill, 2010 56
Muslims: body 78; Judicial Council 63; male migrant 70; marriages 55–57; marriages in South Africa 55–57; migration crisis 69; polygyny 55–57; polygyny in South Africa 61; suicide bomber 78; Tinder 108; veil 68–69
Muttā 26–27
Myanmar (Burma) 85; anti-Muslim sentiments 84–85; Buddhist-only areas 85; illegal immigrants 85; "Muslim-free" villages 85; polygyny 85; Rohingya Muslim minority 85
mystic 1, 19, 31, 98, 114–117, 127, 131

Najmabadi, Afsaneh 44
Nanda, Serena 36
National Association of Evangelicals (NAE) 58
Nation of Islam 97
Native Americans 74; children 74–75; physical abuse at boarding schools 76; spirituality 7–8
Navajo (Diné) culture 12
Neopaganism 116
Nepal 40
Newar Buddhists 41
Newars 40
niddah laws 114
niizh manidoowag (Two Spirit) 12
niqab 70, 78
nirvan 36
nirvana 23–24
nonbinary 12
non-confessional religious 4
non-conforming bodies 113, 120–124
non-consensual treatment 10
non-governmental organizations (NGOs) 106
non-normative sexuality 45
non-royal Kumārīs 42
nuclearization 84, 86

off-reservation boarding school 74
Omar, Rashied 62
Oneida Perfectionists 94–95
oral cultures 6
ordination as Buddhist nun 27
Ordo Templi Orientis (OTO) 115–116
orientalism/orientalist 6–7, 16, 83
Orsi, Robert 122
orthodoxy 60
orthopraxis 60, 65

pandaka 119
Papa Gede 138–140
paranormal phenomena 115
partition of India 118; sexual violence during 118
pass laws 62
Paul, apostle 99–100
pederasty 120, 128
penis 1, 9, 117–120, 122
Pentheus 135
performativity 125
permanent celibacy 33
physical bonds of sexual exclusivity 95
physical violence 80
pleasures 24
plural marriage 96
polygynous unions 55, 57; contraction of 57
polygyny 55–57, 59, 61, 85, 96; in Islam 55; in South Africa 59
Pomba Gira 73–74, 77, 80, 89; independent female sexuality 73
pornography 4, 108
Porres, Martín de 65
postcolonial theory 17
post-menopausal females 112
potential fertility 50
Pratt, Richard Henry 74–75
pre-adolescent betrothals 50
pregnancy 93
pre-pubescent girls 52
Presbyterian 74
profane 1–2, 19–20, 42, 98–100, 102, 107
Promise Keepers 99
Prophet Muhammad 49, 99
prostitutes 73
Protestantism 5, 102
Protestant Reformation 98, 107
Protestants 75
public rites of purification 46
Punk Prayer: Mother of God Drive Putin Away (Pussy Riot) 67
purity: pollution, wholeness, and holiness 45–46; rules 46–47
Pussy Riot 67

Quakers 75
queer: jihad 83; Muslim 83; people 83; religious 88; studies 13–18; theory 16–17
queerness of God 59
queerphobia 77
Qur'an 43, 99
Qur'an and Woman (Wadud) 62

races 14, 79
racial segregation 55
Rādhā 133; *see also* Kṛṣṇa
Radical Faeries 99, 116
Ramaswamy, Vijaya 30

Ramberg, Lucinda 106
rape 76, 81, 118
rapism 81
Recognition of Customary Marriages Act of 1998 55
regulation 40–45; body in menstruation and childbirth 47–48; gender segregation 51–52; gender-variant and intersex people of Iran 43–45; Kumārīs of Nepal's Kathmandu valley 40–42; purity, pollution, wholeness, and holiness 45–46; of sexual body 46–49; sexuality in marriage 48–49; social status and marriage regulations 49–51
regulation-based celibacy 33
reincarnation 5
religio-ethnic cleansing 119
religion: academic study 2–8; as accessory to violence 83–86; for African Americans 97; Big Five 6; as cipher 68–70; controversy and 59–61; defined 8; ecstasy 134; instrumentalization of 116; lived 19–20; metaphysical 97; as resource in violent situations 81–83; as source of violence 78–80; and superstition 7; as target of violence 86–88; violence and 76–78
religious bathing place 47
religious dating 107–108
religious divorce 57
religious impurity 45
religious innovation 96–97, 108; in India 105–106
religious morality codes 80
religious piety 49
religious pluralism 8
religious queers 88
religious regulations *see* regulation
religious specialists 98
religious studies 2–8; descriptive-analytical aspect 7; human phenomenon 3; interdisciplinary field 2; transdisciplinary field 2; world-concepts 3
renaissance 114
renunciant 1, 23, 32–33, 49, 98, 100, 102, 119
reproductive organs 46
reproductive sex 93
Reuss, Theodor 115
Reynolds v. United States 97
Rich, Adrienne 15
ritual impurity 45, 47
ritual inversion 112
ritual of marriage 114
ritual pollution 45, 47
ritual purity 42, 45–46
ritual sex stem 112
Roberts, Rosemary 82
Roman Catholicism 34, 101–102, 126; girls 124
Roy, Arundhati 83–85

royal Kumārī 41–42
Ruether, Rosemary Radford 81
Rushd-Goethe, Masjid Ibn 102
Russian Orthodox 74

Sabbatai Zevi 137, 139
sacrament 114
sacred text 6
Saddleback Initiative 58
Sahajiyā 133
same sex: desire 18, 37, 101; eroticism 4, 44–45,
    95, 101, 116; marriage practices 61; marriages
    59; pairings 15, 35; relationships with 101;
    sexual attraction 34
Sami 87
Sarkozy, Nicolas 70
sati 29
saving: of Native American children 74–75;
    souls 76
scattered corpse 25
Schalow, Paul Gordon 120
scriptural commandments 32
scriptural metaphors 24
seasonal renunciation 33
seismograph 25
self-awareness 24
self-denial 23
self-discipline 49
self-expression 31
self-immolation 29
self-indulgence 23
self-inflicted violence 80
semen 46, 53; offering 112
Sennett, Richard 25
sensationalism 44
sensual gratification 25
servant of Satan 86
Seventh-Day Adventism 98
sex 9–10
sex change surgery 43–44
*Sex Lives of Saints, The: An Erotics of Ancient
    Hagiography* (Burrus) 31
sex magic 114
sexologists 14–15
sexology 17
sex-segregated communal housing 94
sexual abstinence 31
sexual acts 35, 113–116
sexual arousal 112
sexual attraction 24
Sexual Behavior in the Human Female (Kinsey) 15
Sexual Behavior in the Human Male (Kinsey) 15
sexual body, regulation of 46–49
sexual brutalization of bodies 80
sexual desire 18, 24–25, 29, 32, 49
sexual emissions 46
sexual expression 35; in Iran 45

sexual fluids 46, 112; divine nectar of 112
sexual identity and celibacy 34–35
sexual imagination 35
sexual impropriety 100
sexual indulgence 48
sexual intercourse 46, 112
sexual intercourse prior to marriage 49
sexual intimacy with divine beings 131
sexuality 49, 116; in marriage 48–49; for
    Muslims 49; profane 1–2; and spiritual
    power 1–2; studies 13–18
sexualized bodies 113
sexualized violence 118
sexual organs 1
sexual purity 79
sexual regulation 31; in marriage 48–49
sexual renunciation 28, 31
sexual self-control 48
sexual violence 76, 79; against women in
    war 118
sex workers 73, 117
Shabbot 49
Shakers 94–95, 97
shakti 40, 42, 52, 119
Shari'ah law 56
Shia Islam 43–44
Shirazi, Faegheh 45
Shiva 36, 119
Sider, Ron 58
Sikhism 6–7
Silvers, Laury 102
singleness 24
singular presence 24
Siraj, Afisa 34–35
Sirimā 26
Sisters of the Spirit (Andrews) 64
Sita (Hindu goddess) 80, 84
skeletal corpse 25
Slain in the spirit 138
slave trade 105
Smart phones 108
social and religious regulations and celibacy 35
social construction 5, 7, 9–13, 17,
    21–22
social control 48
social hierarchy 49
social illegitimacy 115
social inequality 14
socially conservative Christians 108
socially transgressive sex 116
social power 17
social reproduction of religion 32
social status and marriage regulations 49–51
sodomites 121
sodomy 121
South Africa: Muslim communities 55–56;
    Muslim marriages 55; Muslim Marriages Bill,

2010 56; Muslim women 56; polygyny in 55
South Asian Hinduism 50
Spiral Dance ritual 82
spirit possession 74, 134–135, 140
spiritual ecofeminism 81
spiritual energy 116
spiritual eugenics 96
spiritualists 92–93, 104, 107, 115
spiritualities 7, 81
spiritual power 1
spiritual skills 112
Spivak, Gayatri 77, 79
Starhawk 82, 116
Steilneset Witchcraft Memorial 87
stigmata 65
stole 57, 66
S.T.O.P. strategy 58–59
suffering 24–25
suicide bomber 78
Sumangala 27
Sumedhā 27–28
superstition 5, 7

Talamantez, Inés 126
Tantras 113
tantric practices 120
tantric sex 112–113
tantrikas 112–113; sexual intercourse 112; violation of social norms 112
tantrism 133
Taoism 6
technology 96, 104, 107, 110
Teresa of Avila 130–132, 134, 139
terrorism 78
tertiary order 98, 102
Tertullian's notion of women being 86
testicles 117, 122
Theravada Buddhism 33
Therīgāthā poetry collection 27
third eye 41
third sex 9
Thomas, Tissa Mariam 37
Thriller (Michael Jackson) 70
Torah 6, 114, 117–118, 122
Torjesen, Karen 100
Toronto Unity Mosque 102
transgender 8, 11–14, 16, 36, 68, 101–102, 104, 117, 122–126
transgenders: Jews 122–123; people 101; studies 8–13
transphobia 77
transsexual people 9–10
Trimorphic Protennoia 137
Truth, Sojourner 98
Tunisia 55
Tushnet, Eve 34–35

Ubuntu 76
ulama (religious clergy) 56–57
U.S. War on Terror 79

vaginal corona 119
vaginal emissions 46
vaginal fluids 112
vaginas and uteruses, stabbing 118
Vaiṣṇava 132
veil 68–69; politicization of 69–70
veneration 50
violation of social norms 112
violence 70; boarding schools and First Nation children 74–76; bodies and sexualities 76–77; epistemic 77, 80; physical 77; Pomba Gira in Brazil 73–74; religion and 76–78; religion as accessory to 83–86; religion as resource in violent situations 81–83; religion as source 78–80; religion as target of 86–88
virgin-gift 50
Virgin Mary 67, 103
Virgin of Guadalupe 103
Viṣṇu 132; incarnations (avatars) of 132
visionary experience 130–131
visual art 68
Vodou 138–139
Vrndāvana 132
vulvas 118–119

Wadud, Amina 62, 64, 100; *khutbah* 62–64
Walker, Mitch 116
Wallin, Elisabeth Ohlson 68
War on Terror 79
Warren, Kay 58
Warren, Rick 58
water 46, 124
"water baby rites" 92
Wenger, Tisa 8
Western tantric sex practices 113
White, David Gordon 112
White, Ellen Gould 98
wholeness 41, 45–46, 52
Wicca 82
Wiccan practice 116
Wickedary (Daly) 81
witchcraft legislation in Finnmark 86–87
witch-craze 86
witch-hunt 86
"witch's chairs" 88
woman's sexuality 73
womb 48, 63, 118
women: access to ordination 100; bodies 18; of Buddhist monastic community 26–28; desirability 18; in Islam 79; renunciants 1; second-class citizens 56; self-expression 51;

sexual "purity" 119; South African Muslim
women 56
women–born–women–only Dianic branch of
Wicca 116
Women Healing Earth (Ruether) 81
world–concepts 3, 8, 20, 93
worm–infested corpse 25
writes of kinship 107

Yalom, Marilyn 49
"Yo Mama's Last Supper" 104

Zahed, Ludovic–Mohamed 102
Zajovic, Stasa 118
zelador 74
Zevi, Sabbatai 137, 139
Zumthor, Peter 87